How to Start a
Wedding Planning Business

Sherrie Wilkolaski
Cho Phillips

How to Start a Wedding Planning Business

By Sherrie Wilkolaski, Cho Phillips

Book Cover Design: Garnet Press, Self Published Marketing Group, Inc.

Other Titles by Sherrie Wilkolaski:

How to Get a Job as a Wedding Planner – Copyright © 2005, 2008 by Sherrie Wilkolaski, Garnet Press, Self Published Marketing Group, Inc.

Cookies and Cocktails – Copyright © 2008 by Sherrie Wilkolaski, Garnet Press, Self Published Marketing Group, Inc.

ISBN: 1-4116-6444-2

ISBN-13: 978-14116-64449

Library of Congress Number: Available upon request.

Table of Contents

IN THIS CHAPTER YOU WILL LEARN:
- How wedding planning has evolved
- The purpose of the engagement
- Current statistics for marriage bound couples

IN THIS CHAPTER YOU WILL LEARN:
- The process of the engagement from a bride's perspective
- How wedding planning expenses are traditionally divided
- Traditional meanings behind "Something Old, New, Borrowed and Blue"
- The bride's count down to her big moment
- Bridal Shower Ideas, Groom's Check List and Men's Fashion's
- FAQs

IN THIS CHAPTER YOU WILL LEARN:
- What questions to ask a new bride-to-be
- How to set vendor expectations
- How to set the expectation of the bride and her family
- Wedding Etiquette

IN THIS CHAPTER YOU WILL LEARN:
- How to structure your business based on your marketplace
- How to evaluate your competition when establishing your services
- How to set preliminary marketing objectives
- Tools and tips for organizing your home office and business practices
- Business start-up costs

IN THIS CHAPTER YOU WILL LEARN:
- The importance of documentation
- How documentation of your business practices plays an imperative role in the success of your business
- How to set goals for yourself and your business

IN THIS CHAPTER YOU WILL LEARN:
- Why vendor selection is a key element to the success of your business
- How to identify quality vendors
- What questions to ask when building your vendor network

IN THIS CHAPTER YOU WILL LEARN:
- Contract Law
- The key elements of a contract
- Contract rules to remember
- The importance of having business insurance
- U.S. Chamber of Commerce business resources

planning party

IN THIS CHAPTER YOU WILL LEARN:
- The importance of bridal show participation
- How to research bridal shows
- Essential elements of a bridal show checklist
- How to book a show
- How to work a booth
- How to conduct post bridal show follow up

IN THIS CHAPTER YOU WILL LEARN:
- The importance of having an online presence
- The proper way to construct a web page for online marketing
- The importance of Keywords and placement
- Recommended Web Positioning Companies, software, websites
- Keyword Tools
- How to choose the right keywords for your site
- The importance of having your won domain name
- How to create keyword rich pages
- How to improve the Link Popularity of your site
- How to submit your site to the open directory
- How to become an Open Directory Project Editor
- About frames and how they effect search engines
- The top 10 search engine positioning mistakes
- Glossary of online terms

IN THIS CHAPTER YOU WILL LEARN:
- How to approach the media and position yourself as the expert in your field

- The key elements of a press release
- How to get your press release out on the wire
- How to write your biography
- How to conduct editorial opportunity research
- How to create an editorial opportunity calendar
- How to contact local news and radio stations
- How to get your articles published
- How to create your business press/media kit

    IN THIS CHAPTER YOU WILL LEARN:
- Ways to organize your business and streamline your daily activities
- How to plan your work and work your plan

    IN THIS CHAPTER YOU WILL LEARN:
- How to incorporate additional services and products into your business
- Examples of complementary products and how to start expansion

    IN THIS CHAPTER YOU WILL LEARN:
- What it means to be a certified wedding planner
- How certification can improve your business success
- What certification programs are available and what each has to offer
- How to earn your certification at a discount rate

Relationship Education: Plan for a Wedding…Prepare for a

Dedication

This book was inspired by the entrepreneurial spirit of thousands of women on their quest for independence, creativity, and a passion for planning weddings.

Introduction

Trends

The future for the professional wedding planner has never been so bright. Wedding planners equipped with proper training and experience will benefit from the growing demand for social event planners of lifecycle events such as weddings, anniversaries, bar mitzvahs, reunions, and family celebrations.

Today's brides-to-be come from many diverse backgrounds and experiences. Many have had the opportunity to be involved in a friend's or relative's wedding and are knowledgeable as to what she wants for her wedding day and the support she expects from her consultant. On the other hand, there is the novice bride who is easily overwhelmed and confused as she begins planning her wedding and will need more support and guidance from her consultant. It is the responsibility of the consultant to set the expectations of both parties from the very beginning.

A bride's decision to hire a consultant is based on several factors. For many, the main motivation is lack of time. Most women have full time jobs which do not allow for the time consuming phone calls and visits required to identify the best vendors. Major oversights often occur when time is limited, and the necessity to stay focused and organized creates more problems that add to the overall stresses and responsibilities of planning a wedding. When a bride is new to an area, with few friends or family members close by, planning a wedding can become a too stressful…unless she has help and support from a seasoned consultant. Out-of-town weddings and brides with a limited budget can lend to additional challenges to planning the event.

Without a doubt, a bride's wisest choice is to hire a professional who is competently trained and well acquainted with her local vendors.

Expectations

Good rapport, communication, and a feeling that the bride and family can rely on the consultant are vital to a successful wedding day outcome. A professional consultant will go the extra mile and act as a couple's liaison, smoothing over the rough spots that inevitably manifest themselves during the planning and on the wedding day.

A good consultant can stretch any budget to ensure the bride is receiving all the perks possible, based on her business connections and expertise. From frugal to extravagant the wedding planner will never run out of creative ideas to satisfy the client. As a professional it is your duty to stay within the bride's budget while alleviating financial concerns and is a major part of planning any client's event. An established consultant will have a network of quality vendors with a wide selection of styles, price points and personalities. She will assist the bride by keeping her on a schedule, knowing whom to book and when. Additionally, the wedding consultant will be able to provide price comparisons, oversee vendor contracts, avoid overtime charges and save on unnecessary services. A professional consultant will establish strong relationships with her vendors, resulting in a trust that each vendor will do what is expected, deliver on time, and stay within the budget while maintaining the highest regard for quality and service. Details such as coordinating events, overseeing vendors, supervising the wedding party, cueing the music, and assisting with seating arrangements are only a few of the duties a consultant will assume.

Most brides come to realize an extra pair of hands on their wedding day is priceless. The wedding day itinerary and schedule will be planned in great detail and then distributed to all vendors and the members of the wedding party to ensure a smooth-running event. The bride and groom can rest assured knowing the wedding day will be handled with care, allowing them to relax and enjoy their day.

Careers

Many consultants find themselves in the industry by accident, a result of simply doing what they love. Many professional consultants in the wedding industry have found their calling by assisting friends and family with wedding plans and coordinating additional social events. If this description sounds familiar, then this book is exactly what you have been looking for.

As you read through the following pages you will come to understand the business side of wedding planning and the different ways to start and establish your own business as a professional wedding planner.

How to Best Utilize this Book to Become Certified...

This book is used as a foundation for the industry's best wedding planning educational programs and is structured to walk the student through the process of starting a wedding planning business. At the end of each chapter there are suggested assignments which the reader can choose to complete if they so desire. In the event that the reader does complete the assignments and would like to put their assignments towards their wedding planning certification, they should contact these education resources:

www.weddingacademy.com

www.weddingplanningschool.com

www.weddingplanninguniversity.com

Students will have additional assignments and requirements to fulfill, however this book covers approximately 60% of the certification requirements for achieving a certificate of completion. Check with each individual school for seminar schedules or classes in your local area.

Go to www.howtostartaweddingplanningbusiness.com for more information and downloadable checklists from this book.

Preface: A Recipe for Success

Imagine you own a bakery and a bride-to-be has been referred to your business because you are an excellent baker with a great reputation. The bride is a client who wants a *cake*. She has never ordered a *cake* before and is unsure of what to do, so she asks you to design the *cake* for her. This bride is looking to you for guidance, because you are an expert at making delicious *cakes*. You need to listen carefully as she describes what she envisions for this *"cake,"* i.e. *her wedding day.*

First, you must select the ingredients. (*Think of vendors as the ingredients.*)

1. Quality: Vendors should be dependable and reputable.

2. Freshness: Vendors should be up-to-date on current trends.

3. The best flavor: Vendors should be professionals in the industry.

In order to prepare the most beautiful and delicious *cake* you must first conduct a little research.

Which vendors have the ingredients you require? Do your research. Call, introduce yourself, and ask questions about their business. Tell them what you are looking for and ask if they can provide that service. Tell them about your wedding planning business and the wonderful opportunities you can provide. Ask if they are interested in partnering with your company and building a business relationship.

Work with your vendors as if you are an extension of their business. This is a solid business strategy and allows you to share information on new leads and referrals. This is a professional and unique approach to a successful business partnership, and most vendors will find this idea appealing.

1. Prepare the cake: Select the services.

2. Mix the ingredients: Coordinate the vendors.

3. Bake a delicious and beautiful cake: Coordinate a wonderful wedding with your client's unique personality and you've just produced her signature wedding that her guests will remember for years to come.

As a result, the bride is thankful that she had YOU to handle all of her wedding planning details. She feels confident that her wedding will be perfect. Now that she has tasted the fruits of your labor, she may even hire you for her future occasions. The bride is overjoyed with the great job you have done and tells all her friends how you helped make her day *perfect*.

Summary
The success of your business depends on how good your cakes taste. How good the cakes taste depends on the quality of your vendors. How good the vendors are depends on the amount of effort you put into your business. Never forget, successful businesses are built one happy client at a time!

Once you understand the importance of vendor relationships and marketing, developing your own unique wedding planning style and reputation will be a "piece of cake".

Author Anonymous

Chapter One

10 | Chapter One

Wedding Industry Overview

IN THIS CHAPTER YOU WILL LEARN:
- How wedding planning has evolved
- The purpose of an engagement
- Current statistics for marriage bound couples

History of Weddings

For as long as anyone can remember marriage has existed, and it has acquired many different interpretations through the ages. In the 1800's, marriage was no longer considered necessary to survive. Instead it evolved into a meaningful union between a loving couple, one marked by religious ceremony. Marriage also provided a social opportunity to introduce one community to another, creating the perfect opportunity for celebration!

During this age the wedding consultant was born, and her role was to primarily work with the bride while *the family* made the wedding arrangements. The consultant would help prepare the bride for the wedding day by instructing her on what is appropriate and educating her on wedding and social etiquette.

Until the 1960's the role of the consultant didn't change much, but with the culmination of the sexual revolution the traditional wedding planner was no longer in demand. As a result, wedding consultants took an extended vacation.

The 1970's brought forth a divorce era and it was not until the 1980's that marriage became fashionable again. Wedding consulting reemerged...ready for a big comeback.

The working woman also helped establish the wedding planning industry. With women putting in more time at the office, they had more money to spend but less time to spend it.

According to the Association of Bridal Consultants, the wedding industry was a 17 billion dollar industry in 1981. It grew to 32 billion dollars in 1992 and in 2003 was a 72 billion dollar industry.

Engagement

It is easy to understand why the Victorian Era was filled with romance, for what is more romantic than two people in love, pledging their lives to one another? It was not considered proper for young single men and woman to spend much time alone or frequently interact. An engagement provided a perfect excuse for two lovers to be together in public. Once a couple was engaged, they were encouraged to spend more time together at parties and social functions, a practice that evolved into what we now consider the engagement party.

Throughout the engagement, the couple would save money and receive gifts in order to prepare for their life together.

Brides Today 2005

The Wedding Industry is one of the fastest growing markets today as new trends and non- wedding industries begin to add to the overall cost of pre-wedding activities and preparations. Brides today have more money to spend but less time to spend it with full time careers and responsibilities. More and more rely of the assistance of a consultant or full-time wedding planner to execute her vision of the perfect day.

Industry Statistics

Projected U.S. weddings for 2006: 2.2 million.*

• Average cost for a wedding and reception: $26,400*

• Cost will increase about 2.3% over already high 2005 prices.*

• **Wedding Planner Fee***

$2,640.00 at 10%

$3.960.00 at 15%

• Average ages of wedding couple: 27, bride; 29, groom**

• Receptions: Approximately 71% of all wedding receptions take place at a hotel, country club or catering facility.**

Source: The Wedding Report

**Fairchild Bridal Group*

There are also many brides who are getting married for a second time. Because it is their second marriage, they want to do it right, and will most likely have a traditional-type wedding.

Research from the Institute of American Values reports 75% of divorced individuals remarry and try it again. Like first weddings, these events can range from small quaint get-togethers to full traditional extended family celebrations.

Wedding Seasons

It is important to realize wedding planning is a seasonal business. Be conscious of the busy wedding season in your area, as this can be good for your business. Many people desire a June wedding while very few care to be married in January. You do the math. Plan ahead for Memorial Day, Labor Day and those long Fourth of July weekends. And of course, don't forget about those June weddings.

Your location will also determine how seasonal your business will be. Warmer climates tend to have a longer wedding season while those of colder climates may be shorter.

The Budget

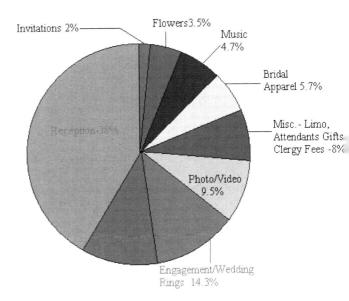

Most couples today will be contributing financially to their own wedding, and the bride and groom will most likely have dual incomes. It is no longer the sole responsibility of the bride's parents to assume the huge financial task of paying for their daughter's wedding. The groom's parents may also offer to contribute, although they typically pay for the rehearsal dinner, the bride's bouquet and bridal attendants' flowers.

The average price for a wedding in the US, is $26,400* and has an average engagement of ten months to one year.

Source: The Wedding Report

Chapter One

End of Chapter Suggested Assignments

First Objective

Contact your local city hall to research how to obtain your business license in your area. Call your local SBA (Small Business Association) for business resources and tax information for new businesses. You must have all of your papers in order and in accordance with your local city and state laws before you start running your business.

Second Objective

Develop a list of local business and networking organizations you should consider becoming a member. (Chamber of Commerce, Association for Wedding Professionals International, Women in Business groups, NACE-National Association of Catering Executives, Better Business Bureau, local wedding groups, etc.) You will use this information when developing your annual business and marketing plans. Keep in mind that you don't have to join EVERY organization. Compare annual membership rates and benefits and see which programs best fit your business plan.

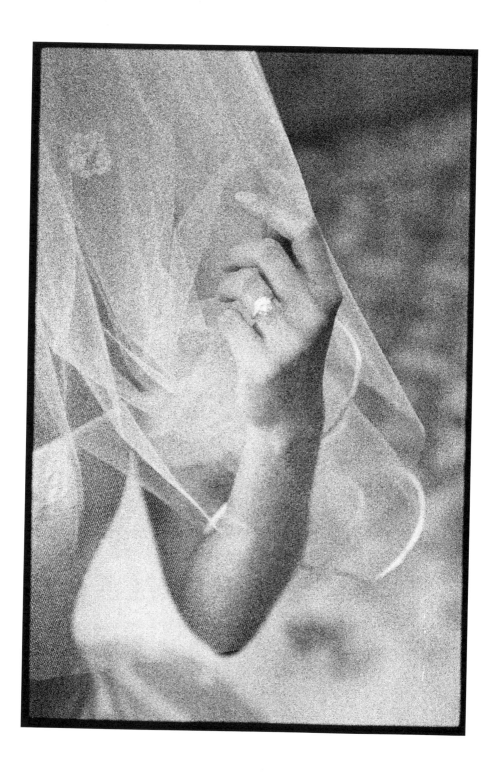

Chapter Two

Engagement

IN THIS CHAPTER YOU WILL LEARN:
- The process of the engagement from a bride's perspective
- How wedding expenses are traditionally divided
- Traditional meanings behind "Something Old, New, Borrowed and Blue"
- The bride's count down to her big moment
- Bridal Shower Ideas, Groom's Check List and Men's Fashions
- FAQ's

"Will you marry me?" the nervous boy asks the young girl, one knee on the ground, anxiously awaiting the response. "YES!" she excitedly accepts his proposal. He slips a diamond ring on her finger to symbolize their engagement and the promise of marriage. From this moment forward, their lives will never be the same. This is the beginning of their lifelong journey, and the first step, the engagement, is already complete.

The Engagement Party

This is the first of many parties and events leading up to the wedding, a sort of kick-off party for the big day. If you establish contact with the bride at this early stage, take advantage of the opportunity to help plan the couple's engagement party. Traditionally, the parents of the bride host the engagement party. It can range from a small gathering of close family and friends to a large gala.

Depending on the size of the event and the budget, an engagement party can include everything from invitations to a cake. Engagement gifts are part of the festivities. The couple probably hasn't registered at this point, but guests usually had an idea that the engagement was probable and may have gift ideas already planned. This is also a time for family heirlooms to be passed down.

The couple can also throw their own engagement party; this is usually a less formal event. The popular practice of gathering friends together for a surprise announcement is another wonderful way to celebrate.

Does a girl need an engagement ring to be engaged?

No. If a couple is in love but cannot afford a ring, that doesn't make them any less committed to each other.

Newspaper Announcement

Find out what your local paper requires to run an engagement announcement. It is a good idea to have the engagement forms or rates already printed out for a new couple. Your job is to make the couple's experience simple and seamless. You can also provide examples of what other couples have put in their announcements or make photo copies to give to the bride so she will have an idea of what to include in her own announcement.

Engagement 101

The following articles are written to the bride and/or groom. Include these ideas in the marketing information you give your couples. They are basic wedding planning ideas and provide the couple with an overview of what they should be doing and what they can expect.

Some Things to Consider

Don't let the upcoming event and responsibilities cause great stress to you and your future mate. It is a fact that wedding planning alone has played a major part in creating stressful situations, disagreements and lifelong grudges. Don't get caught up in all of this. The most important thing to remember is the two of you need to stick together, compromise when necessary and stay focused on the reasons for it all, i.e. what made you decide to get married in the first place.
Family is sure to be involved in wedding planning and decisions. Be conscientious to consider each other's family and traditions and be open to negotiate so that no feelings are hurt in the planning process.

These days there is really no right or wrong way to get married. It is your decision as to which traditional customs you want to include and which you feel could be left out. Check with your wedding consultant about rules of etiquette and ethnic customs.

First Things First

Register for pre-marital education. This will be your most important task when planning a wedding. The choices you make before you wed will determine the success of your marriage and relationship. While "Love Is Blind" is a nice phrase, the divorce rate is a statistic that disproves this saying all too well.

You and your fiancé need to take active responsibility for the future of your marriage. Unless you have been well trained and educated in relationship 101 or marriage "boot camp", the chances your marriage will be a success depends on your level of communication.

*Think of it this way...*marriage is like flying a plane. You would never take the controls and fly a plane without flight school and training. The plane doesn't just take care of itself. It is inevitable that as a pilot you will encounter turbulence, rainy days and stormy weather, but this does not make you a bad pilot. How you handle yourself in these trying situations will determine your career as a whole. It only makes sense to be prepared with skills and education so that when you experience turbulence in your relationship you are prepared as a couple to weather the storm.

Workshops and weekend getaways are available nationally from several resources, possibly including your own church or parish. Taking advantage of opportunities such as these may very well help to save your future marriage.

Set the Date

The wedding date you set will determine where you plan to hold the ceremony as well as the reception. It is important to decide on the location before an official date is set. If you don't have a place in mind, talk with family and friends to find out what weddings they enjoyed the most and where they were held. Your wedding consultant will also have suggestions. Remember to set a date early enough to adequately plan both the ceremony and the celebration. Each requires extensive attention to detail in order to allow you to plan the event of your dreams.

Introductions
You and your fiancé should arrange a meeting of your parents and future in-laws as soon as your engagement is announced. The groom's parents usually make the first move to become acquainted. Inviting them to dinner is usually a good place to start if you and your fiancé are making the arrangements.

Set the Budget
Try to be realistic when setting a budget. Traditionally, parents contribute to the cost of the wedding, so this should be discussed with all parties involved. Remember to account for every aspect of the event, including head count, gratuity, tax, and miscellaneous. By sitting down with everyone involved you can decide who will contribute to what and how much. This will give you a realistic idea of how much you will need and when to cut corners in order to stay within your budget. If working with a wedding consultant, they should be able to help plan within your budget.

Wedding Budget
Who Pays for What?

The Groom

- Wedding ring for the bride
- Wedding gift for bride
- The marriage license
- Gifts for the best man, groomsmen, and ushers
- Fee for the officiant
- Gloves, ties or ascots for the men in the wedding party
- Personal physical examination
- The honey moon

The Bride

- Wedding ring for the groom
- Wedding gift for the groom
- Accommodations for her out-of-town attendants
- Personal physical examination
- Gifts for the bridal attendants

The Groom's Family

- Wedding gift for the couple
- Travel expenses, hotel bills
- Wedding attire
- The Attendants
- Rehearsal Dinner

The Bride's Family

- Invitations, announcements and mailing costs
- Bride's wedding attire
- Ceremony, including rental of sanctuary, fees for organist, soloist, choir, and/or sexton, aisle carpets and/or canopy and any other additional costs for decorations
- Bridesmaids' bouquets
- Engagement and wedding photographs and video.
- Transportation for bridal party to the wedding ceremony and from the ceremony to reception
- The bridesmaids' luncheon
- The reception, including food, wedding cake, beverages, gratuities for the bartenders and waiters, decorations, music, flowers
- Wedding gift for the newlyweds

Wedding Traditions

Your religious beliefs and traditional customs will predetermine how the ceremony is conducted. When couples share a common faith, the planning is usually less complicated than when a couple has separate religious beliefs. You should try to make every attempt to respect the traditions of both families. It is very common for couples to extend the wedding ceremonies into a full weekend of events in order to recognize the customs of both families.

Talk to your grandparents and older family members to learn about traditions they honored at their weddings. Learn about your history and incorporate what is most important to you.

Did you ever wonder???
Something Old, Something New, Something Borrowed, Something Blue...

Something Old: Continuity
Something New: Optimism and Hope
Something Borrowed: Happiness shared from happily married couple
Something Blue: Fidelity, Love, Purity
Lucky Sixpence for Her Shoe: Ensures a Life of Fortune

Groom's Checklist
What's a Guy to Do?

Getting married can be an exciting and overwhelming time. While your bride is busy with all the fine details of planning the wedding, you should be preparing for your personal responsibilities...

- ➤ Buy an engagement ring.
- ➤ Draw up a wedding guest list and have your family make theirs.
- ➤ Choose and invite your best man and ushers for the wedding.
- ➤ With your bride, choose formal wear for you and the ushers.
- ➤ Choose gifts for ushers to be given at the rehearsal dinner.
- ➤ Choose your bride's wedding present; usually it is something personal like jewelry or lingerie.
- ➤ Select a wedding ring with your bride. This should be engraved on the inside with each of your initials and the date. An additional personal message is always special.
- ➤ Plan the honeymoon several months before the big day to ensure reservations.
- ➤ Traditionally, the groom pays for the bride's bouquet, corsages, and boutonnieres.
- ➤ Apply for the marriage license several weeks in advance and give it to the best man the day of the wedding.

- Check to be sure you and your bride have all the necessary papers, birth certificates, blood tests, baptismal certificates, etc.
- Make insurance provisions for your new status.
- Notify your attendants of the time and place of rehearsal.
- Provide the clergyman's fee, which is given to the best man to hold on the wedding day.
- Send a thank-you telegram to your bride's parents the next day saying how enjoyable the event was.

Countdown to "I Do"
Moment by moment as the day unfolds...

The night before:
Sleep, sleep, sleep. You have the biggest day of your life ahead of you. You want to look and feel your best. Be sure to make time with family, especially parents in order to share memories and say thank you. Take photos of your last hours at home as a single person. Take some time by yourself to relax. Close your eyes and visualize every step of the coming day. This will help to relax you and prevent unforeseen incidents.

The morning of:
Have a small meal before leaving for the church. Don't bring too many personal items to the church; the less to worry about, the better. Stay calm. If you run behind schedule, take a deep breath and remember that the ceremony will wait for you!!! Your family and friends want to see you shine, not be frazzled because you are running late, so relax. Looking and feeling wonderful and radiating your happiness is what counts.

Countdown to "I Do"

2 hours till "I Do": Groom, best man and groomsmen get together to begin dressing.

45 minutes: Ushers arrive at the wedding sight, pick up boutonnieres and programs, go over seating plans and wait at the entrance to the church for the guests to arrive.

30 minutes: Organ or other music begins. Final check of marriage license. Mother and attendants leave for the wedding site, ushers begin seating guests.

20 minutes: Groom and best man arrive. Father (or bride's escort) and bride leave for the ceremony site.

10 minutes: Bridal party and parents wait in the back of church while other relatives are seated.

5 minutes: Mother of the groom is escorted to her seat (unless it is a Jewish ceremony). Groom's father walks behind the usher, then takes his seat beside his wife. Mother of the groom enters the pew first with the father sitting on the aisle. Bride and father arrive at ceremony site while mother of the bride is escorted down the aisle.

* 1 minute: If there is an aisle runner, two ushers walk in step to the front of the church and unroll the runner then walk in step to the back of the church, unrolling runner as they go. They then take their place in the procession. Now the moment you have waited for: the minister, priest or rabbi takes his/her place along with the groom and best man. (In Christian tradition, the groom and best man enter from chancel door and stand, at an angle, facing the congregation. The groom stands nearest the minister and the best man one step behind the groom. In Jewish tradition, the groom and best man are part of the wedding procession. As the ceremony begins, the guests will rise to watch the bride make her entrance. Smile... this is your moment!!!

Men's Fashion
The Latest in Tuxedos and Formalwear

For the groom, picking out what to wear is easy, right? Well, not quite. There are many styles of formal wear for men. The time of day your wedding is held, how formal the wedding is, and what your bride is wearing all help determine how you should be dressed. If you're having a formal evening wedding you could wear a white tie and tails or a standard tuxedo. For afternoon formal weddings there are cutaway coats (morning coats) and strollers. Be sure that whatever you choose fits the mood and season of your wedding.

Bow ties and ascots are the two most popular choices of neckwear, though regular neckties are appropriate as well. Because the pattern you choose will also appear on your cummerbund, select something that will look good around both your neck and your waist! Remember that the pleats on cummerbunds always face upward. If you don't like cummerbunds you may decide to wear a vest. Your vest and bow tie don't have to match exactly, but do be sure they don't clash. Tuxedo shirts usually are pleated, but you can decide what type of collar looks best on you. Your shirtsleeves should hang one-half to one inch out of your jacket. French cuff sleeves are popular among many men.

Traditionally, the groom wears black patent leather oxfords. This is your big day, so make sure that your socks match each other and your shoes!

When Honeymoon Dreams Come True
Smart ideas and a few fun locations

If you want to preserve the romance in your honeymoon, make sure your honeymoon planning is practical, realistic and a little street-smart. Here are a few guidelines to get you off to a good start.

Start as early as you can. Last minute honeymoon plans lead to miserable honeymoon experiences.

Find a specialist. Honeymoons are not the same as business travel. The nice folks who helped you line up hotel and flight reservations for your business conference won't be much help, despite their best intentions. Find someone who will sit down with you in person or take the time to talk on the phone (for at least an hour) in order to gather important information about you and discuss your options in detail. You can also locate many online honeymoon travel companies with representatives who specialize in honeymoons. They will be able to help you book your romantic getaway right from your computer.

Clarify what you want to do on your honeymoon (besides the obvious!) so it's easier to identify a suitable location. In between the extremes of catatonic beach bums and die-hard mountain climbers lies a multitude of choices -- shopping, sight-seeing, fine dining, aquatic sports, etc. The best honeymoon specialists begin by having husband and wife each fill out a questionnaire. News flash! You and your spouse-to-be might have different ideas on what constitutes a "great" honeymoon.

Be realistic about what you are prepared to spend. That way, your travel agent doesn't waste time with packages that are unsuitable to your budget. While you're at it, ask your travel agent about setting up a honeymoon registry. That way, it's easy for friends and relatives to contribute to your honeymoon budget (and reduce your inventory of surplus kitchen appliances!).

Know your destination. This is especially true if you plan to travel -- or hold your marriage ceremony -- outside the United States. Every country has its own rules, its own government, its own bureaucratic idiosyncrasies -- you get the idea. Your experienced honeymoon specialist should be all over this stuff like a magnet, knowing what offices to contact, what forms to fill out, what permissions to obtain, etc.

Make lists. (If you're not a "list person," jump into a phone booth and transform yourself immediately!) Bring those lists when you visit your honeymoon specialist so you can write down new things right then and there. With the myriad of details you'll have to manage, lists will not only reduce the risk of forgetting something important, they'll boost your morale as you triumphantly check off item after item.

Consider the pros and cons of travel packages. If you're both adventurous and experienced, they may limit your options. Otherwise, they can solve the problem of keeping yourself fed and beveraged, thus reducing the risk of confronting a five-dollar soda pop when you only have three dollars left.

Get smart advice about spending money. ATM's are convenient, but are they reliable at your location? Traveler's checks are convenient, as long as using them isn't a hassle. Money conversion storefronts are convenient but might be a rip-off. While you're at it, find out the conversion rate for whatever foreign currency you will need.

Include one or two changes of clothing (especially underwear and socks) in your carry-on luggage. Believe it or not, airlines have been known to misroute or lose luggage.

Invest in a document holder that will work with your carry-on luggage. The best honeymoon specialists provide them. Fumbling for paperwork when you're standing in line facing an impatient bureaucrat is a miserable experience.

Parents of the Groom
The role of the grooms parents

When you are the parent of the groom, you're sometimes left out of most of the major decisions made regarding the wedding. The role of the groom's parents traditionally has been to support the groom and the bride's parents by planning around the bride's decisions. Traditionally the groom's parents are responsible for some of the financial responsibilities. Today more and more parents are taking a more involved and active role in this area. Below are some guidelines to keep in mind when you find yourself about to become an in-law.

The parents of the groom should make an effort to meet the bride's family before the engagement is officially announced. Send a note to the bride welcoming her into your family as well as a note to the bride's mother expressing happiness about the couple's engagement.

It's recommended to establish who is paying for what early in the planning process. Tradition tells us that the groom's family's expenses consist of their wedding attire, travel expenses, rehearsal dinner, lodging, and the couple's gift. As tradition meets with modern times more and more financially able families of the groom are assisting with additional costs of the wedding such as flowers and beverages or splitting the cost for the reception dinner. This is more common when the number of guests continues to grow past the couple's budget.

It is extremely helpful to the bride and those involved in the planning process when you compile your guest list promptly and completely. Traditionally the bride or her mother will keep you updated as to responses or wedding gifts received from your family or friends If the father of the groom is also the best man, he should arrange to be fitted for his formalwear as soon as the bride and groom have decided on the style and fashion for the men in the wedding party.

When planning the rehearsal dinner, remember that each member of the wedding party should be included along with their spouses. It is also recommended to invite grandparents and out of town guest if space permits.

Traditionally, the groom's mother is escorted and seated before the bride's mother. The groom's mother sits in the first pew on the right side of the aisle. If her husband in not part of the wedding party, he sits in the same pew.

At the end of the ceremony or during the reception the groom's parents may be asked to participate in the formal receiving line with the bride's parents.

Bride

Congratulations! You are about to embark on a whole new stage in your life: love, engagement and marriage. This will be one of the most stressful, overwhelming, and high points in your life, so enjoy every minute. In this section, you will find several resources to help the bride plan the event of a lifetime as well as unique wedding ideas and suggestions from our experts to help you develop a wedding signature (what makes your wedding different than anyone else's in the world).

The bride sets the mood, theme and tone for the wedding by the dress that she wears. The beauty she radiates and the unique details she incorporates will pull it all together.

When getting married, there are some important issues that need to be addressed right away. The first one is setting a date. The date you set, most of the time, depends on where you plan to hold the ceremony as well as the reception. It's important to determine the location before an official date is set. If you know where you'd like to hold the event, secure the date as soon as possible.

You'll want to decide how many guests you'll be able to invite after determining your budget. Having a master list on hand with total head count will help when pricing for caterers. Usually the bride compiles a list for her side of the family with her parents and the groom with his. You should also compile a "wish list" together, in order to invite additional guests as others decline. The last important list is a Master

Wedding Announcements list. This includes all of your acquaintances not invited to the wedding but with whom you wish to share the news of your marriage. There are several ways to express yourself in your invitations and announcements. Most companies provide suggestions as well as styles. In your area there are certain to be several sources to choose from.

Finding THE Dress

One of the most fun and exciting parts of planning a wedding is finding the right dress. The bride's gown will set the style for the entire wedding. You can start by looking through bridal magazines to determine a style that catches your eye. Once you have an idea of the basics about the dress it's time to browse through the dresses available at a bridal shop. Here you will determine if the style you like in a magazine is the style that looks best on you. There are several bridal shops that carry all of the latest fashions to accommodate all of your needs from head to toe.

After you have an idea of the dress style, you should consider the type of flowers that will compliment your dress. The flowers for the wedding day should have the same uniqueness and creative touch as every other detail of your wedding. You should choose a florist early in the planning process as the best ones book up quickly.

You will most definitely want to capture the entire day on film whether it's pictures or on video. Most couples elect to have both because pictures are tradition and a video of the day captures the mood, music and will be a precious keepsake to view in years to come. It's important to find a reputable photographer; if the film turns out fuzzy or dim you will never be able to precisely reenact the celebration. We suggest you preview the work of any photographer or videographer before making a final decision.

Some photographers provide a video service as well. If you choose a photographer that does not have a video service there are independent video companies you can contact.

The Perfect Flowers

To work a wonder, God would have her shown, at once, a bud, and yet a rose full-blown. - (R. Herrick)

If you have ever had the delicious pleasure of drifting through daffodils and daisies in a springtime field or strolling lazily among the high-hung roses and elegant orchids of a botanist's dream, the exquisite ambience of flowers has not been lost on you.

However, you may feel unsure of how to create the perfect floral experience that will both caress your senses and embrace your emotions. Do you put your trust, as well as a decent portion of your budget, in a professional designer? Do you utilize the vast knowledge of your neighborhood florist while intimating your style and tastes into the selections? Or perhaps you could set out on your own, culling jewels of floral delights from local nurseries.

Aside from the lifelong memories, flowers signify the celebration of your love and new life together. From choosing the boutonnieres and the bridal bouquet to orchestrating a mesmerizing display in the grandest of ballrooms, making the right decisions early in the process will do wonders to ensure your vision becomes a reality on your wedding day.

Depending of the grandeur of your wedding, as well as the scope of your budget, you may employ the services of a professional floral designer. These true artists bring an appreciation for each flower and a working knowledge of the nuances that combine different flora into a beautiful masterpiece of color and fragrance.

If you prefer a more hands-on, less costly approach, your local florist can supply not only a seemingly endless array of flowers and accessories, but also invaluable experience gained from years of helping people realize their visions. Finding a creative florist who is attentive to your wishes and respectful of your budget should be your priority. Locating the right florist early will allow you to establish rapport and benefit fully from the professional advice you will receive.

Perhaps you tend towards the more independent and wouldn't mind shifting resources from your flower arrangement fund to that of your honeymoon. If you enjoy a creative streak that begs for expression, you will be pleasantly surprised with the abundance of fresh flowers available through farmer markets, wholesalers and nurseries in your area. Although you will be hard pressed to find good wedding advice, you will discover the raw material you will need to compose a symphony of sensual delights.

Hair and Makeup Tips

Your makeup should not fulfill "something new" on your wedding day. Practice your makeup several weeks in advance or have a professional makeup artist give you some wedding day tips for looking natural and radiant.

Do not overdo your makeup for photographs and video. You do need to wear more than usual, but your over-all goal is to keep it looking natural. The number one rule for make up is to "Blend, Blend, Blend." Blending helps to achieve a natural look, by avoiding demarcation lines and uneven color.

Use a matte color for your foundation to avoid any extra light reflection showing up in your photographs.

Keep your powder compact accessible all day. You'll want to touch up throughout the entire event (especially since the photographer usually sticks around to catch some of those last minute candid shots of the event).

Do a trial run of your makeup before the big day.

Avoid trying new makeup or skin care within the last two weeks before your wedding.

Remove stray hairs that fall below the brow. When plucking eyebrows, the arch of the brow should line up with the outer circle of your iris.

Define you eyebrows by using a slightly darker shade than your natural color. If you make them too dark, tone them down with a yellow eyebrow powder or use your face powder.

Avoid pink, light blue or frost on the eyes. It will create a tired appearance.

Avoid matching eye shadow to eye color, as diminishes rather than enhances your natural eye color.

For blemishes and pimples, use a concealer one shade lighter than your skin tone and blend evenly.

Gift Giving

It is customary for the bride and groom to start receiving gifts as soon as the engagement is public knowledge. For this reason it is important to have the wedding gift registry available for your family and friends. Many department stores, specialty stores and catalogs allow the bride and groom to list their preferences into the company computer. This helps to ensure you receive exactly what you picked out, right down to the number, style and color of a particular item. It also makes it easier on guests when trying to find the perfect gift for you.

It is customary for the bride and groom to provide gifts to each of the attendants as a token of appreciation and as a memento of your special day. These do not have to be expensive but should be an item that will have lasting memory. Traditionally each bridesmaid and usher receives the same gift. Honor attendants usually receive something more special. Newer trends suggest you customize each gift to the attendant.

It is tradition, but optional for the bride and groom to exchange gifts besides the wedding rings. *Something memorable and special like jewelry is appropriate.*

Bridal Shower Ideas

If you're looking to have a unique bridal shower, themed showers have become very popular in recent years. You can always drop hints to your maid of honor, as it is customary for her to throw the shower.

Lingerie/Personal

Personal showers are a lot of fun. Gifts usually include personal items of lingerie that people don't seem to buy for themselves. A bride needs to have every part of her trousseau, and that especially includes lingerie for the honeymoon. Gifts may include sexy underwear, bras, lacy nightgowns, camisoles or a silky robe. Other personal items include lotions, bath salts, perfume, or a basket full of massage gifts.

Kitchen Showers

There are several companies that will help in hosting a kitchen themed shower. The Pampered Chef and Tupperware are the most popular. Gift ideas become endless and can range from large appliances to inexpensive kitchen utensils. A fun idea for this shower is to have each guest bring a favorite recipe with a gift that will help prepare the recipe.

New Home Showers

A great co-ed shower idea, this is an opportunity to get the groom and his friends involved. The theme of this shower is all about the home. If the couple is moving into a new home after the wedding, have guests hit the local Home Depot or Lowe's and pick up gifts that both the bride AND groom will appreciate, such as charcoal grills, lawnmowers, hammers, etc. The possibilities are endless.

Shower Tips

In order to avoid the possibility of duplicate gifts, it's important that a bride and groom register at two or more department or home furnishing stores. This helps your guest pick out the right colors or theme you are planning to use in your new home. Another way to eliminate duplicate gifts is to assign each shower guest to buy a gift for a specific room in your new home.

The highlight of the shower is opening the gifts. A seat should be specially prepared for the bride. Either her maid of honor or the hostess should sit next to her to record who gave each gift; this helps the bride when she's writing thank-you notes. A new way to do this is to use instant photos. Have the bride pose with each guest and her opened gift. The record-keeper can write the guest's name and a description of the gift on the back of each photo. Later, the photos make a great keepsake for the bride or a lovely token to include with each thank-you note.

Frequently Asked Questions

Every bride wants the most important day of her life to be perfect! To help you plan your perfect day we have compiled a list of the most frequently asked questions. Answers have been compiled from authoritative sources on wedding etiquette, from the engagement to the wedding reception.

Q: If this is a second marriage for the bride and first marriage for the groom, is it proper to give the bride-to-be a bridal shower?

A: Yes, it is proper to throw a shower for a bride even if it is a second marriage. The shower gifts are for both the bride and groom. Without a shower, the new groom would be missing out

Q: Is it proper for the bride on a second marriage to wear white?

A: Usually a bride that is getting married for a second time will wear off white, although the newer fashions have first time brides wearing off white as well. Be sure to wear an off white shirt under your tux; when standing next to your bride for pictures you want to match and you don't want her dress to look yellowed when standing next to you. Brides sometimes wear white for second and even third marriages. Age of the bride will play a role. If she is a younger bride, i.e. under 30, white wouldn't be questionable. If she is older, a classier bride would wear the traditional off white and still look just as beautiful.

Q: Is an engagement ring necessary?

A: No, However, the wedding ring is, as it is an integral part of the wedding ceremony.

Q: *Are engagement presents given?*

A: They are not necessary but on occasion the families or close friends may give small gifts.

Q: *May relatives give showers for the bride?*

A: This is not considered appropriate.

Q: *Should the church and reception invitation be sent out by the bride's parents on the second marriage for the bride or should it be sent out by the bride and groom?*

A: This depends on several factors such as age and financing. If the bride is under 30, you should mention the parents on the invitations, especially if the parents are helping with the wedding plans. If the bride is over 30 it depends on how much the parents are involved in the wedding. If they are contributing financially they should be mentioned in the invitation. If they are not and will be attending as a guest, the invitations should be sent out by the bride and groom.

Q: *When should invitations and announcements be ordered?*

A: Approximately two months prior to the wedding.

Q: *When are invitations for a formal wedding mailed?*

A: Approximately three to four weeks prior to the ceremony.

Q: *Does the fact the groom has been married before affect the bride's wedding plans?*

A: No, plans do not differ.

Q: *If the bride is a young widow, does her family send invitations?*

A: Yes.

Q: Are reception cards included with invitations?

A: Yes, along with reply cards and envelopes with the home address printed on the reply envelopes.

Q: Should invitations be engraved?

A: If the bride wishes. However, simulated engraving is very satisfactory and less costly.

Q: When should announcements be mailed?

A: Approximately a day or two following the wedding.

Q: When are at-home cards mailed?

A: Normally with the announcement.

Q: Are announcements sent to anyone who has been invited to the ceremony or reception?

A: No. Announcements are sent to acquaintances of the bride and groom who are not attending the wedding.

Q: May guests be invited to the reception and not the wedding?

A: Yes, if the ceremony is to be attended by only relatives and close friends.

Q: If the bride's parents are divorced, who handles the invitations and plans the wedding?

A: The bride's mother.

Q: Does the formal invitation to a church wedding require an answer?

A: No.

Q: Are wedding invitations sent to those in mourning?

A: Yes.

Q: How are envelopes of invitations addressed formally?
A: No abbreviations except for Mr., Mrs., Jr., Dr., etc.

Q: Is it proper to use "and family" on invitation envelopes?
A: No. Separate invitations should be mailed to adult sons and daughters. Small children's names should be listed on the inner envelope with only first names under the parents' names.

Q: How should the invitation be inserted into the envelope?
A: The invitation is folded with wording outside and placed in the inner envelope (unsealed) with the folded edge down. The inner envelope is placed in the outer envelope facing the flap.

Q: Who provides the wedding and reception?
A: The parents of the bride.

Q: What does the bride give the bridesmaids?
A: A small lasting gift such as a piece of jewelry.

Q: What does the groom present to his bride as a gift?
A: Usually a personal gift such as jewelry.

Q: How are the wedding bands engraved?
A: Inside the band, first with the bride's initials, then the groom's and then the date of marriage.

Q: How many ushers are needed?

Engagement | 41

A: Usually figure one usher per 50 guests.

Q: Is it required to have the same number of ushers as bridesmaids?
A: No.

Q: Where can receptions be held?
A: The bride's home, the home of a friend, hotel or club.

Q: Where does the bride sit at the Bride's Table?
A: Always on the groom's right.

Q: Do parents sit at the Bride's Table?
A: Yes, or they may have their own table.

Q: If the reception is given by the bride's divorced father, what is the mother's position?
A: The mother is an honored guest, but if this poses a problem, she should refrain from attending.

Q: Are gifts brought to the reception?
A: No.

Q: Are identifying name cards placed with presents on display?
A: No.

Q: Are checks displayed with other wedding gifts?
A: No, but they can be noted on a card.

Q: Is it correct to exchange duplicate gifts?

A: Yes.

Q: Who should read congratulatory telegrams for the guests?

A: The best man.

Q: Who gives the first toast to the bride?

A: The best man.

Q: Which side of the church is to be reserved for the bride's family and friends?

A: The left is for the bride, the right for groom. In some synagogues this procedure is reversed.

Q: If the church has two center aisles, what should be done?

A: Choose one aisle only and conduct the wedding as if it were the only aisle. If you wish, you may use the right aisle for the processional and the left aisle for the recessional.

Q: Is wearing black acceptable by any of the feminine members of the wedding party?

A: Traditionally not, but today black and white weddings are very popular.

Q: Are divorced parents of the bride seated together?

A: No, the mother is seated in the front row with her new husband, if remarried; the father in the third left-hand pew.

Q: Where do the groom's parents sit if they are divorced?

A: The mother in the front right-hand pew, the father in the third pew.

Q: Does the groom always kiss the bride following the ceremony at the altar?

A: This is ruled by the church ceremony. The clergyman will advise the couple.

Q: *Does the groom always kiss the bride following the ceremony at the altar?*

A: This is ruled by the church ceremony. The clergyman will advise the couple.

Q: *Who handles the clergy's fee?*

A: The groom pays the fee, but the best man presents it to the clergy either before or after the ceremony in a plain white envelope.

Q: *Is the clergyman invited to the wedding reception?*

A: Yes, along with his wife, if married. He is seated at the parents' table.

Q: *Do ushers and best man stand in the receiving line?*

A: No.

Q: *Should the bride and groom smoke or hold drinks and food in the receiving line?*

A: No.

Q: *Should the groom dance with others?*

A: Yes, with his mother, mother-in-law and the maids of honor.

Q: *What is "boxed" wedding cake?*

A: Individual pieces of cake in small white boxes for guests to take home. This is done at very elaborate weddings.

Q: *Can a home wedding be as formal as a church wedding?*

A: Yes, but usually there are not as many attendants.

Q: How is a recessional conducted at a home wedding?

A: The couple simply turns around after the ceremony to receive the best wishes of the guests.

Q: How are wedding gifts displayed if a home reception is not planned?

A: A tea or cocktail party may be held for close friends several days prior to the wedding.

Q: Who cuts the first piece of cake?

A: The bride with the groom's right hand over hers. They then break the slice and eat it together. A friend or a waiter then slices the rest of the cake.

Q: How is the reception dance begun?

A: The bride and groom should be honored with the first dance. However, if guests have already started when the couple enters the dance floor, the dancing stops and the couple dance once around the floor alone.

Chapter Two

End of Chapter Suggested Assignments

First Objective

Contact your local newspaper to find out what is required to submit engagement and wedding announcements.

Second Objective

Create five unique bridal shower themes. Put your ideas together so you can use them when you meet with a new bride. You will ultimately want to help coordinate the showers in addition to the wedding.

Third Objective

Make a list of 10 ways to make the groom feel special; it's his day too!

Chapter Three

Your Role as a Wedding Planner

IN THIS CHAPTER YOU WILL LEARN:
- **What questions to ask a new bride-to-be**
- **How to set vendor expectations**
- **How to set the expectations of the bride and her family**
- **Wedding Etiquette**

Bridal Expectations

A bride's wedding day is one of the biggest days of her life. It is the one day in her life when she is guaranteed to have all eyes on her and can be "Cinderella" at her own personal ball. As a young girl, she dreamed of someday walking down the aisle with her prince, and along with that dream comes the expectation of perfection.

The goal of any good wedding planner is to offer the bride and her family peace of mind by staying on top of the planning. A bride and her family should be able to enjoy the occasion, leaving details and hassles to the consultant.

The bride has found her Prince Charming; now she needs to find the perfect dress, those beautiful flowers, a romantic jazz band and the perfect romantic wedding location. In a flash, her dream has turned into panic, and she's not quite sure where to start. Her family and friends offer their assistance and before you know it, she's officially in a wedding planning nightmare and is looking for a professional third party to keep her dream alive.

As a professional wedding planner, your ultimate goal is to assist the bride and guide her in the "right" direction, "right" being relative for each individual bride. You must be a good listener and know how to ask the right questions. Think about yourself and what you would want from a personal assistant. Have the bride explain her vision of the ideal wedding day and pay close attention.

Questions to Ask

You will need to gather basic information such as names of the bride and groom, the wedding date, time, estimated budget and number of guests. You can begin by asking if the couple has already decided on a theme or if they have an idea of the style of wedding they desire.

Instruct the bride to list her most important items first, and then ask what she is flexible on. She may not care about the flowers, but a live band is a must. Utilize a bridal client profiling form to help gather this information and to remind you of all the appropriate questions. A profiling form details the items she needs and leaves room for specific notes and details. Develop a form that works best for the way you work. It should be a tool to streamline the process if you are speaking with a bride over the phone by entering her information directly into an online document or PDF form. This enables emailing of documents to and from your bridal clients. You should invest in Adobe Acrobat or MS Word to create documents you can email or print out for your clients. The need to streamline communication will become apparent very quickly.

Many wedding planners develop a formula of questions to ask each bride during the interviewing process. This formula helps to guide the consultant as she creates the bride's vision and adds the consultant's special touch of creativity to help express the bride's and groom's unique personalities.

Once you have planned her day, you can start researching the market for her treasures.

Vendor Expectations

So you have your bride's blueprint for a perfect wedding, but now what? It's time to start calling on vendors.

Vendors like to deal with a professional who knows what the bride wants. Even if you're not sure exactly what is needed, at least you've done enough research that you have some idea of which direction to go in.

When dealing with a vendor keep in mind that the vendor is the expert in their field. If you work with the best vendors, your business will be a success; your brides will be happy with your service and the outcome.

Do your research. The key to a successful consultant is her network of vendors who provide excellent service. Talk to more than one vendor in each industry, get samples, get price lists and obtain references. Know your market. Vendors want to work with consultants they can trust to understand the wedding business as well as their own business. Remember, you cannot present a vendor to a bride if you haven't taken the time to research each vendor and the packages and/or styles offered. Be professional and learn as much as you can from your vendors. Your bridal clients will appreciate your wealth of knowledge and the expertise of the vendors you chose to help represent your business.

Hint: Your business is only as good as your worst vendor, so be selective.

Family Expectations

Even though the marriage is a commitment between the bride and groom, whether they like it or not they are also marrying into each other's families. This starts with the engagement. A bride's decision to use a wedding planner may cause tension with family members and even close friends.

Everyone has their own expectations of how they believe Suzie's wedding should be and will probably voice their opinions and advice. A wedding planner is there to help the bride and to sometimes ward off opinionated loved ones. Keep in mind you are working for the bride, and during your first meeting with her it's a good idea to ask about family expectations and her feelings about them. This will alleviate any problems throughout the planning stages.

Wedding Etiquette

As the wedding planner, your clients will rely on your knowledge and expertise when it comes to proper wedding etiquette. Today's contemporary couples find many non-traditional ways to take their vows, and it is up to you, the consultant, to guide them towards the most respectful and tasteful ways.

Use Good Judgment

If you find yourself in a position where your views are not in line with the desires of your couple-to-be, remember to use good judgment when giving your advice. Many couples will throw tradition and proper etiquette to the wind in order to express their own vision of the perfect day.

Build a Library

There are hundreds of books on the market that cover the proper do's and don'ts of a wedding and the process leading up to the big event. As a professional wedding planner it is your responsibility to brush up on all traditional wedding etiquette. Start by building a library of books that cover etiquette for many ethnicities and also include suggestions and ideas on how to incorporate different ethnic backgrounds into a wedding. You will find such books to be a valuable resource of information right at your fingertips whenever you need it. As you build your business you will also build your fund of knowledge through experience and research as you plan for each couple's wedding.

Resources

- *Wedding Etiquette* - by Peggy Post

- *Etiquette, 4th Edition*- by Emily Post

- *The Perfect Wedding* - by Maria McBride-Mellinger
- *Multicultural Celebrations* - Today's Rules of Etiquette for Life's Special Occasions - by Norine Dresser

- *Wedding Question & Answer Book* - by Diane Warner

- *I do, I do, America's Wedding Etiquette of Yesteryear* - by Suzanna A. Driver

- *The Traditional Irish Wedding* - by Bridget Haggerty

- *Irish Wedding Traditions: Using Your Irish Heritage to Create the Perfect Wedding* - by Shannon McMahon-Lichte, Patricia Brentano (Illustrator)

- *The Booke of Betrothal: Verses, Vows & Etiquette for the Romantic, Renaissance Couple* - by Laura Crockett

- *The Catholic Wedding Book* - by Molly K. Stein, William C. Graham (Contributor)

- *Viva el amor: The Latino Wedding Planner, A Practical Guide for Arranging a Traditional Ceremony and a Fabulous Fiesta* - Edna Bautista

- ❖ *Bride's Book of Etiquette* - by Bride's Magazine, Millie Martini Bratten

- ❖ *Polish Weddings Customs & Traditions* - by Sophie Hodorowicz Knab

- ❖ *The Little Giant Encyclopedia of Wedding Etiquette* - by Wendy Toliver

- ❖ *Getting Married When It's Not Your First Time: An Etiquette Guide and Wedding Planner* - by Pamela Hill Nettleton
- ❖ *Wedding Etiquette for Divorced Families: Tasteful Advice for Planning a Beautiful Wedding* - by Martha A. Woodham

- ❖ *Miss Manners on Weddings* - by Judith Martin

- ❖ *The Everything Jewish Wedding Book* - by Helen Latner

- ❖ *Emily Post on Second Weddings* - by Elizabeth L. Post

- ❖ *The Bride's Etiquette Guide: Etiquette Made Easy* - by Pamela A. Lach

- ❖ *Weddings, a Family Affair: The New Etiquette for Second Marriages and Couples With Divorced Parents* - by Marjorie Engel

- ❖ *The New Book of Wedding Etiquette: How to Combine the Best Traditions with Today's Flair* - by Kim Shaw

Chapter Three

End of Chapter Suggested Assignments

First Objective

Create your own Bridal Client Profile Form, which you can utilize when first meeting a prospective client. The form should include a checklist of items including contact information and a general outline of the basic items the couple is looking for. This form will help you get organized as you move through the planning process.

Second Objective

Using your library of wedding etiquette books develop a list of duties for each responsible bridal party member outlining specific duties to perform throughout the planning process, wedding day and post wedding day.

Include each of the following:

Best Man

Maid of Honor

Bridesmaids

Groomsmen and Ushers

Flower girl

Ring bearer

Mother of the Bride

Father of the Bride

Mother of the Groom

Father of the Groom

Provide simple instructions for each member to follow. Use these as handouts so that each person is aware of their role at the wedding.

Tip: Leave a blank area for notes so that specific directions can also be added to tailor your templates to each individual wedding.

Third Objective

Start building your wedding etiquette library. Your first selection should be the Emily Post's "Wedding Etiquette, 4th Edition". It is a wonderful etiquette book that covers the basics for the new wedding planner. Read it cover to cover.

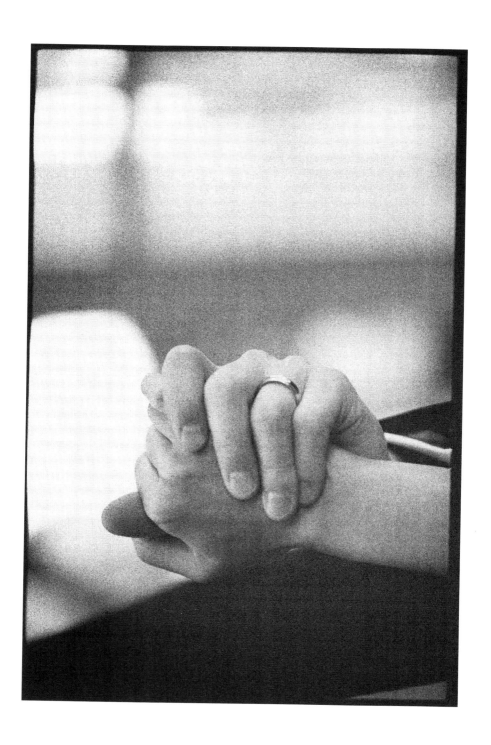

Chapter Four

Running Your Own Business

IN THIS CHAPTER YOU WILL LEARN:

- How to structure your business based on your marketplace
- How to evaluate your competition when establishing your services
- How to set preliminary marketing objectives
- Tools and tips for organizing your home office and business practices
- Business start-up costs

The decision you have made to start your own business is one to be proud of. Many successful people have come to realize working for yourself and building your fortune is time well spent. You may have come to this decision for several different reasons. It may be a time of taking control of your independence, a major life change such as a new child or job loss, or just a decision that now is the time to take charge and work for yourself. Nothing is more motivating and empowering than knowing you are your own boss. You control what you will and will not do each and every day. The gift of flexibility and time for your family is priceless.

Whatever your decision is to start your own business, aim high and strive to achieve your own personal goals. Dreams can come true if you keep your focus, enthusiasm and passion.

Marketplace

Weddings are big business and no matter where you live, couples are getting married. If you plan your business carefully and your business model is solid and well structured, you will be positioned for success in a fruitful yet competitive industry.

Every market area is different. You will discover through trial and error the tools that are best suited to your marketplace, your business goals and lifestyle. It is possible to apply different aspects of a traditional business model with a referral-based system, or you can strictly stick with one or the other. Keep in mind that as a business owner, you will have to change with the economic times, and what works for you today may not work six months or six years from now. As your business grows, your initial business plan will need to grow with it. As you start to develop your own vision you'll understand how to apply your business model in your day-to-day business practices and marketplace.

Your Local Wedding Market

Run the numbers. Run the numbers. Run the numbers. Start running the numbers and never stop researching. Estimating your income potential and the number of weddings you can anticipate booking and attending through the year is all based on the number of weddings taking place in your market. You will need the answers to the following questions in order to project revenue for your business for the coming year:

How many weddings take place in your local market per year?
This obvious question will help you determine what piece of the pie you can take. If there are 10,000 weddings per year in your city and currently 50% (5,000) are using wedding planners and there are only three bridal consultants in your market…your business has the potential to be very successful! Divided evenly would give you a potential target market of over 1,000 brides per year. Realistically, if you are a one-person operation, you will be hard pressed to capture and handle 1,000 brides in a year's time, so scaling that number back further still provides for a successful wedding planning business. Realistically you will plan one wedding a weekend until you hire additional help.

Keeping in mind that these numbers are only offered as an example, you should approach your research in this manner and start running the numbers! Remember to use realistic figures and research to see how many weddings per year the competition is doing. This will give you a better view of what you can realistically capture for your business. Contact your local marriage license office for an accurate count of marriage ceremonies in your local area.

When is the busy wedding season?

Summer is going to be your busy season if you live in the North East. If you live in the South your wedding season will be longer, especially for those couples looking to have their ceremony outdoors. Southwest weddings are more popular in the winter months due to the extreme heat during the mid-summer. If you live in Alaska... well, you get the idea. Find out when you'll need to plan on attending more weddings and performing your day-of-service.

What is the off-season?

Off-season is when it is slow; less wedding ceremonies take place during the off-season. Just because it's called the "off-season" doesn't mean you won't be busy. Your off-season may involve more pre-planning for your brides that will then keep you busy during the "busy" season. When creating your business plan, keep in mind what your focus will need to be during particular months of the year based on local wedding activity. Most wedding businesses use this off-season time to market themselves more heavily and build up their business for the busy season.

When are the local bridal shows?

Start researching NOW! Bridal shows will be a staple in the success of your business, and by planning ahead you can incorporate the shows in between your wedding dates. Don't wait until the last minute to book your first bridal show booth as they go quickly and most shows limit the number of vendors per category. If there are other wedding planners in your market be sure to stay on top of what shows are more popular and successful in your market. You will want to ensure you have booth space at these. Take this opportunity also to introduce yourself to other wedding vendors and set appointments to meet them following the show in order to learn more about their services.

Research Bridal Show Producers International www.bspishows.com. There is sure to be a show producer in your area. Call them up introduce yourself, you may find them to be a great source for networking. Another source for bridal shows to exhibit or attend is: www.bridalshownearyou.com.

Competition

As a wedding planner you will be competing with other independent wedding planners in your market. As stated above, you'll need to do your research. Find out who your local competition is and who they are working with; again, aim high. Look at how other consultants work in your area and structure your business model accordingly. Then think about what will make your business unique; think outside the box. Ask yourself the following questions:

How many wedding planning businesses are in your market?

Once you research the number of weddings and the seasons, etc., you should apply that number to the number of wedding planners currently working in your market to calculate your potential earnings.

What does your competition charge?

Get their rates and wedding planning packages. Structure your fees accordingly and see where you can get creative. You want to keep yourself profitable, but also price yourself to be competitive.

Typically wedding planners charge 10-15% of the total budget for their services.

This includes a combination of pre-planning and day-of-services.

Costs of Pre-Planning vs. Day-of-Service?

Find out what your competition charges for their pre-planning vs. their day of charge for attending the wedding. What is included in their services? How many hours are included? Is there an additional charge for the busy season? What other services in addition to wedding planning do they offer? Many will charge an hourly rate although you may find charging a flat rate to be more accommodating to your client's needs. Your local market will dictate the going rate for your services. Do your research and price yourself accordingly.

You can enhance your business with additional services that other consultants may not have available. Invitations, discounted rose programs, wedding music CDs, etc. Find out what they are offering and then see how you can use your skills and resources to benefit and entice brides to want to work with your business. Make your business unique.

Who are the vendors your competition is working with?

There are always going to be premier or high dollar vendors, and then there will be those less expensive vendors, but regardless of the cost of using a caterer or DJ...everyone has a reputation. As you grow your business you will find that you may prefer to work with one vendor instead of another and you'll develop relationships, which will hopefully help to blossom your own business. GOOD VENDORS WILL HELP YOU GROW YOUR BUSINESS. Check out who your competition is using and search for vendors with a reputation for quality and service.

Where is your competition marketing?

Did you ever notice that fast food restaurants are all located in the same area? It's no accident; it is called marketing. If you want a Big Mac and your sister wants a Whopper...you can both be satisfied. There is sure to be a McDonalds and a Burger King within several hundred yards of each other. A person looking for a fast food lunch only needs to decide which drive thru window to choose.

It's the same in the wedding planning business. You're sure to find your competition at the local bridal shows, advertising in local bridal magazines and in the yellow pages. Don't give them an unnecessary advantage. You'll need to put your business into the mix and then also find ways to introduce innovative marketing strategies to put you above the rest. You'll learn more about how to be a strategic marketer in the coming weeks.

What business organizations does your competition belong to?

Just as it's important for McDonalds to be on the opposite street corner as Burger King, successful businesses must take advantage of local industry organizations and networking opportunities. Find out which local wedding associations and business organizations they belong to and join them. You will find the sooner you establish yourself with the competition, the quicker your business will grow.

How many weddings do they handle each year?

Don't be shy. It's not possible that a competing wedding planner can possibly handle ALL of the weddings in your local market, so just ask. Birds of a feather stick together, so go ahead and introduce yourself to the competition. You may be able to utilize her services when you are double-booked for the same wedding day. If your competition gets sick one Saturday, they may be looking for someone to cover for them and vice versa.

Finding Business

Start working smart. Always look at the big picture, whether you are planning on a full or part-time business. Take the time to research your market so that you can apply the upcoming lessons to your advantage. Work at your own pace and don't worry; you can never have done too much research. The industry is always changing, and keeping abreast of what's going on in your market will be a good habit to start right out of the gate.

Get started by putting together a preliminary marketing itinerary for the first month of your business. It will ensure a successful start.

Example: Sample Sue One-Month Marketing Objectives

Purchase a marketing list of 1000 brides in my area.

Order and mail postcards to brides on my marketing list offering my wedding planning services.

Attend the next bridal show in my area as a vendor.

Begin networking with other vendors.

Being organized and having your home office in order is crucial to the success of your business. If you can't find the phone because it's under a stack of papers, you're going to miss out. Here are the basics to help you stay organized:

Computer

High-speed Internet access

Printer

Fax/copier

Standard supplies (file folders, paper clips, file cabinet.)

Phone, cell phone, voice mail, email, website.

Office or home office work space

There are excellent printer/copier/fax machines for under $200 that provide great quality and come in one unit, which saves on space. Your initial business expenses should include a solid education, business licenses and membership fees to your local networking organizations. Don't let yourself get trapped into buying an expensive desk and office supplies since you'll be meeting most of your brides at your vendors' place of business. Invest in what counts.

Information Organization

To simplify your organization, you should keep detailed records, preferably in a contact management software program like ACT! or Outlook. These inexpensive software programs keep track of all the details for every client, vendor and event. A resource you will not want to work without. Be sure to research the capabilities of each program before making your purchase.

Don't expect that you will remember everything for every wedding, but you can be certain that a client will expect you to remember everything for <u>her</u> wedding. You must have some sort of software or filing system which will allow you to juggle numerous tasks with ease, keep your details straight and keep your stress level to a minimum.

ACT! can be found at most office supply stores or on the web at www.act.com.

Wedding planning software is also available, and it's a great way for you to keep your bridal timelines in order and keep you on track for each couple you work with. There are many to choose from that will offer a 30 day free trial. Start by doing a search online using the keywords: "Wedding Planning Software". Research which program will best fit your needs and style of planning.

Start-up Capital

The investment in your education and certification should be your first business expense.

You will then need to take care of any office equipment, accounting software like Quickbooks, and you'll need, marketing materials, association memberships, advertising expenses, etc.

How quickly you start your marketing and networking efforts will determine how quickly your business will be up and running. Look at your time and effort as part of your "investment capital" in addition to any monetary investment. Your hard work will help you reap financial rewards in the future.

One piece of advice: set a budget and stick to it. It will take you about a year before you have true understanding of what works, what's important to invest your capital in and what your return on investment will be. Planning for business expenses is just like helping a bride budget for her wedding. Pay attention to detail. The little things add up.

Here is a breakdown of the estimated basic start-up costs for a wedding planning business that is run from a home office. If you are planning on having a storefront, add the additional cost for office/space rental. This will depend on your location and market. Most companies will charge you per square foot. The average rate usually falls between $50.00 to $100.00 per square foot. These costs are estimates and are only provided as an example. Contact your local commercial real estate company for details.

Education
- Wedding Planner Certification $895
- Sales and/or marketing classes/books $300

Legal Fees $300

Business License $ 50

Insurance $200

Office Equipment and Furniture
- Computer $800
- Printer/Fax/Copier $200
- Software
  - Accounting $200
  - Wedding Planning $200
  - Contact Management $200
- Phone/voicemail (flat rate plan) $ 50
- Desk $100
- Filing cabinets $ 50
- Bookcases $100

- Chair(s) $ 60
- Work table $ 50

Marketing Materials

- Letterhead $100
- Envelopes $ 50
- Business cards (vistaprint.com) $ 50
- Fax and copy paper $ 30
- Media kits and folders $500
- Brochures $300
- Miscellaneous $100

Website

- Domain registration $ 10
- Design $600
- Hosting (per month) $ 35

Business Associations

- Association for Wedding Professionals $175
- Better Business Bureau $375
- Local Wedding Association $150

Monthly Advertising Expenses

- Wedding Planning Network (co-op marketing) $100
- Phone book listing $100
- Newspaper classified advertisement $100
- Wedding Magazine classified ad $200

Miscellaneous
- Miscellaneous $270

Estimated Start-up Costs = $7,000.

Tips:

> - If you already have your home office established, you can eliminate those specific expenses.
> - Get a flat rate phone line so you know what your expenses will be every month.
> - Space out when you enroll into different associations and business organizations so that you are not paying your membership dues simultaneously. You will be glad you did when it comes time for your annual renewal.
> - Purchase your marketing materials from a reputable vendor who can provide you with all your marketing materials. It will lessen on logo and printing charges and you should save in the long run.
> - Stick with a one-color logo. It is expensive to have more than one color, and black *is* considered a color. Choosing pink and black would count as two colors.
> - Don't skimp on your marketing efforts. Cut corners in other areas before deciding to not market at all. Even during the slow seasons, it should be one of your monthly expenses, just like your phone bill. Marketing drives sales and revenue. If you cannot afford to spend at least $250-500 per month on marketing, you should not be in business.

Reputation

How can you have a reputation if you're a new player in the market?

You need to build it.

This is where becoming a member of local business organizations such as a local wedding association or Chamber of Commerce and having your wedding planning certification by a nationally recognized organization like Wedding Planning University will lend credibility. Even though you may be the new kid on the block, you can show that you mean business by associating yourself with the best professional organizations.

Once you're in the door, you'll create a name for yourself by being professional, reliable and knowledgeable about your craft. Continue to educate yourself in the coming months and years, take it upon yourself to keep up with changes in your market and stay abreast of wedding trends that return or become outdated from time to time.

Accounting

Accounts receivable, accounts payable and invoices…oh my! What's a consultant to do? You do what you love to do: plan weddings. Find a reputable accountant, invest in accounting software such as Quick Books or find a service which can handle your accounting needs. Keeping good financial records is a must. Running a business is all about the bottom line, i.e. what is on the books. You should always stay within your budget, pay your bills on time and be sure to pay yourself.

Personal Appearance

Image IS everything, whether it is the look of your website, the delivery of your voicemail message or the look of your marketing materials. Uphold the highest standards.

When you meet a bride, you should be dressed in a professional manner. Whether a bride spends $20,000 or $200 on her wedding, she should be given the red carpet treatment. Your personal appearance will lend credibility to both the bride and vendors.

Ladies, make sure your hair is neat, your make-up is professional, your stockings are run free and your nails are nicely groomed. Gentlemen, see that your shoes are polished and your tie is pressed. Everyone please be aware of your oral hygiene. You will lose business if your breath is not fresh.

Image also includes your presence in a meeting and how you converse. Your language should not include slang or profanity. Be respectful at all times; you never know who you are speaking to. Be timely for meetings, call when you will be late, send thank you notes, and email a follow up after each meeting with both couples and vendors.

A Road Map to Success: Your Business Plan

Most new business owners become uneasy when it comes to writing a business plan. Where to begin, what's included, projections, research, market analysis and financial calculations inspire many people to leave this key business tool to chance. It is important to understand that a business plan is an ever-changing document that will develop and evolve as you uncover the recipe for success in your business. Writing a business plan helps to organize your thoughts, goals and objectives over a period of time. In the same way you organize and plan a vacation to make sure you visit and experience all there is to do on your trip, you will want to do the same with your business plan. Preplanning helps to uncover potential problem so you can prepare ahead of time and anticipate changes to the original plan.

In the beginning, a business plan is more of a vision of what you anticipate you business to look like in one, three or five years. You can start by describing your business and business model in one to two paragraphs. Later you can plug in additional information as you piece your plan together. The following is an outline to follow when writing a business plan.

1. Executive Summary
    a. Objectives
    b. Mission
    c. Keys to success
2. Company Summary
    a. Company Ownership
    b. Company History
    c. Past Performance
3. Services
    a. Service Description
    b. Competition Summary
    c. Sales
    d. Fulfillment

e. Future Services
4. Market Analysis
    a. Target Market
    b. Market Need
    c. Market Trends
    d. Market Growth
5. Strategy and Implementation Summary
    a. Marketing Strategy
    b. Positioning Statement
    c. Promotion Strategy
    d. Pricing Strategy
    e. Sales Forecast
    f. Competitive Edge
6. Management Summary
    a. Organizational Structure
    b. Management Team
    c. Management Team Gaps
    d. Personnel Plan
7. Financial Plan
    a. Important Assumptions
    b. Key Financial Indicators
    c. Break-Even Analysis
    d. Projected Profit and Loss
    e. Projected Cash Flow
    f. Balance Sheet

There are many software programs on the market to help create a business plan by utilizing an existing template that best fits your business. One we recommend is Business Plan Pro by Palo Alto Software.

http://www.palo-alto.com

Entrepreneur.com is also an excellent resource to learn more about the structure of a business plan. The site walks you through the process of structuring your business plan from start to finish.

http://www.entrepreneur.com/howto/bizplan

Chapter Four

End of Chapter Suggested Assignments

First Objective

Research your local competition. Compile a list of competition and provide names, phone numbers, addresses, etc. Include any additional information you may find, such as years in business, how they charge their clients, etc. The phone book and online research will be your best resources. Create files or a "Competition Manual" so that you can quickly reference competitive information as necessary. When speaking with brides or vendors you will have the knowledge at your fingertips.

Second Objective

Contact your local marriage license office to find out how many licenses are applied for annually in your local market. This will give you an idea of how many weddings take place in your area. This office may also be able to provide you with additional information, depending on your market.

Third Objective

Find out what the process is to obtain a marriage license. You should keep up with the local procedures to ensure your couples are prepared and all their paperwork is in order in time for the big day.

Fourth Objective

Research and compile a list of the local bridal shows in your market.

Fifth Objective

Is your home office in order? Get your home office organized so that will be ready to run down the aisle at a moment's notice!

Sixth Objective

Write the beginning of what will eventually be your business plan. First step: write your mission statement. You can't start a business without putting your thoughts and ideas down on paper. Let this be your first draft; it will develop as you move through each chapter. A simple paragraph on why you want to start this business is a great place to begin. What do you plan on getting out of this experience? Fame? Fortune? Freedom? Personal happiness? Write down your goals and objectives as you see them with regards to the "big picture".

Your final business and marketing plan will include all the specific details of your one, two, five year plan, etc. This first objective is something you will have to help you design and structure your ideas so you have an overall vision on where you are going.

You should be finished with your business plan outline summary by the time you are done with this book. The details of the plan will be a work in progress and will continue to change as your business grows.

Chapter Five

Documentation and Goals

IN THIS CHAPTER YOU WILL LEARN:
- **The importance of documentation**
- **How documentation of your business practices plays an imperative role in the success of your business**
- **How to set goals for yourself and your business**

Where do you want to be five years from today?
If you are starting your business today, what do you want your business to look like in five years? How many clients will you have? How many events or weddings will you be planning? How much money will you be making? How will you spend your day? What will your competitors say about you? What will your clients say? What reputation will you have established?

Having a specific goal and working each day to move closer to it is your road map to success. Just like a builder who works by his blue prints, you need to have a plan to follow to lead you in your desired direction.

Ask yourself: where do you want to be in 10 years?

Will your business goals today be the same 10 years from now? Probably not. To run a successful event planning business, or any business, you must accept change. When you start out, YOU ARE the business. You need to lay the foundation by getting your name out there and developing a reputation and your referral base. This process can take anywhere from six months to two years. Most traditional wedding planners fail because they stay in the early construction mode and never move up to "running" their business. They ARE the business. When the owner stops...the business stops.

You cannot BE the business.
Understanding that your business must be able to function without you is one many small business owners never comprehend. You are only one person and there is only so much time in a day to accomplish what needs to be done. What happens to your business when you want to

take a vacation? What happens as you get older? You may want to slow down. Will that mean the business will also slow down or even stop? Not if you have the right plan.

You Reap What You Sow.

As the old adage goes, we reap what we sow. In other words, your hard work today will pay off in the years to come.

Begin now to build your business with the idea that others will work for you as wedding and social event planners. Your name and reputation for producing fabulous signature events will be the business, not you personally. Your unique style and the designer weddings you create will all be documented so that others in YOUR business can perform the day-to-day tasks just as you want it, keeping you free to manage the business. For example, if your recipe for a French country outdoor wedding includes favor boxes made from twigs with exactly four inches of ivy, then that is exactly how you should document it so that others in your business can duplicate your recipe, style and signature events.

This allows you to work ON your business...not IN your business. What are the three most important things when buying real estate? If you have ever purchased a house you know they are **location, location, location.**

The three most important things to remember when building a business is **documentation, documentation, documentation.**

That's right: the best thing you can do for your business is to document how you do things and put down on paper exactly how you want them to be done.

Look at your business as a one-story building when you first start out. You've invested in the structure and blueprint designs by reading this book, because you know and trust the experts, the writers...the "construction company". An education will provide you with the tools to help lay the foundation, provide the beams for your structure and help to erect the interior and exterior walls.

As the business owner and partner, you need to make your business unique. You're the interior designer. Fill it up with your own style and creativity. When you're ready, you can add on another floor, you can duplicate your original first floor design or create a whole new second floor look. It's up to you. It's your vision that will make it special.

So how do you get your vision across to someone else?

Simple. Create manuals for each process, each style of wedding, and each social event. Include anything that needs to be repeated so that others in your company can perform these tasks exactly, *right down to the number of petals sprinkled on each table top.* If you capture this information as you develop and build your business you will be prepared when you are ready to bring on additional help.

Success comes in many shapes and sizes...only YOU can make it happen!

Chapter Five

End of Chapter Suggested Assignments

First Objective

Create a list of items you see that will be important to be documented. Outline each department (accounting, marketing, sales, day-to-day operations, etc.) Your processes and procedures will change as your business grows, but with everything documented from the beginning, it will be easier to update in the future.

Chapter Six

Vendor Selection

IN THIS CHAPTER YOU WILL LEARN:
- **Why vendor selection is a key element to the success of your business**
- **How to identify quality vendors**
- **What questions to ask when building your vendor network**

A professional wedding consultant builds her business on reputation, one wedding at a time. The secret to this business is your relationship with your vendors. You should be able to explain and present your vendors' services, packages and styles to your brides well enough so it is as if you worked for each vendor directly.

Vendor Relationships: The Key to Your Business

Developing positive relationships with vendors will give you a wonderful start to building your business. Select vendors who can offer you special services your client needs. They will choose to work with you because you can provide them with the customers their own business requires. Bringing a vendor business makes them happy. Providing the bride with quality services makes her happy, and creating a lasting relationship makes your business grow. If this happens, *everyone* wins!

Hint:

Your business is only as good as your *worst* vendor, so **be selective**.

Questions for Professional Vendors...

Asking the right questions when researching your area for quality vendors is the first step to building a solid vendor network to support your bridal consulting business.

Vendor Questions

> ➤ Interviewing your vendors will help you select the best vendor for each individual job. For every professional you need to possess basic knowledge regarding the services they provide.
> ➤ General questions you should ask of all vendors include the following:
> ➤ How long have they been in business?
> ➤ What is their pricing structure?
> ➤ What makes their service unique from their competitors?
> ➤ Have they received special awards or acknowledgements?
> ➤ Have they worked at this facility before?
> ➤ Can they provide references?

You should also have specific questions for different categories of vendors.

Bakery

> ✓ Are their cakes made fresh daily? (Some bakeries will freeze cakes and decorate when it is time to fill the order)
> ✓ Are they familiar with the latest trends?
> ✓ Do they deliver and set up?
> ✓ Do they have a nice variety of flavors for cakes as well as unique fillings?
> ✓ Are they able to recreate a cake from a picture?
> ✓ Do they have a design book with ideas?
> ✓ Do they offer cake tastings? Is there a charge?
> ✓ Can they provide references?

Florists

> ✓ Where do they get their flowers?
> ✓ Do they do their own designing?
> ✓ Do they deliver and how far do they travel?
> ✓ Will they set up the event or do they send assistants?
> ✓ How many weddings/events do they do in one day?
> ✓ Have they decorated at this facility before?
> ✓ Can they provide references?

DJ

- ✓ It is particularly important to determine how long they have been doing weddings. A club DJ and a wedding DJ are **not** the same.
- ✓ What types of music do they play?
- ✓ Do they have a nice variety that can please a diverse crowd?
- ✓ Do they provide a song list to the bride and groom?
- ✓ Do they bring assistants?
- ✓ Do they have props or special games?
- ✓ Will they be attending your event or will it be another DJ?
- ✓ Will they act as MC for the event? If yes, is there an additional fee?
- ✓ Do they have any special electrical requirements?
- ✓ Do they have a wireless microphone?
- ✓ How much room do they need for set-up?
- ✓ How much time does it take to set-up and take down?
- ✓ Can they provide references?

Bands

- ✓ It is particularly important to determine how long they have been doing weddings. A band that only plays clubs is not a good sign.
- ✓ What type of music do they play?
- ✓ Do they have a nice variety that can please a diverse crowd?
- ✓ Do they provide a song list to the bride and groom?
- ✓ Have they worked at the selected reception site before?
- ✓ Do they have props or special games?
- ✓ Will they act as MC for the event? If yes, is there an additional fee?
- ✓ Do they have any special electrical requirements?
- ✓ Do they have a wireless microphone?
- ✓ How much room do they need for set-up?
- ✓ How much time does it take to set-up and take down?
- ✓ Obtain a list of events they are playing so you can see them live BEFORE making a final decision.
- ✓ Can they provide references?

Photographer

- ✓ Have they worked the facility before? (This is very important for lighting and selecting locations to take the pictures.)
- ✓ What is their photographic style?
- ✓ Do they take a photojournalism approach to their photography?
- ✓ Do they bring an assistant with them?
- ✓ How many cameras do they use?
- ✓ Do they take black and whites? Sepia tones?
- ✓ How long will it take to get the proofs back?
- ✓ Do they charge for proofs?
- ✓ Do they have online viewing and ordering?
- ✓ Do they offer an "a la carte" package?
- ✓ Do they give you the negatives?
- ✓ How long do they keep your negatives on file?
- ✓ Do they do their own developing?
- ✓ Do they have their own studio?
- ✓ Do they do engagement photo sessions as part of their package?
- ✓ Can they provide references?

Videographer

- ✓ Have they worked the facility before? (Important for them to know for set-up.)
- ✓ Do they bring an assistant?
- ✓ How many cameras do they use?
- ✓ How long before the video is ready?
- ✓ Do they do their own editing?
- ✓ Do they use digital cameras?
- ✓ Can they provide references?

Limousine Service

- ✓ Will they be the driver attending the service?
- ✓ Do they contract out to other limo companies?
- ✓ How many cars do they have? What sizes?
- ✓ Do they have vintage cars?
- ✓ Do they share cars with other limo companies?
- ✓ Are the cars available for viewing?
- ✓ How many drivers do they have? What do their drivers wear?

- ✓ Do they offer any special touches such as red carpet, roses, keepsake photos, champagne, etc.?
- ✓ Can they provide references?

Caterers

- ✓ Ensure the ingredients are fresh. Obtain a reference list of events they have worked.
- ✓ Ask if they are a preferred vendor for any local sites. Which ones?
- ✓ Have they worked the site you have reserved?
- ✓ Do they do on-site cooking and food prep?
- ✓ What are their specialty dishes?
- ✓ Ask for a copy of the banquet menu.
- ✓ Do they offer a nice variety of dishes?
- ✓ Do they have a specialty? What is their style of cooking?
- ✓ Are they able to create ethnic, vegetarian, diabetic meals, etc?
- ✓ Do they offer tasting? Is there a charge?
- ✓ Are they willing to work within your budget to provide you with a menu that satisfies your needs?
- ✓ How many staff do they require? What is their attire?
- ✓ Do they have bartenders who work with them?
- ✓ Do they provide rentals? (Dishes, china, flatware, linens, tables, etc.)
- ✓ Do they utilize food stations, buffets, and/or sit down?
- ✓ Is there a set-up or tear down charge?

Bridal Shops

- ✓ What are the local going rates in your market?
- ✓ Compare and contrast one shop to the next.
- ✓ Where you can get discounted bridal gowns for the bride who cannot afford designer gown rates?
- ✓ Does the shop do alterations?
- ✓ Do they send their gowns out to be altered at another location?
- ✓ Can they recommend a good seamstress if they don't have one on staff?
- ✓ What is their turnaround time on orders?
- ✓ How long do alterations take?

- ✓ Do they charge extra for alterations in addition to gown costs?
- ✓ Does the shop offer bridesmaid gowns, shoes and accessories?
- ✓ How much of a deposit is required to order a gown?
- ✓ When is the final payment due? Does the shop require an appointment?
- ✓ How many people are allowed to join the bride for her appointment?
- ✓ How many fittings are included with the price of her gown?
- ✓ Is there an extra charge if the bride would like to have her portrait taken in her dress?
- ✓ How long will the shop hold her gown before the wedding date?
- ✓ Is there a discount on bridesmaid gowns if the bride purchases her wedding dress here?
- ✓ Can they provide references?

Reception Halls

- ✓ If the bride is utilizing a unique location, such as a museum or outdoor theatre, etc., has the location been the site of weddings before?
- ✓ What type of deposit is required?
- ✓ When is the final payment due?
- ✓ What EXACTLY is covered in the cost of the hall?
- ✓ Are linens, china, chairs, tables, silverware, etc. included in the basic cost?
- ✓ Is the wait staff included?
- ✓ Will the bride be charged a gratuity on top of her final total?
- ✓ Is alcohol allowed?
- ✓ Can alcohol be brought by the couple? If the couple purchased a special bottle of champagne that they would like to toast with, you need to know if they can bring it into the facility.
- ✓ Will the couple have to apply for any liquor licenses or is that covered by the reception location?
- ✓ Set-up and break-down: is this included or is there an additional charge?
- ✓ Is there a fee if the reception goes over the scheduled allotted time?
- ✓ Who, from the reception hall, will be working the day of the wedding?
- ✓ How many weddings have they handled?

- ✓ Can they provide references?
- ✓ Is it cheaper to buy a la carte or to purchase a wedding package?
- ✓ Compare buffet to sit-down dinner…sit down is usually more cost effective.
- ✓ If the couple chooses a buffet, can they limit what is served or will the reception location continue to bring out food as long as the guests are eating? (This will greatly affect the cost.)
- ✓ Does the reception hall allow off-site caterers to be brought in or do they have their own catering staff?
- ✓ Do they have a preferred list of wedding vendors they allow into their hall?
- ✓ Can the bride bring in her own vendors?
- ✓ Will there be any other events on the day of the wedding?
- ✓ Do they have pictures of previous events?
- ✓ Do they provide a dance floor?
- ✓ Is there an additional charge for the dance floor?
- ✓ Are they equipped for a DJ?
- ✓ Are they equipped for a band?
- ✓ Do they provide bartenders? If so, is there an additional charge for them?

Guidelines to Establish and Maintain Vendor Relationships

Introduce Yourself. Contact local, reputable vendors and introduce yourself. Learn as much as you can about their business and the services they offer. Ask them to send you a brochure to keep on file.

Document the process that works best for you. (Example: Contact vendors in three steps. 1. Send an email 2. Follow up with a phone call 3. Schedule a face-to-face meeting.)

Stay in Contact. Knowing what is going on in your market is the key to your success. Touch base with your vendors no less than every two weeks.

Follow-up. Be sure to follow-up on every call or email from your vendors. Good customer service will bring you additional business. When you are professional with a vendor they will be confident when sending you a bridal referral and will be assured you will treat their bride the same way you have treated them…as a professional.

Network. It is important to continuously network with your vendors. When you can, attend functions that you know your vendors will also be attending and networking. For example: if you are not participating in a bridal show by renting a booth, it is still important to attend the show and touch base with vendors you already know as well as introduce yourself and your business services to new vendors.

Chapter Six

End of Chapter Suggested Assignments

First Objective

Use the list of questions to introduce yourself and your new business to vendors in your market. Speak with 1-2 vendors per category/industry. Learn as much as you can about their business and explain you are just getting started and may need to call on them in the coming weeks when working with bridal clients who may be looking for their type of service.

Remember, the key is to learn as much as you can about their business so you can explain what a vendor can offer your brides. Utilize the category questions to help you when talking to a vendor.

Second Objective

Request three contracts from different vendors in three different industries. Once you receive these contracts you should examine them soundly. Mark the contracts with your notes on potential issues or circumstances that may arise if a bride did not read the entire contract. Look especially at the fine print and cancellation policies. If after reviewing them you still have additional questions, contact the vendor for clarification.

Chapter Seven

Contracts

IN THIS CHAPTER YOU WILL LEARN:

- *Contract Law*
- *The key elements of a contract*
- *Contract rules to remember*
- *The importance of having business insurance*
- *U.S. Chamber of Commerce business resources*

Your Responsibility as a Professional Wedding Planner

Although many brides skip hiring a wedding consultant in an effort to save on expenses, the truth of the matter is that many professional consultants actually save a bride money and many headaches when it comes to planning. Be sure to have your contract in place and do not start working for a client before they sign a contract with your business. Be sure to consult an attorney regarding your local contract law.

Contract Law – Information provided by Cornell University

Contracts are promises that the law will enforce. The law provides remedies if a promise is breached or recognizes the performance of a promise as a duty. Contracts arise when a duty does or may come into existence, because of a promise made by one of the parties. To be legally binding as a contract, a promise must be exchanged for adequate consideration. Adequate consideration is a benefit or detriment which a party receives which reasonably and fairly induces them to make the promise/contract. For example, promises that are purely gifts are not considered enforceable because the personal satisfaction the grantor of the promise may receive from the act of giving is normally not considered adequate consideration. Certain promises that are not considered contracts may, in limited circumstances, be enforced if one party has relied to his detriment on the assurances of the other party.

Contracts are mainly governed by state statutory and common (judge-made) law and private law. Private law principally includes the terms of the agreement between the parties who are exchanging promises. This private law may override many of the rules otherwise established by state law. Statutory law may require some contracts be put in writing and executed with particular formalities. Otherwise, the parties may enter into a binding agreement without signing a formal written document. Most of the principles of the common law of contracts are outlined in the Restatement Second of The Law of Contracts published by the American Law Institute. *See* Restatement (Second) of Contracts. The Uniform Commercial Code, whose original Articles have been adopted in nearly every state, represents a body of statutory law that governs important categories of contracts.

"**Agreement**" means the bargain of the parties in fact as found in their language or by implication from other circumstances including course of dealing or usage of trade or course of performance.

Contract" means the total legal obligation which results from the parties' agreement as affected by the applicable rules of law.

General Obligations of Parties. **The obligation of the seller is to transfer and deliver and that of the buyer is to accept and pay in accordance with the contract.**

Termination of a contract by one party except on the happening of an agreed event requires that reasonable notification be received by the other party and an agreement dispensing with notification is invalid if its operation would be unconscionable.

Contract Details

Most wedding vendors have standard contracts prepared. It is wise to ask all new vendors for a copy of their standard contract so you have it on file and can become familiar with each vendor's policies. Be sure to advise your bride and groom to read over every detail before they sign any contracts. When reviewing any contract, make sure it includes the following items:

> ➢ Day, date and time the contract is signed

- Day, date, time and location of wedding ceremony and reception
- Delivery dates, times and locations
- Complete list of services to be provided, including the number of hours, breaks, etc.
- The length of their service. When will they start and when will they finish. Be sure that they include setup and breakdown of their equipment.
- Overtime rate
- The appropriate attire for the vendor
- The name of the contact person or person in charge of the wedding
- The bride's name and contact number
- The groom's name and contact number
- The mother of the bride's name and contact number
- The name of the wedding consultant and contact information
- Alternative service or merchandise in case of a problem
- Amount of deposit paid and payment schedule
- Cancellation and refund policy
- Last date to make changes to services or provide final guest count

It is very important to read all fine print and ask questions on ways to save money with each package. Vendors sometimes may not disclose alternative options to lower the cost. Some examples include a three-hour reception vs. a four-hour reception.

Rules to Remember

<u>Make Sure Everything Agreed To Is Written In The Contract</u>

Make sure everything that you and your bridal client agree to is written in the contract - every single detail. The most common complaint from brides is related to something they were "promised" by a wedding vendor but did not receive, even though there is no mention of it in the contract. Wedding vendors work with hundreds of brides and just like any of us, they can forget things and make mistakes. The best way to keep track of all the details is to get them in writing with a signature.

Read the Fine Print

Always read the entire contract including the fine print. If you have any questions or changes you need to make to the contract have the bride or groom initial them before signing the contract.

Don't Forget to Sign and Date the Contract

You should also make sure that both the bride and the vendor date and sign the contract. If the vendor doesn't sign the contract, you can't hold them liable if there is ever a problem. Be sure to get a copy of all contracts for your records and be sure the couple has a copy.

Don't Give the Vendor ANY Money without a Signed Contract

In many cases, just the exchange of money constitutes an implied contract so you should NEVER instruct your bride to give a wedding vendor a check to hold a date without a written and signed contract. If your bride decides not to use a vendor she can lose her money, even if she has not yet gone over the details in a tangible contract.

For Increased Protection, Use a Credit Card for Deposits

Instruct your bride to put the deposits on a credit card whenever possible. There are special federal consumer protection laws that protect all payments made with a credit card.

Company Insurance

In addition to having your contracts in order, make sure you have business insurance. Just like you will be suggesting to your couples that they invest in wedding insurance, you shouldn't operate your business without the necessary insurance.

Insurance can be purchased for a small business on an annual basis and should cost only a few hundred dollars. Consult your local insurance agent for more details. The agent you use for your mortgage and auto insurance should also be able to help you or refer you to the rep at their firm who can help you.

The U.S. Chamber of Commerce

For more information on how to keep your business in order and deal with issues from contracts to insurance to taxes, you can learn more at The U.S. Chamber of Commerce's website. They offer a wealth of resources on where to obtain the necessary local information and provide tips, tools, information and regulations.

http://www.chamberbiz.com

Here is a list of resources the U.S. Chamber of Commerce can provide to a new and/or existing business owner:

Starting Your Business
- First Steps
- Business Plans
- Financing

Managing Your Business
- Bookkeeping
- Employees
- Financing
- Office Management
- Taxes

Expanding Your Business
- Sales & Marketing
- Recruiting & Hiring
- Government Contracts

Resources
- Economic Analysis
- Association Resources
- Finding a Chamber
- Research Publications
- Business Documents

Government & Regulations

- Issues Index
- Legal Policy
- State by State Resources

Chapter Seven

End of Chapter Suggested Assignments

First Objective

Research your local city and state small business contract law. Head to your local library, call your local city government, and consult a local attorney.

Second Objective

Consult your local insurance company and find out what type of business insurance is necessary to protect your wedding planning business.

Third Objective

Take the time to read everything the U.S. Chamber of Commerce has to offer on their website. It is a wonderful reference tool for any new or existing business owner. http://www.chamberbiz.com/

Fourth Objective

Develop a contract for your "day of" services. Provide details on what your services cover, what they do not cover, cancellation policies, and any other details you would like to include. This assignment, once completed, will be used again in our chapter on traditional wedding planning packages.

Chapter Eight

The Traditional Wedding Planner

IN THIS CHAPTER YOU WILL LEARN:
- **Traditional Wedding Planner vs. Contemporary Wedding Planner**
- **How to create wedding packages as a traditional wedding planner**
- **Role of wedding planner, wedding coordinator and wedding director**
- **How to work with a prospective bridal client**
- **Tools and suggestions for initial consultations**

There are not many differences between a traditional wedding planner and a straight commission/referral wedding planner. The only difference is that traditional wedding planners do not receive commissions from vendors they have booked with their bridal clients. The revenue for a traditional wedding planner comes from the bride directly and the additional services she includes in her business for the bride to purchase such as invitations, flowers, makeup, favors, etc. The key to deciding whether you will establish your business as a traditional wedding planner or a referral-wedding planner depends on the market you plan to establish your business.

If you plan to begin a wedding planning business where over 80% of the vendors in your market are booked 100% of the time, you will find it difficult to convince them that they need your services and representation. As with most industries, you will find most of the time vendors are very open to commissioning for business. However, there are some markets where the traditional method is the only acceptable method. If this is the case you will need to set up a pricing structure for the services you plan to offer.

IT IS UNETHICAL TO RECEIVE MONEY FROM A BRIDAL CLIENT FOR WEDDING PLANNING AND ALSO TAKE A COMMISSION FROM THE VENDORS YOU USE TO ORCHESTRATE HER WEDDING.

It is not good business practice to be unfair to your bridal clients and the vendors who help you to service your clients. However, your fees for wedding direction for "day of" services will still apply when receiving commissions from vendors for booking the bride.

Setting Up Your Wedding Packages as a Traditional Planner

When setting up your service packages, be sure to include three options, with the middle option being the better value. When making a buying decision, most people choose the middle of the road option.

Example: You can begin by offering your smallest package to include help with planning and advice but not with coordinating or directing. Be sure to understand the difference between a wedding planner, coordinator and director as you begin to put your menu of services together.

Keep in mind how much time you will spend with each service you offer and how much your time is worth so you can price appropriately. Remember to set limits on the amount of time for each package. As you will quickly find out, one bride can easily become high maintenance and monopolize your time, leaving you with less time to work with other clients. Avoid falling into this trap by setting up limits ahead of time.

Wedding Consultant - Works in partnership with the couple and guides them through the process of wedding decisions. Couples working with a consultant are very much in control of their wedding plans but can rest assured that they have professional guidance and assistance when needed. This allows the couple to enjoy the wedding planning process, making it as fun and stress-free as possible.

Wedding Planner - A professional who takes charge and plans the details of a wedding from start to finish. The couple is still involved, but most of the leg work is left to the planner, and the couple can trust a professional to make the arrangements for them.

Wedding Director - Coordinates the details, vendors and itinerary on your wedding day. All concerns are placed on the shoulders of the wedding director. The couple doesn't need to get caught up in the small details and can enjoy their big day.

Calculating Your Fees

When a couple hires a wedding planner, they should expect to pay 10-15% of their total wedding budget. If you are a new wedding consultant, start off at 10% and move to 15% as you gain more experience and become more recognized in the market.

You should also calculate your fees for brides who are not looking for a full package from start to finish. For example, a couple may want to do all the planning on their own but still need guidance. Create a smaller consulting package that will give you an opportunity to provide them with a roadmap to planning their perfect day. Include a list of your preferred vendors, give them a bridal timeline based on their wedding dates, promote your other services (invitations, favors etc.) and charge a flat fee for a limited amount of services. For this type of service list exactly what you will be doing, limit the number of hours worked and stick to it.

Set your rates for your day-of-services only. There is always that opportunity to pick up additional business for the couple who have planned everything themselves, but decide to bring in a consultant for the day of the wedding. Specify exactly what you will be doing for the couple, the hours your services will be needed and your fees. You can charge a flat fee based on the total number of people attending the wedding, the total wedding budget or the total number of hours you'll be coordinating. Specify exactly what you will be doing and note any additional fees for anything outside of your standard package. Be sure to establish expectations up front.

If you are planning on being commissioned on the pre-planning from your preferred vendor partners, be sure to notify your couple of how they can save on your cost by utilizing your list of preferred vendors.

Example: If a couple has a budget of $20,000, your fee should be set at $2000 for all pre-planning details, coordination and directing. Your couple can choose to utilize these vendors who pay the commissions of 10% to you and subtract that amount from the total fee they owe you of $2000. An example is below:

$2000	Consulting fee
- 250	Commission from vendor package of $2500 (Musicians)
- 600	Commission from vendor package of $6000 (Catering)
- 100	Commission from vendor package of $1000 (Flowers)
- 300	Commission from vendor package of $3000 (Photographer)
- 90	Commission from vendor package of $900 (Reception)
- 40	Commission from vendor package of $400 (Invitations)
- 10	Commission from vendor package of $100 (Gifts)
- 60	Commission from vendor package of $600 (Videographer)

$550   Balance Due for Entire Consulting package.

This remaining balance covers day of service responsibilities.

This example shows the bridal couple will only pay the consultant $550.00 for planning, coordinating and day of services, because the wedding consultant planning fees were covered by the consultant's preferred vendors that were booked.

The following pages represent a few examples of Traditional Wedding Consulting Packages.

Acme Wedding Planning Inc.

- Wedding director services on the wedding day include, but are not limited to:
- Follow-up that all deliveries are made on time, and action to ensure vendors are present
- Assist the bridal party in getting ready, and ensure everyone is aware of their roles, cues, etc.
- Ensure decorations and details are in place at the ceremony and reception sites
- Ensure marriage license and rings are present for the ceremony
- Coordinate the processional order, timing and spacing
- Coordinate transfer of ceremony decorations to reception site
- Provision of a wedding day emergency kit (with nearly everything you could ever need!)
- Ensure events continue to flow according to pre-arranged itinerary
- Assist the bride with bustle, veil, and other attire difficulties
- Supervision of all onsite vendors to ensure everything is provided according to contracts
- Assist with unexpected situations - vendor no shows, missing items, etc
- Assistance with setting up cake cutting for photo opportunities
- Ensuring the bride and groom have a chance to eat and drink
- Supervision of clean-up and monitoring that all gifts go to the right place
- Deal with the overall details so that the couple, family and friends can enjoy the special day
- Free one-hour consultation for all couples

Hourly Consultation

Three referrals, pricelists and information packets for all vendors to include wedding ceremony and reception venues, photographers, entertainment, florists, bakeries, officiates or churches, transportation, men's formal wear, bridal wear, guest accommodations, invitations, decorations, etc.

Additional Hourly Services

Schedule appointments and site inspections with vendors, create and type itinerary, secure fees and costs, and accompany you to scheduled appointments and site inspections - **$350.00**

Wedding Blueprint Only - $150

Prepare an estimated budget, outline and guide for the couple looking for a roadmap. The couple will plan the wedding, on their own.

Destination Wedding Packages - $500+

Acme's knowledge of incredible ceremony locations such as breath-taking sun-set views, beautiful outdoor courtyards, historic homes or a private island all offer brides unique locations for their ceremonies.

We offer packages for the couple looking to elope or for traveling parties of up to 300. Whatever the destination…we will get you there!

Rehearsal and Wedding Day Coordinator - $650

Provide each vendor a typed wedding itinerary.

One week prior:

Confirm all vendor arrangements, times and discuss in-depth the details of their responsibilities, ensuring there are no last minute questions

Three (3) days prior:

Prepare ceremony outline to include order of procession and recession and song list. Coordinate details of ceremony rehearsal (i.e. how to seat family and guests and explain responsibilities of ushers, best man and maid of honor).

One hour prior:

A coordinator will arrive at your ceremony to coordinate your guests and your ceremony on the day of the wedding. The coordinator will be your personal bridal consultant for your ceremony and reception by helping you with your dress, pinning on corsages and honoring any other request you may have. Our goal is for you to enjoy the most important day of your life.

Diamond Package - Fees to be discussed at time of consultation.

Three referrals, pricelists and information packets for all vendors to include wedding ceremony and reception venues, photographers, entertainment, florists, bakeries, officiates or churches, transportation, men's formal wear, bridal wear, guest accommodations, invitations, and linen and special décor rentals.

Schedule appointments and site inspections with vendors, create and type itinerary, secure fees and costs and accompany you to scheduled appointments and site inspections. Negotiate all vendor contracts and secure deposits.

Prepare an estimated budget and guide you to ensure you remain on budget.

Send each vendor a typed wedding itinerary

One week prior:

Confirm all vendor arrangements, times and discuss in-depth details of their responsibilities, ensuring there are no last minute questions.

3 days prior:

Prepare ceremony outline to include order of procession and recession and song list. Coordinate details of ceremony rehearsal (i.e. how to seat family and guests and explain the responsibilities of ushers, best man and maid of honor).

One hour prior:

A coordinator will arrive at your ceremony to coordinate your guests and your ceremony on the day of the wedding. The coordinator will be your personal bridal consultant for your ceremony and reception by helping you with your dress, pinning on corsages and honoring any other request you may have. Our goal is for you to enjoy the most important day of your life.

– Fees to be discussed at time of consultation.

Optional Recommendations

Rose Special 300 Roses for - $300

Music Book and CD - $30

Wedding Day Makeup Bride - $50

Invitations – Save 10% on top of already discounted prices

Bronze Wedding Consultation Package - $150.00

A great package for those who just need help getting started, or at any other point where you just need a little assistance!

Up to three hours of consultation regarding your planning

Referral to reputable vendors and advice regarding contracts

Unlimited basic email and telephone questions (long distance excluded)

10% discount on catalogue invitations (optional)

Full payment required at signing of contract

Silver Wedding Directing Package - $475.00

Perfect for those wanting professional assistance ONLY on the day of their wedding!

Review of all vendor contracts and confirmation of vendor services 1-2 weeks prior to your wedding day

Assistance in development of a wedding day itinerary

My services on your wedding day for a maximum of 10 hours

Provision of complete wedding emergency 911 kit

Personal management of your wedding day itinerary, vendors and you!

$150.00 deposit at signing of contract, balance due on wedding day

Gold Wedding Consultation Package - $475.00

Need full assistance with your plans, but not wedding day directing services?

FREE wedding planning binder with tip sheets, questions for vendors, worksheets and timeline guides, including pockets for your contracts, pictures and other important information!

Up to ten hours of consultation regarding your planning

Referral to reputable vendors, review of vendor contracts, and confirmation of vendors (1-2 weeks prior)

Assistance in developing your wedding day itinerary

FREE- Wedding Style Consultation

One visit to your ceremony and reception venue prior to your wedding (travel charges may apply)

Unlimited email and telephone questions (long distance excluded)

10% discount on tent / canopy rental (optional)

10% discount on rentals from some of Edmonton's major suppliers (optional)

20% discount on catalogue invitations (optional)

$150.00 deposit at signing of contract; balance paid one week prior to the wedding day

Platinum Wedding Coordination Package - $725.00

For the all-inclusive wedding package, this is for you!

Includes all the details of the Gold Wedding Consultation Package

My attendance & assistance at your wedding ceremony rehearsal

My services on your wedding day for a maximum of 12 hours

Provision of complete wedding emergency 911 kit

Personal management of day's itinerary, vendors, and YOU!

$200.00 deposit at signing of contract; balance due on wedding day

Wedding Emergency Package

Have all your planning done, but now you want a coordinator or someone else to stress over all the details? Acme Wedding Planning Inc. can come to the rescue before you lose your mind!!

Provision of as little or as much consulting and coordinating assistance you require!

Including personal management of day itinerary, vendors, and YOU!

Packages customized to your needs and requirements to ensure you have a stress-free day after all.

How to Work with a Prospective Bride

After you have received a referral or a lead from your marketing efforts, what happens when you get that bride's information? If you are nervous with your first bride, don't worry, it's entirely natural. Take advantage of the adrenalin rush and jump right in. If you don't know the answers to her questions, just tell her you will research and find out. The best part about your job is that you have the time to research. Research is so important. It will also help you learn.

Bridal leads are a hot commodity, so don't let them sit too long or they will get cold and you will lose the sale. Call your bride AS SOON AS YOU GET HER INFORMATION. Don't dawdle; introduce yourself and your services right away. You will receive most leads from a list service, bridal show or online registration. They will provide you with the bride's work, home and email or a combination of one or two. The best way to introduce your service is via the telephone. However, catching a bride during the day will prove to be difficult, as the majority of brides today are working women. If you find you are not connecting via the phone an email is the most appropriate next step. Snail mail is also a nice touch, and regardless if you reach the bride by phone or email, send her your marketing materials and/or a hand written note in the mail. Never drop the ball. Below you will find a sample phone introduction script, as well as an email introduction.

Here is a sample phone introduction:

Hi Anna,

My name is _____ *and I am a wedding consultant with Acme Weddings, Inc. I am calling because you were referred to me and I understand you have a wedding in your future.*

First let me say congratulations on your engagement! Have you given much thought to how you're going to handle all of the details and arrangements? (Wait for a response, reply, warm up)

Here you should ask her questions about her wedding and if she has considered help from a wedding planner. Probe with additional questions to see where your expertise can be of help to her.

Finally, if you have built her confidence by answering her questions she will want to know more about you and your services.

Let me explain how our company works and then you can see if you feel we could be a benefit to you. I am the owner of Acme Weddings, Inc. and am a certified wedding planner. We have been designing weddings for five years and handle weddings of all budgets.

Our services vary from helping with the pre-planning details to handling day-of-services. I can help give you a plan to work with on your own, or I can help you with as many details as you like. My job is to help you create your own "perfect" wedding, whatever that means to you and your fiancé.

My consultation is free of charge and I also give each couple a free wedding planning calendar as my gift. Additionally, I work with only the most reputable vendors and will be happy to offer suggestions as you need. If there is a vendor you would like to use that is not on my preferred list, I will be sure to research and check their references to ensure they provide quality service.

My role includes meeting with you, researching vendors, coordinating calendars, getting the best rates and packages, presenting my research to you and helping you with wedding ideas for your wedding signature. In other words, just helping you to decide what you want.

Most of the engaged couples I work with think of me as their personal assistant. It's nice to have some help when you need to juggle your everyday responsibilities while planning such a big event in your life.

Let's try to meet sometime this week to go over some of the details I can help with. Let's meet at my office on _____. I'm looking at my calendar and I have _____ open. Does that day work for you? Great; see you then!

Email

In today's world of fast-paced communication using the phone sometimes leads to a game of phone tag. Many people respond more quickly through email. As you work with prospective brides many will fall into this category, as it is an efficient way to communicate and provides documentation that can be filed and referenced at a later time. This is especially true when creating a contract of services and expectations.

Example Email Introduction

Dear Anne and Mark,

Congratulations on your upcoming wedding.   My name is _____ and I am a wedding consultant with Acme Weddings, Inc. I am emailing you because you were referred to me and I understand you have a wedding in your future.

Have you given much thought to how you're going to handle all of the details and arrangements?

Let me explain how our company works and then you can see if you feel we could be a benefit to you. I am the owner of Acme Weddings, Inc. and am a certified wedding planner. We have been in business for five years and handle weddings of all budgets.

Our services vary from helping with the pre-planning details to handling day-of-services. I can give you a plan to work with on your own, or I can help you with more detailed preparations. My job is to help you create your own "perfect" wedding, whatever that means to you and your fiancé.

My consultation is free of charge, and I also give each couple a free wedding planning calendar as my gift to you. Additionally, I work with only the most reputable vendors and will be happy to offer suggestions as you need them. If there is a vendor you would like to use that is not on my preferred list, I will be sure to research and check their references to ensure they provide quality service.

My role includes meeting with you, researching vendors, coordinating calendars, procuring the best rates and packages, presenting my research to you and helping you with wedding ideas for your wedding signature. In other words, just helping you to decide what you want.

Most of the engaged couples I work with think of me as their personal assistant. It's nice to have assistance when you need to juggle your everyday responsibilities while planning for such a big event in your life.

I am available Tuesday and Thursday of this week and can also meet in the evenings and/or on Sundays. If you think this is something you would like to explore in more detail, please email me back at consultant@acmeweddings.com or call me at 555-5555.

I know this can be an overwhelming time, but that's why we're here... to help with the details and assist you with your plans.

I look forward to hearing from you.

Sincerely,

Sample Sue

Certified Wedding Planner

Acme Weddings, Inc.

123 Maple Drive

City, State 12345

(555)555-5555

consultant@acmeweddings.com

Your influence and follow-up will lead you to success.

Once you receive a response from a bridal lead you should contact the bride with additional information on what you have to offer.

Think Smart

Proof read your letters, marketing pieces and anything you send out to the public. Use spell check and be sure to tailor the letter to each bride when you can. Keep your template letter on your computer desktop for easy access.

Keep an email file and record all correspondence in ACT! or the alternative contact management software you are utilizing. Start off on the right foot. Schedule your follow-up calls.

What if don't have an email address? In this day and age you won't make it in this business without an email address, computer or internet access. Call her or send a letter via snail mail until you can get yourself online.

What if you don't hear back from a bride? There could be a million reasons why the bride does not get back in touch. Regardless, if you do the research and email or snail mail her information based on what you could ascertain from her registration or lead then don't dwell on it. If she is interested, she will be in touch. In time, you will get a feel for how much follow-up is needed and what method works best for you in closing the sale and acquiring a couple's business.

Follow-up. Be persistent when trying to get in touch. If it takes longer for her to return your call or email than you would like, use that time to do the research for her so that you're prepared when she does call you back. Don't go overboard in doing your research, but if you know your market and your vendors you will already be prepared to talk to her when you make that first initial contact.

Don't ever forget…the client is the bottom line to your success!

Initial Meeting or Conversation

The initial meeting is the information gathering session, which can be held at your office, a local coffee shop, or over lunch. You should always treat the bride to coffee or lunch prior to her becoming a client. Once she has signed your contract then all expenses should be her responsibility. Don't get nit-picky if you meet for coffee again and you go Dutch, as you can always write off your café latte as a business expense. This meeting will give the bride a chance to put a face to a name as well as get to know you. The bride will need to go over the basic details outlined in your initial paperwork. Here is an example of the initial information required to move forward on developing the specific plans for this couple's wedding.

Fill out the form completely by asking each question and opening up the conversation to provide details of how she envisions the day of her wedding. Be sure to offer ideas and suggestions to help her create a unique wedding signature. At this time you can explain Day-of-Services and how they are different from the research and planning prior to the wedding day. Explain your packages and what you have to offer. This is the time to sell your services.

When the bride has made the decision to employ your services, don't move forward until both the bride and the groom have signed your contract. This will protect you if there is any question in the future of what your responsibility is. It also gives you the authority to work on behalf of the couple. At this time, you should request a deposit for your service. It can be a small fee if the couple has not yet decided which of your packages they are interested in. The fee can be applied to the cost of the package they choose. This way you can reserve the day for the couple and let them know that with their deposit, their wedding day is booked with you and no other weddings will be taken that day.

This form can be used in conjunction with your contract.

☐ Yes, I would like to participate in Acme Weddings, Inc. wedding planning services. I understand there is a cost to me for utilizing the personal assistant services of planning the wedding details.

☐ I would also like to employ the services of the Acme Weddings, Inc. for the "day-of-services" for my wedding at $_____X_____
Please sign here for the day of service agreement.

Please fill out the following information completely.

Bride's Name: _____

Wedding Date: _____ City of Wedding: _____

Street Address/ P.O. Box: _____

City: _____ State: _____ Zip: _____

Phone: _____ Work Phone: _____

Email: _____ Budget: _____

Number of Guests: _____

Indoor: _____ Out door: _____

Seated: _____ Buffet: _____

Specific Request: _____

_____

_____

Notes: _____

_____

_____

Please check the items you are interested in getting more information from to help plan your wedding.

☐ Bridal Shops	☐ Entertainment —Type_____
☐ Alterations	☐ Limousines
☐ Looking Good	☐ Photographers
☐ Wedding Cakes	☐ Videographer
☐ Caterers	☐ Jewelry
☐ Reception Hall	☐ Honeymoon Packages
☐ Decorations	☐ Tuxedos
☐ Invitations	☐ Events
☐ Gifts	☐ Specials
☐ Florists	☐ Real estate
☐ Rental	☐ Insurance
☐ Hotel Accommodations	☐ Loan Information
☐ Officiate	☐ Relationship Education
☐ Ceremony Sites	☐ Lovegevity Newsletter
☐ Consultants	☐ Subscription to

*Provide Payment information below **only** for the reservation and payment of wedding "day-of- services".

Authorization Signature:_____   Date:_____

☐ Visa   ☐ Master Card   ☐ AMEX   ☐ Discover _____

Card #:_____   Exp Date:_____

Acme Weddings, Inc. Representative:_____   ID#_____

I understand I am utilizing Acme Weddings, Inc. to help in my wedding plans. I also understand a 25% deposit is required and final payment is due one week prior to the wedding date. I can cancel at anytime or change my contract at anytime and agree to pay all fees, if any. I acknowledge that Acme Weddings, Inc. and its representatives are not liable for the products services and warranties of participating vendors. I understand that it is my responsibility to purchase my own wedding insurance, if I so desire.

Chapter Eight

End of Chapter Suggested Assignments

First Objective

Develop a unique wedding signature for a bride who is Chinese but has lived in America her whole life. In what way can she acknowledge her family traditions and pay respect to her parents? Her husband to be is American and wants a traditional American wedding for his bride.

Second Objective

Create your menu of services using the example in your reading as a guide. Provide pricing details as if you are setting up your business as a traditional wedding planner. Include your day-of-services contract.

Chapter Nine

The Bride

IN THIS CHAPTER YOU WILL LEARN:
- **The bride's timeline**
- **How to educate your bride on what to expect from a wedding planner**
- **The importance of a bridal registry**

A smart entrepreneur knows that any good business must have a solid foundation.

By now, you've done your market research, applied for your business license and put into words, your personal goals and objectives. You have started creating your map for success. Keep all that in mind as we move through the next few chapters. Try to put yourself in the bride's shoes so you can get your first taste of this big celebration called...the wedding.

A wedding planner must approach a client's wedding with the objective of creating their vision and at the same time provide guidance and advice to help steer her in the right direction when it comes to budget, personality and family. A professional wedding planner will tend to the bride's needs and make the couple feel as if they are the planner's most important client. By doing so, you will enjoy a greater level of personal and professional success.

Wedding planning tips and advice to give to your clients.

You may want to give a copy of the following pages to your bride as hand-outs at your initial meeting.

What's A Girl To Do?

The Bride's Checklist

12 Months Before the Wedding

- Select a wedding consultant to help you avoid wasting time or money
- Confirm ceremony date, time, and site with officiant
- Set a preliminary budget
- Select attendants
- Reserve the reception site
- Select and book caterers, photographers, videographers, florists, musicians, cake creators and other service providers
- Begin compiling guest list
- Select wedding dress, headpiece, and bridesmaids' dresses
- Start thinking about your honeymoon

9 Months Before

- Attend premarital classes
- Choose and order your dress accessories
- Register for china, gifts, etc
- Shop for a new home

6 Months Before

- Place deposits and sign contracts for wedding services
- Choose bridesmaids' dresses and accessories
- Choose flower girl's dress
- Make sure your visas and passports are up to date, if you're traveling
- Complete honeymoon plans with groom
- Discuss rehearsal dinner with groom

4 Months Before

- Verify that the wedding gown, bridesmaids' dresses, and flower girl's dress have been ordered
- Make sure addresses for guest list are up to date
- Order invitations, announcements, and any other personal stationary
- Choose and order formal wear for groom and attendants
- Make sure all out-of-town male attendants have submitted their measurements to your formal wear provider
- Verify that both mothers have selected and ordered their dresses
- Investigate requirements for medical tests and other records for your marriage license
- Design a map to direct guests to the ceremony and reception sites
- Finish registering
- Shop for trousseau

2 Months Before

- Schedule final fitting
- Finalize bridal registry
- Confirm ceremony details with your officiant
- Finish addressing invitations and announcements
- Finalize wardrobe for showers, pre-wedding parties, and honeymoon
- Shop for gifts for bridal party
- Shop for accessories such as shoes, stockings, garter, purse, cake knife, candles, and guest registration book
- Choose wedding rings and arrange for engraving
- Plan your bridesmaids' party

- Schedule an appointment with your hairdresser and make-up consultant
- Finalize and verify all details with contracted service providers
- Order wedding cake

6 Weeks before

- Mail invitations
- Confirm all male and female attendants have been fitted for formal wear
- Schedule rehearsal and inform all who need to be there
- Make final menu decisions
- Discuss wedding photo shots with photographer and videographer
- Send announcement to newspaper
- Write thank you notes for gifts

2 Weeks Before

- Pick up wedding gown and confirm that it fits properly
- Take care of blood and medical tests and marriage license
- Finalize musical selections for the ceremony and reception
- Finalize seating chart for reception
- Finish addressing announcements to mail on wedding day

1 Week Before

- Pick up wedding rings
- Give final guest count for the reception to your caterer
- Practice applying make-up for the wedding day if you're doing it yourself
- Confirm details with all service providers

- Verify all bridesmaids and groomsmen have picked up their formal wear
- Confirm that all attendants know when to arrive at the rehearsal, rehearsal dinner and wedding ceremony
- Confirm honeymoon plans
- Make a list of names and their correct pronunciation for the Best Man to mention in his introduction, if appropriate
- Cancel newspaper and mail for the time you'll be away
- Pay upcoming bills that will be due while you are away
- Pack for honeymoon and purchase traveler's checks
- Arrange to move belongings to new home

1-2 Days Before

- Review any special seating arrangements with ushers
- Groom picks up formal wear
- Make sure to have marriage license
- Check all final details with caterer, florist, musicians, etc.

The Night Before

Sleep, sleep, sleep. You have the biggest day of your life ahead of you. You want to look and feel your best. Be sure to make time with family, especially parents in order to share memories and say thank you. Take photos of your last hours at home as a single person. Take some time by yourself to relax. Close your eyes and visualize every step of the coming day. This will help to relax you and prevent unforeseen incidents.

The morning of

Have a small meal before leaving for the church. Don't bring too many personal items to the church; the less to worry about, the better. Stay calm. If you run behind schedule, take a deep breath and remember that the ceremony will wait for you!!! Your family and friends want to see you shine, not be frazzled because you are running late, so relax. Looking and feeling wonderful and radiating your happiness is what counts.

Countdown to "I Do"

2 hours till "I Do": Groom, best man and groomsmen get together to begin dressing.

45 minutes: Ushers arrive at the wedding sight, pick up boutonnieres and programs, go over seating plans and wait at the entrance to the church for the guests to arrive.

30 minutes: Organ or other music begins. Final check of marriage license. Mother and attendants leave for the wedding site, ushers begin seating guests.

20 minutes: Groom and best man arrive. Father (or bride's escort) and bride leave for the ceremony site.

10 minutes: Bridal party and parents wait in the back of church while other relatives are seated.

5 minutes: Mother of the groom is escorted to her seat (unless it is a Jewish ceremony). Groom's father walks behind the usher then takes his seat beside his wife. Mother of the groom enters the pew first with the father sitting on the aisle. Bride and father arrive at ceremony site while mother of the bride is escorted down the aisle.

* 1 minute: If there is an aisle runner, two ushers walk in step to the front of the church and unroll the runner then walk in step to the back of the church, unrolling runner as they go. They then take their place in the procession. Now the moment you have waited for: the minister, priest or rabbi takes his/her place along with the groom and best man. (In Christian tradition, the groom and best man enter from chancel door and stand, at an angle, facing the congregation. The groom stands nearest the minister and the best man one step behind the groom. In Jewish tradition, the groom and best man are part of the wedding procession. As the ceremony begins, the guests will rise to watch the bride make her entrance.

Smile... this is your moment!!!

After the Honeymoon

Congratulations, Mrs. X! In today's modern society, women are still taking the last name of their groom. To make things easier for the new bride, find out what she needs to do in your local city and state to change her name. Provide her with all the necessary contact information, forms, etc.

She will also need to report her name change to Social Security. Call 1-800-772-1213 or go online at www.ssa.gov.

Good advice can save you more than money

Getting the right amount of help . . . a look at wedding coordinators:

"Cinderella had outside help," protests the poor insomniac princess-to-be in "Once Upon a Mattress", the famous Broadway musical version of Hans Christian Anderson's "The Princess and the Pea".

If you don't believe that planning a wedding can be a huge pain in the under-bustle, take a look at a bride's checklist. While there are many wedding planning resources out there and enough information available for a bride to do it all herself, we know wedding planning isn't for everyone. Just as your groom's purchase of a "Chilton's Guide" for his late model automobile doesn't keep him away from his favorite mechanic, your investment in your own planning research should not deter you from choosing a qualified wedding coordinator if you determine that you need one.

The following thoughts on wedding coordinators should help you decide.

The best wedding coordinators are very flexible

Forget any notions you may have had about "all or nothing" or "one size fits all". Today's wedding coordinators can assist you with as much or as little as you prefer. Because many of today's brides are already busy with their careers, it's logical for them to obtain wedding coordinator assistance in the same manner that they would "delegate" or "outsource" projects at work. A typical scenario is for the coordinator to do all of the "leg work", like checking in with the bride at regular intervals via e-mail to get answers and/or new instructions. You can let your coordinator handle everything or pick and choose specific areas for him/her to handle. They will be involved as much or as little as you prefer. The best wedding coordinators know how to skillfully guide you through the entire process without taking control.

The best wedding coordinators help smooth family tensions

Whose wedding is this anyway? While common sense would say it's the bride and groom's big day, parents and others can be very demanding, particularly if they are the ones footing the bill. A wedding coordinator can be very helpful by "sticking up for the bride" and ensuring that her preferences are honored or by proposing creative solutions that satisfy a variety of concerns.

The best wedding coordinators understand wedding economics

In this day and age weddings can get very expensive before anyone really understands what they're buying. Today's wedding coordinators stay on top of prevailing market conditions, vendors costs, etc., so they can give sound advice about different price ranges, what to expect in return for what you spend, etc. Additionally, most wedding coordinators maintain information for several vendors at different price points. If you can't afford established stars, your coordinator can steer you toward emerging talents who can provide great service but aren't going to charge top dollar.

The best wedding coordinators exert their own measure of quality control on vendors

In the eyes of a vendor the biggest difference between you and a coordinator can be summed up in one word: tomorrow. Because she coordinates weddings for a living, your coordinator is someone your vendors can expect to see a lot of in the future. They offer the benefit of being an overall "larger" client of the vendor. They are also seen as the expert, so vendors will respect the fact that you, the bride, have chosen to work with someone who is certified and trained. A bride who works with a coordinator is more likely to get better overall service.

The best wedding coordinators are there on your big day

Ask any of your married female friends about their state of mind on their wedding day. If any tell you they were cool, calm and collected throughout, beware: like the man who claims he's head of the house, they may not be 100% honest. Like any roller coaster ride, your wedding day will be a magnificent memory tomorrow, but a huge load to process right now. It might even scare you a little. That's where a coordinator can be a huge help by generally overseeing all of the vendors, vendors' employees, your relatives and friends, etc. This will leave you free to concentrate on getting yourself prepared. Even if you decide you want to handle all of the pre-planning on your own, you may want to consider bringing in a wedding coordinator to oversee your day-of services.

Wedding planning isn't for everyone. The perfect recipe for your wedding planning support system will depend on you: your schedule, your organizational skills and your personality. And yes, your vision as you prepare for that magical day. There is no right way or wrong way to utilize a wedding planner; you decide what is right for you.

Happiness Is a Bridal Registry

"Find out what they like and how they like it, and let 'em have it just that way."

When he wrote these lyrics for a Fats Waller tune many years ago, lyricist Andy Razaf probably never imagined they would become the golden rule of wedding gifts.

Look at it from another angle: can you find a constructive purpose for 40 toasters in one house? Perhaps you could get 80 hot breakfast pastries to jump up at the same time and make a music video (Jump! Jump! etc.) That's probably a simpler solution than trying to return all those toasters.

But seriously, one of the benefits of life in this enlightened age is that bridal couples get to choose what they want for wedding gifts and can be confident that family and friends would much rather buy something the couple wants than contribute one more cast member to the "Toaster Rockettes". The modern mechanism created to document those preferences and their purchase is called a bridal registry.

Believe it or not, J.C. Penney and Tiffany's do have something in common: a highly evolved computer-oriented registry system. In fact, these computer registries are popular with many retailers across the United States. The concept is simple. The bridal couple walks into one branch of the store, meets with a representative and then walks around identifying those items they wish to receive as gifts. A list of these gifts and their prices is entered into a main computer database under the bride's name. Thereafter, anyone wishing to purchase one or more gifts for the couple can telephone a toll-free number, place the order and probably pay for it using their chosen major credit card. Meanwhile, the couple can call in at any time to check the status of their registry to learn which gifts have been purchased.

Keep in mind that there is no rule that says the couple can only visit the store once. For many couples, the "information overload" of looking through 250,000 items and trying to anticipate their needs over the next ten years is just too much. The remedy is simple: break up the gift selection process into two or three visits.

Chapter Nine

End of Chapter Suggested Assignments

First Objective

Put yourself in the bride's shoes. Compile a list of questions you would ask a wedding planner if YOU were the bride. Think about what you would be looking for and expect only the best.

Second Objective

Put together packages for engagement parties, showers and Bachelorette parties as additional services you can offer through your business. These can range from simple to extravagant and can help increase your revenue throughout the planning process and in the off season.

Third Objective

Create a list of 15 local places where a couple can register for wedding gifts.

Chapter Ten

Traditional and Non-Traditional Wedding Ceremonies, Wedding Party Responsibilities, Insider Tips

IN THIS CHAPTER YOU WILL LEARN:
- **The key elements of traditional, non-traditional and civil ceremony weddings**
- **What questions to ask when planning a specific type of wedding and venue**
- **How to delegate bridal party responsibilities and who is responsible for what**
- **How to keep abreast of wedding trends and fashion**
- **Emergency tips and what is included in a wedding day emergency kit**

Today's bridal couple is not much different from couples who have married over the last 50 years. Couples can still chose to have a traditional wedding to honor their family heritage or religious beliefs or a non-traditional ceremony in a back yard or on the beach. Whatever your bridal clients' imagination can think of, you will need to be in tune with their style and preferences to maintain their confidence in you.

Traditional Wedding Venues Include:

Church

Synagogue

Chapel

Wedding Facility

Family Home

If you are directing a traditional wedding it is important to remind your bride to check with her officiant for approval on her location. For example, Catholic weddings are only performed in a Catholic church.

She may also need to provide church documents in order to fulfill her traditional requirements to enter into marriage.

With a traditional church wedding, as the director, you will need to learn what the church will and will not permit and ensure that your vendors have appropriate access on the big day. A common mistake for some brides is assuming anything goes when it comes to the floral decorations in a church. Just because your bride spent money on flowers for the church doesn't mean the church will allow her to display them as she intended. Always check to avoid a preventable wedding day disaster.

Questions to ask:

→ Will there be another service or wedding on the same day as the wedding I am coordinating?

→ Where are the parking accommodations? Are there restrictions?

→ Is there a separate area or dressing room for the bride and her maid of honor?

→ Can the flower girl drop rose petals down the aisle? Who is responsible for cleaning up afterwards?

→ What fees are required for the officiant and/or use of the facility?

→ Are there any decorating restrictions or rules?

→ How do you arrange access for the decorators and florist?

→ What is the policy for disposing of the decorations and/or flowers after the ceremony?

→ Can we use an aisle runner? Does the facility have one to use?

→ Are there rules for the brides dress? (i.e. no bare shoulders) What about the guests?

→ Is photography permitted during the ceremony? Video?

→ Is there a type of music that is not allowed?

→ Can the bride and groom write their own vows?

Non-Traditional Ceremony Settings Include:

Family home

Backyard

Park

Beach

Drive through chapel

Museum

Outdoor Theater

Extreme ones include:

Scuba diving

Parachuting

Hot air balloon

You may not have as many rules and restrictions to be concerned about when directing a non-traditional ceremony; however, it can bring other issues to be concerned with.

Examples could include:

Rentals: tents, chairs, altar, etc.

Equipment

Safety

Weather

The Civil Ceremony

You may be asked to help with the arrangement for a simple civil ceremony. This is usually held at the justice of the peace or at city hall. Some preparation is needed for this simple service, such as legal requirements and two witnesses.

Delegating Responsibilities to the Bride, Groom, Best Man & Maid of Honor

When directing a wedding, you are assisting the bride. There are several others in the wedding party with responsibilities they may have never had before. This could impact your bride and wedding day festivities if wedding party members are not clued in regarding the importance of their role on such a special day.

Wedding plans are stressful to both the bride's and groom's families. You will want to help by delegating certain responsibilities to the appropriate individuals. With the help of your bride, examine her list of "to do's" and assign some of the tasks that can be performed by others who are close to her.

The Maid of Honor (single)
Matron of Honor (married)

The maid of honor is one of the legal witnesses for the ceremony, but her duties begin the moment she accepts the offer from the bride.

A maid or matron of honor is responsible for:

- The bridal shower and pre-wedding get-togethers
- Helping the bride to chose the bridesmaids' dresses
- Addressing invitations and if necessary, helping to create favors
- Supervising the attendants for fittings and rehearsals
- Holding the groom's ring at the ceremony
- Tending to the bride's needs and her gown
- Holding the bride's bouquet at the ceremony
- Overall, helping to reduce the stress of the bride

The Best Man

The best man is also a legal witness to the marriage and is responsible for:

- Planning the bachelor party
- Helping with the gift to the groom from the ushers
- Attending the rehearsal dinner
- Getting the groom to the ceremony on time
- Delivering the payment to the clergy
- Holding the bride's wedding ring
- Coordinating the ushers
- Offering the first toast to the bride and groom
- Decorating the newlyweds' car and readying it for the bride and groom after the reception.

Trends and Wedding Fashion

As a professional in your business it is imperative to keep up with the changing trends and latest fashions in the wedding industry. Your bridal clients will look to you for advice and direction regarding gift selection, unique favor ideas and bridal attire. Use industry magazines and trade publications to keep abreast of what's new.

Utilize your vendor relationships with your local bridal shop owners and gown designers to learn what is hot and happening. This also applies to other categories, from dresses to flowers to music. Your wedding vendors will know what the hottest trends are and be aware of what is going on in their industry.

Emergency Tips & Industry "Insider" Trade Secrets
Did you know ...

You can remove a fresh lipstick stain by rubbing it with white bread? How about removing a red wine stain with white wine and cool water?

You can dry up acne pimples with Colgate tooth paste?
Reduce the swelling under your eyes with Preparation-H.

How do some people just know what to do under circumstances that seem hopeless? Life experience? Maybe their grandmother is related to "Heloise" (America's most trusted household-hints advisor) or they just have too much time on their hands. Either way, their timely advice is welcomed with sighs of relief that someone has it under control. As a professional wedding planner, that someone should be you.

Brush up on industry "insider" secrets to fast, safe and unconventional solutions to everyday problems. The following is a list of suggested books and references with tips, hints and secrets you can pass along to your clients when necessary.

Tiptionary by Mary Hunt

Have you ever wished you could remember all those great tips your grandmother told you or the ones you've heard somewhere along the line but have no way of remembering? Have you wished there was a cheap and effective way to do something? Well, this book will help you with quick tips for how to do an assortment of things.

Talking Dirty Laundry with the Queen of Clean

Most of the chapters are devoted to various types of special problems, such as colors that ran, stain and odor removal, and cleaning large items like bedspreads and lampshades. Explanations for when to dry-clean and how to make your own spot cleaners using household items like club soda, cream of tartar, and denture-cleaning tablets are also included, alongside ironing techniques and the definitive way of color sorting. Particularly helpful are the A-to-Z guides to fabric care and stain removal at the end of the book. Each type of fabric--from delicates like chiffon and velvet to rugged corduroy and denim--has a preferred treatment and certain chemicals that it just can't handle.

Heloise from A to Z

An encyclopedia of trusted hints featuring such topics as removing stains from clothing and more.

Joey Green's Clean It Fix It Eat It

100's of wacky and amazingly helpful uses for ordinary brand-name products!

Professional Consultant's Emergency Kit

Whether you are coordinating "day of" services or preparing your bridal client for her "Big Day", you will need to reference your emergency kit and make sure you have all items covered between you and your bride or maid of honor.

As a true professional you should always be prepared and plan ahead for mishaps and mistakes so that you can handle them discreetly and avoid disaster

Remember to keep your cool when emergencies arise. You are in control and should never seem as if you don't have a handle on the day's events, good or bad.

The following list is a general guideline of items to include in the "Consultant's/Bride's Emergency Kit". The kit can take many forms, from apron, overnight bag, paper bag, basket, or a big purse. In general, the kit is left in the bride's dressing/changing room for easy access at the wedding site.

Consultant's/Bride's Emergency Kit

- ☐ Antacid
- ☐ Antihistamine, cold remedy
- ☐ Any prescription medications
- ☐ Aspirin, Tylenol, or Advil
- ☐ Band-Aids
- ☐ Hard candy (better than medicinal scent of cough-drops)
- ☐ Pepto-Bismol or other antacid/upset stomach aid.
- ☐ Smelling salts
- ☐ Tampons, pads
- ☐ Sunscreen (if significant activities will be outdoors)
- ☐ Beauty/Grooming
- ☐ Dusting powder for before pictures are taken
- ☐ Hair spray, brush, barrettes and/or bobby pins
- ☐ Hand lotion, Handy-Wipes
- ☐ Kleenex
- ☐ Makeup
- ☐ Perfume
- ☐ Nail polish in shade worn by bride and remover
- ☐ Small hand towel
- ☐ Toothbrush and toothpaste
- ☐ Attire
- ☐ 'Throwaway" garter
- ☐ Clear nail polish for runs in hose
- ☐ Earring backs
- ☐ Emergency buttons
- ☐ Flat shoes or ballet slippers (if necessary)
- ☐ Iron

- ☐ Pantyhose (extras in case anything happened)
- ☐ Safety pins
- ☐ Masking tape (last-minute ripped hems)
- ☐ Small sewing kit, including thread for all dresses, wedding party
- ☐ Miscellaneous
- ☐ Directions to reception: extra copies
- ☐ Phone numbers of all service folks
- ☐ Small flashlight
- ☐ Cell Phone
- ☐ Bottled water

Chapter Ten

End of Chapter Suggested Assignments

First Objective

Order your annual and local wedding magazine subscriptions.

Tip: *Annual bridal magazine subscriptions starting at $3.95...check out* *www.bestdealmagazines.com.*

Second Objective

Just for fun, imagine you are working with several different brides who each have different ideas of the "perfect" wedding. Compile a list of questions that you should be prepared to ask and answer for each venue and setting. Church, family home, backyard, park, beach, drive through chapel, museum, outdoor theater, scuba diving, parachuting and hot air balloon could be some of the different options.

Third Objective

Contact your city hall to find out the requirements for a civil ceremony.

Chapter Eleven

The Wedding Gown: Elements of Style

IN THIS CHAPTER YOU WILL LEARN:
- How to select the best bridal gown style for your bridal client and how to advise her when searching for the right gown
- Basic gown styles
- Basic veil styles
- The Top 50 wedding dress designers

A bride's gown is the first thing anyone thinks of when a girl gets engaged: "What will the gown look like?" The newly engaged bride-to-be has probably dreamt about the gown she would wear on her wedding day for years. The mother of the bride probably has her own ideas of what her daughter should wear. The bridal gown is always at the center of the wedding. All eyes and interest are on the bride when she steps onto the aisle runner to make her appearance.

The gown sets the tone for the rest of the wedding details and is usually one of the first things a bride researches if she hasn't already chosen the gown before she is engaged.

Gowns change with the seasons and your annual bridal magazine subscriptions will show you what is hot and what is not. Regardless of what styles come and go, there are some basic guidelines to gown styles.

There are several wedding magazines dedicated to wedding gowns and a few good books. We recommend Vera Wang's book "Vera Wang on Weddings". This is one to include in your library of wedding books for your business. This book is more than just a pictorial of beautiful gowns; it is also a wedding planning book from Vera's perspective.

Have some fun and go out to your local bridal shops and see what styles are available. You should take the time to meet with all local bridal shop owners so you know what quality of service they will provide your brides. Learn what the local going rates are and compare and contrast one shop to the next. Find out where you can get discounted bridal gowns for the bride who cannot afford the designer gown rates.

Find out if the shop does alterations or if they send their gowns out to be altered. Can they recommend a good seamstress if they don't have one on staff? What is their turnaround time on orders? How long do alterations take? Most shops charge for alterations on top of what the gown costs. Does the shop offer gowns, shoes and accessories? How much of a deposit is required to order a gown? When is the final payment due? Does the shop require an appointment? How many people are allowed to join the bride? Some shops limit a bride to one or two guests. Is there a discount on bridesmaids' gowns if the bride's wedding dress is purchased from the same location?

Remember, the gown will set the tone for the rest of the wedding. Pull details from her dress when appropriate and incorporate them into the wedding. If she chooses a Victorian style gown, then sachets and pearls are great accents to use as favors or decorations. If she is a bit more contemporary with, for example, a white gown with a red accent, then take that element and lace that red tone throughout, using red roses, red tablecloths, etc. It is also your job to advise the bride on topics like the fact a full, traditional style gown is not ideal for a beach wedding or that an evening wedding is most appropriate when a formal event and requires a formal length gown, etc.

After the bride chooses her gown, she will be ready to select her veil. A veil is not always required so don't force it on your bride if it is something she is not willing to wear. Suggest she try on several different styles; she may have one thing in mind but could be surprised that a totally different look turns out to be perfect. Consult your local bridal shop and designers for veil ideas. If a bride does not want to spend a lot on her veil or can't find what she is looking for, she may want to have it made. Find out who the best veil designers are in your local market.

Here are a few popular gown and veil styles you should become familiar with. Be prepared, as brides will ask your advice on styles in season and trends for wedding gowns.

Ball gown: "Cinderella" style gown with a big pouf skirt.

A-Line: In the shape of an A; slimmer at the bodice and widening from the bodice down.

The Empire:
A high waist that is cropped just below the bust, where the skirt begins to flare.

The Basque
The waist is several inches below the natural waistline, giving the illusion of a long torso by forming a U or V shape.

Veils

The **Cathedral Veil** is long and trails from one to three yards away from the gown, as shown in this picture.

The **Chapel Veil** is similar but only trails one to two feet from the gown

The **Sweep Veil** is also long but just touches the floor and sweeps the ground.

Veils: Mantilla

The **Mantilla Veil** is scarf-like
and drapes over the head
and shoulders.

Veils: Fingertip

This veil falls to the tips of the fingers.

The Top Wedding Dress Designers:

Alfred Angelo www.alfredangelo.com	Eden www.edenbridals.com www.saisonblanche.com	Maggie Sottero www.maggiesotterobridal.com
Alfred Sung www.alfredsungbridals.com www.loriann.com	Emme www.emmebridal.com	Marisa www.marisabridals.com
Alvina Valenta www.alvinavalenta.com	Fashion 1001 Nights www.fashion1001nights.com	Melissa Sweet www.melissasweet.com
Alyce www.alycedesigns.com	Forever Yours www.foreverbridal.com	Mon Cheri www.moncheribridals.com
Amy Lee www.amyleebridal.com	Guzzo www.guzzobridal.com	Monique (or Monique Luo) www.moniquebridal.com
Avica Bridal www.avicabridal.com	Ian Stuart www.ianstuart.com www.sinceritybridal.com	Montique www.montique.com www.ginnis.com
Anjolique www.anjolique.com	Impression Bridal www.impressionbridal.com	Moonlight www.moonlightbridal.com
Bari Jay www.barijay.com	Jasmine Bridal www.jasminebridal.com	Mori Lee www.morileeinc.com
Belsoie www.jasminebridal.com	Jacquelin Bridal www.jacquelinbridals.com	New Image www.newimagebridesmaids.com
Bill Levkoff www.billlevkoff.com	Jessica McClintock www.jessicamcclintock.com	Paloma Blanca www.palomablanca.com
Bonny MT www.bonny.com	Jim Hjelm www.jimhjelmoccasions.com www.jimhjelmcouture.com www.jimhjelmvisions.com	P.C. Mary's www.marysbridal.com
Bridal Originals www.bridaloriginals.com	Jordan Fashions www.jordanfashions.com	Private Label www.privatelabelbyg.com www.ginza.com
Champagne Formals www.champagneformals.com	Lamour Bridals www.lamourbridals.com	Pronovias www.pronovias.com
Christos www.christosbridal.com	Lazaro www.lazarobridal.com	Sweetheart Gowns www.gowns.com
Demetrios www.demetriosbride.com	Lestella www.lestella.com	Venus Bridals www.lotusorient.com
Designer Collection/Rena Koh www.renakohbridal.com	Little Angels www.usangels.com	Vera Wang www.verawang.com
Dessy www.aftersix.com www.dessy.com	Lizette www.lizettecreations.com	Victoria's Bridal www.victoriascollection.com
Diamond www.diamondbridal.com		Watters & Watters www.watters.com

Chapter Eleven

End of Chapter Suggested Assignments

First Objective

Create a reference book of local bridal salons and include their price sheets. Most salons will be able to provide you with catalogs for each designer. Another option is to contact dress designers directly in order to have their information on file so your brides have everything they need at their fingertips. Update your gown reference catalog each season as the fashions change. Be sure to include a section on accessories such as jewelry, purses, shoes, etc.

Include a bridesmaid section or create a catalog specifically for bridesmaids and mother of the bride gowns.

Chapter Twelve

Music

IN THIS CHAPTER YOU WILL LEARN:
- **How to incorporate music into wedding day activities and events**
- **How to create a wedding day soundtrack or musical score**

The music is the foundation of any wedding, from start to finish. Incorporating the music and creating a musical wedding score to map out the feel, mood and signature is what makes the event flow. Music can evoke sadness, joy and excitement.

There are two women who are THE wedding music experts. Barbara Rothstein and Gloria Sklerov write wedding music for soap operas and have put their technique in a wonderful book called "How to Set Your Wedding to Music". It comes with a wedding music CD and ***it should be one of the first books in your wedding library.***

It will show you how to create a wedding day soundtrack or musical score and so much more- it is a must have! www.weddingmusiccentral.com

Making Your Wedding Music Decisions
By: Barbara Rothstein and Gloria Sklerov

MusiConcepts

You've been busy. From the minute you set the date it's been about your gown, the wedding location, flowers, bridesmaids, ushers, honeymoon, registering, shopping and on and on . . .

But thank goodness you've hired a great band or a fabulous DJ. At least your music is taken care of.

Or is it?

Don't count on it. Sadly, hundreds of thousands of couples do their entire wedding planning so carefully only to let the ball drop where the most emotional and critical part of their wedding is concerned: the music.

Until now, not enough information and guidance has been available to brides and grooms in the process of hiring bands and DJs or for the final meeting with the musicians just before the wedding. (That's when you actually plan and "choreograph" your wedding program.) Because you'll be asked so many questions and have to make multiple on-the-spot decisions, you'll want to have enough time beforehand to think and imagine how these choices will affect your wedding. When you don't have a good idea of what you want, the band or DJ's choices rule. That's not to say that they won't have good ideas, but remember: it's not their wedding. It's yours. The ideal situation is when you come to the planning sessions with an open mind and a clear vision.

If you're wondering how to avoid last minute problems, and if you'd like to make your wedding a fabulous success (measuring success by how good a time you and your guests have) we're here to help with some suggestions of what to do first.

Step One

First you dream. Believe it or not, visualizing your dream is one of the most important parts of planning, for behind every successful creation is an idea...a heart's desire. Everything starts with an idea, whether a dream, a home you're building, a honeymoon you're planning, or your own wedding.

The clearer your vision, the easier you'll find the process of making it a reality.

At the beginning, it's important to allow yourself the time to explore your own personal preferences and consider many different options.

Remember: this is a creative process. Let your ideas flow and your natural creativity take flight.

Think of your wedding as a film. Like any successful film, a great wedding has an interesting and meaningful opening with dramatic moments that build in intensity up to an exciting climax and satisfying ending. But a great film, though beautifully directed and produced, only comes alive when the composer adds the musical score. The soundtrack is the greatest single influence on the feeling and pacing of a film.

Pretend that you are the composer and the music you choose is the soundtrack of your wedding. Take an imaginary journey through your wedding, scene by scene. Imagine how beautiful you'll feel at the moment. Now imagine music that expresses all these feelings. Play your favorite music and songs, trying different selections and styles as you imagine the 'scenes' of your wedding. Picture yourself and others in each scene as you play the different selections.

Successful wedding planners, consultants and musicians instinctively conceptualize different parts of the wedding as "scenes" and they use certain definitions that you may not be familiar with yet. These definitions will be very helpful to you at the beginning when you are gathering information and interviewing caterers, catering halls or hotels, etc., and dealing with musicians or DJs.

Step Two

Keep a small notebook just for planning your wedding music. Start a list of music ideas. Using the definitions we just gave you, keep a separate page for each one and write down several songs you would consider using for the 'scenes' of your wedding. Jot down titles of songs you particularly like as they occur to you and when you hear them in films, on radio and TV and at other weddings and affairs.

Just as you would want to highlight the emotions of the ceremony, the same is true of the reception, whether it's a small intimate dinner, or a full-blown party. Recognizing and honoring your family and friends and other important people in your lives through special pieces of music during the reception adds warmth and closeness and can make all the difference in the world to the success of the wedding. As you're visualizing the scenes of your wedding, keep these special people in mind. A great way to do that is to find out the special song some of your friends and family members played at their weddings. They will love hearing 'their' song at your wedding.

Now that you know how important it is to visualize your dream wedding, give yourself permission to spend time doing just that and to luxuriate in your daydreaming. The ideas and pictures forming in your mind will be the foundation of your wedding program. There's much to do, but it's a time to enjoy and remember for the rest of your life. We encourage you to take the time and to give all your dreams the attention they deserve.

We wish you a beautiful wedding, and may music and love fill your lives forever.

With love from,

Barbara & Gloria

© 2000 MusiConcepts®
www.weddingmusiccentral.com

GLORIA SKLEROV and **BARBARA ROTHSTEIN** are co-founders of MusiConcepts®, an independent record label and music production company. As professional songwriters and producers, Gloria and Barbara have had many years of experience writing music and special songs for movies and TV, including music for wedding scenes, for which Gloria has won 2 Emmys (with 5 nominations).

Their web site, *weddingmusiccentral.com* offers the "SET YOUR WEDDING TO MUSIC" CD series, the only line of wedding music CDs created *exclusively* for weddings by Grammy and Emmy Award winning artists, writers and producers. We think these CDs are the finest recorded wedding music out there. Many of the classical recordings found on their ceremony album, "FOR YOUR WEDDING CEREMONY", have been used for wedding scenes in "PASSIONS" (NBC TV). This CD features updated favorite classical selections with a movie 'soundtrack' approach, created by Gloria Sklerov, and her contemporary approach to these arrangements are a breath of fresh air for today's formal and informal weddings. The site also features song lists and song suggestions and samples of different choices of music to listen to as couples visualize their wedding 'scene by scene'.

Brides and grooms search for the perfect song for special wedding dances with their fathers and mothers and other significant relatives and friends. Your brides and grooms (and their parents) will appreciate you that much more for leading them to these very special songs written by Gloria Sklerov and Barbara Rothstein for father/daughter dances, mother/son dances and many more, all a part of their CD "YOURS, MINE & OURS".

Gloria and Barbara are also the authors of the #1 wedding music planning guide, "HOW TO SET YOUR WEDDING TO MUSIC". Until Gloria and Barbara introduced their book and developed *weddingmusiccentral.com*, there was very little guidance and advice available for music planning, despite the widespread popularity of wedding web sites.

One of the most common mistakes couples make is in thinking that once they've hired a band or DJ and chosen their favorite songs, their wedding music is taken care of. But *selecting* the music is only the beginning. This momentous event needs thoughtful planning if crucial mistakes are to be avoided and guests of different generations, families and ethnic backgrounds are to feel included and part of every special moment.

"Having seen too many weddings where the music was not only monotonous and ineffectual, but actually detrimental to the success of the wedding (even with expensive bands and DJs), we're thrilled to have had the chance to share our unique planning system with you, and with all the couples you'll be guiding as you help them 'choreograph' the wedding of their dreams" says Gloria.

We know you'll appreciate how easy it is working with couples who have read "HOW TO SET YOUR WEDDING TO MUSIC" and are more aware and focused on what they want for their wedding.

Chapter Twelve

End of Chapter Suggest Assignments

First Objective

Read "How to Set Your Wedding to Music" from cover to cover and complete all assignments. Create a timeline and musical score.

Chapter Thirteen

Signature Weddings

IN THIS CHAPTER YOU WILL LEARN:
- **How to create a signature wedding**
- **Sample wedding themes for each season and ideas for seasonal weddings**

A signature wedding is created from a couple's personality and is conveyed through the smallest details of the day's events. Something as small as the mint leaves, frozen inside the ice cubes or the music leading up to the processional gives a wedding the substance and ambiance that is remembered by guests for years to come.

Creating this memory is the purpose and goal of every wedding planner. An experienced planner will have many suggestions and unique ideas to fit each couple's personality. Think of your job as more of a wedding designer, in charge of developing and creating a unique day that is tailored specifically to each individual couple's hopes and dreams. Making their day, perfect.

A few suggestions are listed below:

Chocolate covered bride and groom strawberries

Wedding favor music CD

A dove or butterfly release

Donation to your favorite charity

A monogram wax seal on each invitation

Edible flowers

A cake and champagne wedding *only*

Most weddings have all the basics: the ceremony and the celebration with all the makings of a party such as music, food, dancing, etc. The details of a wedding are what defines it as a bride's wedding. Only she can decide how her signature wedding will reflect her vision of a perfect wedding day.

Begin with the season your couple plans to be married and incorporate details of the season into the couple's and your ideas. Many inexpensive ideas can really make the difference. Use your imagination and creativity, as a signature wedding is not synonymous with an expensive wedding. Remember: it is the small details that differentiate one wedding from another and makes it special for every individual couple.

Ideas for a Winter Wedding

ATTIRE

White gown for the bride

White, gray or black tux for the groom

Replace your bridal bouquet with a faux fur-lined muff

Compliment your dress with a faux fur-lined cape

CAKE

A snow globe cake topper

Create a "snow" effect and place the cake on top a pile of fabric (such as silk or satin)

An all-white cake accented with icicles

CENTERPIECES

Miniature ice sculptures on each table

A 3-wick pillar candle surrounded by an evergreen wreath

Snow globes.

COLORS

White

Midnight Blue

Silver/ Platinum

DECORATIONS

Use ice sculptures on dessert or buffet tables

Balls of vine wrapped in white lights

FAVORS

Bride and groom chocolate covered strawberries

Christmas ornaments

Potpourri sachets

Christmas bells

Small evergreen trees

FLOWERS

All white roses

White gardenias

White gladiolas

INVITATIONS

Reflect your winter theme using snowflakes or snow

Use a holiday theme

RECEPTION DECORATIONS

Lots of green or white garland

White poinsettias

White twinkle lights

Icicle lights

White lights entwined with balls of dried vine

White branches decorated white twinkle lights and tulle

Plants or small trees decorated with white lights.

TRANSPORTATION

A white sleigh

A white carriage

A white stretch SUV

Ideas for a Spring Wedding

ATTIRE

Wear a wreath of flowers in your hair, along with the bridesmaids and flower girl

Choose a dress that is strapless or has spaghetti-straps

CAKE

Decorate a white or ivory frosted cake with fresh flowers to match bouquets

Use edible flowers

CENTERPIECES

A simple arrangement of cut flowers to match bouquets

A group of individually potted herbs or potted flowers

Flowering potted plants in baskets

Sprinkle flower petals on the tables, chairs and floor

COLORS

Pastels

Pink

Light Green

White

Yellow

Blue

Lavender

FAVORS

Tree seedlings

Seed Packets - if seeds are pre-wrapped, simply tie a colorful ribbon around them. If you are wrapping them yourself, place the seeds in pretty glassine bags then accent with a colorful ribbon. Place seed packets in a large specially decorated terra cotta flower pot.

Using a 2" or 3" small terra cotta pot, place a small envelope of flower seeds and a small envelope of dirt inside. Decorate a Popsicle stick to read "Everywhere you go, love blooms". For presentation, you can decorate the pots in your wedding colors, and you can place the seeds and dirt in small, separate glassine bags.

FLOWERS

Use hand tied bouquets

Tulips

Iris

Hyacinths

Lily of the Valley

Roses

Lilacs

Ivy

INVITATIONS

Fun, spring flower theme like white daises

Invitations made from seeded paper/pressed flowers

LOCATIONS

Botanical gardens

English gardens

Rose gardens

A friend's (or your own) backyard

A historical site with plenty of flowers

OTHER IDEAS

Hire a string quartet to play during the ceremony or the early part of the reception

Trellises decorated with fresh flowers

Instead of using bubbles or rice for a sendoff, use fresh flower petals

Fresh flowers and petals EVERYWHERE!

Another spin on this theme would be to do an individual flower theme such as a daisy theme or a rose theme

Ideas for a Summer Wedding

ATTIRE

Weave strings of pearls into your hair

Pearl or crystal tiara

CAKE

Have your baker create a wave effect with blue curved icing

Have shells decorate your cake (your baker can make realistic ones)

Have a white or ivory frosted cake decorated with colored sugar to simulate sand and decorate with sugar or chocolate seashells

Use a glass cake top shaped into something that matches your theme (dolphins, mermaid, etc.)

Have your baker make the top layer of the cake in the shape of a shell and decorate it with chocolate in the shape of various shells

CENTERPIECES

Fill a hurricane or glass globe with sand and shells then insert a candle votive within the center and tie with coordinating ribbon

Decorate large and small pillar candles with small seashells (just press the shells into the candles). Pour some sand on a mirrored tile, then place one large pillar candle in the center and surround it with smaller pillars of varying sizes. You can also tie all the candles together with some raffia ribbon. Place some small pieces of driftwood and/or larger seashells, dried starfish, etc. around the candles.

Fill large jars with sand; place shells, etc. inside and then close with a cork. Decorate with ribbon.

Fill terra cotta pots with sand and push several taper candles in at uneven heights. Decorate the candles with small seashells

Fill a large clear bowl with water. Place sand on the bottom, and add shells, etc. Place floating candles and/or some flower blossoms to float on the top.

Display large conch shells with flowers coming out of them (cornucopia-like)

Place a large piece of driftwood on a mirrored tile; scatter sand on the mirror and arrange small candles around the driftwood

Fishbowls with sand and shells in the bottom with floating gardenias (perfect for a day wedding!)

COLORS

Blues

Greens

Silver

Creams

Apricots

Warm shades of yellow

FAVORS

Decorative soaps (seashells, seahorses, etc.)

Chocolate shapes (shells, etc) wrapped in tulle or small gift boxes

Fill coconut shell halves with sand and then place a votive in each one

Fill coconut shell halves with candle wax

Fill a white sea shell with candies and white and dark chocolates. Wrap with white tulle and a color coordinated ribbon.

Make candles from scallop shell halves

Bubbles tied with raffia ribbon with small shells glued onto them.

FLOWERS

Yellow and cream roses

Flowers in shades of blue; use silver accents

MENU IDEAS

Lobster boil buffet

Seafood buffet (shrimp, crab, lobster, etc.)

Offer a seafood-plated dinner

Offer a buffet with at least one or two seafood choices

Crab and lobster stuffed mushroom appetizers

Shrimp cocktail appetizers

Plated surf and turf meal

RECEPTION DECORATIONS

Make place cards by making cookies into sea shapes (starfish, fish, shells) and write each guests name on them in icing (also great favor idea!)

Another place card idea: cut blue poster board into sea shapes (starfish, fish, shells). Write on them using a silver pen.

Yet another place card idea: use large actual seashells that you either found or purchased. Print the guests' names on a clear label and attach to the shell.

Hang swags of blue/green/silver iridescent material around the walls or pillars, and then decorate with small silver sea creatures and shells.

Use seashells and shiny pebbles in floral decorations

Name the guests' tables after sea creatures (or something that relates to your theme)

OTHER IDEAS

Have your guests blow bubbles during your first dance

Name your tables after famous beaches

Book a boat for the ceremony and/or the reception

Ideas for a Fall Wedding

ATTIRE

Cream colored or beige wedding gown

It may be cool, so either have a wrap or have your gown made from a heavier fabric such as brocade or velvet

Have the bridesmaids wear different colored dresses that continue with the fall theme

CAKE

Have your baker decorate your cake with fall leaves

Decorate the base of your cake table with leaves and harvest items

CENTERPIECES

A hollowed-out pumpkin used as a vase, with fresh flowers inside

Baskets accented with leaves and filled with fall flowers

Pumpkin-colored candles in varying sizes atop a pile of shimmering white tulle

Arrange gourds, pumpkins and Indian corn on a bed of leaves.

White pillar candles on white shimmering tulle, accented with small miniature pumpkins (gourds)

Baskets filled with apples and cinnamon sticks accented with bows in your wedding colors

Dried flowers in a crystal vase tied with a raffia bow in your wedding colors

Hurricane lamps surrounded by a grapevine wreath and decorated with fall leaves or flowers

Cornucopias sitting on fall leaves or surrounded by fall flowers

COLORS

Burgundy

Buttercup

Dark Orange

Deep Red

Gold

Hunter green

Navy

Pewter

Rust brown

Shiny silver

Wine

DECORATIONS

Mix flower petals with fall leaves and sprinkle over the reception tables and floors

FAVORS

Small baskets filled with potpourri, nuts, etc. wrapped in tulle and tied with a ribbon in your wedding colors

Candy corn wrapped in tulle or placed in small gift boxes wrapped with raffia

Small splits of wine, decorated with fall leaves or flowers

FLOWERS

Dahlias

Gerbera daisies in fall colors

Hydrangea

Mums

Sunflowers

Yellow, peach or coral roses

LOCATIONS

Park

Bed and Breakfast

Winery

Farm or ranch

Apple orchard

Nature Preserve

Country inn

Chapter Thirteen

End of Chapter Suggested Assignments

First Objective
Create a list of 10 items to include at a wedding to help create a unique wedding signature.

Second Objective
Develop your own special signature packages, and break them down by budget, from low to medium to high.

Chapter Fourteen

Marketing Your Business

IN THIS CHAPTER YOU WILL LEARN:

- How to partner yourself and your business with the right associations
- The importance of marketing your business and establishing a mission
- Key elements of your business image
- How to network your business

The following material focuses on marketing and offers ideas and suggestions to help get your business off to the right start.

Associations & Memberships

Simply being associated with the Chamber of Commerce, Association for Wedding Professionals, International, Better Business Bureau or a local wedding association helps to market your business. With every association membership you should be listed in their directory and have the option of receiving a discount on other marketing promotions and events. Take advantage of their cross-promotions and network marketing events. Just being associated with a recognized organization is a form of marketing. This shows you are a professional business owner and it also helps to brand your business. A BBB membership logo on your front door or website lends credibility, showing you are recognized by a national business watchdog. This is an effective part of marketing your business.

For the first time business owner, you may not realize the importance marketing plays in the success of your business. It's as important as having a phone, fax and Internet access. Marketing your services is a necessity. If you do not announce your presence, who is going to know about the services you offer? The old saying is true without marketing, it's like having a billboard out in the desert...no one knows it's there but you.

Marketing 101
Do ONE thing EVERY DAY to market your business.

Why should I market and what am I marketing?

You are marketing yourself and your services to brides and vendors. Tell your target audience what you have to offer and that your business exists. Marketing is a necessity and it can make or break a business. Keep your message simple. The purpose of marketing is to drive clients to your business and build revenue.

Your Mission Statement

A mission statement is part of how you market your business. When a bride and groom read your mission statement, it should make them feel assured that they have made the right decision select your wedding planning services. The mission statement is the first step in your business plan but also a large part of your marketing plan as well.

Think about what drives you to make the decision to buy one product over another or to use the services of this particular vendor. There is a lot of competition out there, but if you position yourself properly, you'll have the advantage and be savvy enough to succeed in your market.

You will need a plan to market your business and services.

How do I get started?

Television, radio, magazines and bridal shows…where do you begin? You don't have to be a big spender to be a huge success. The easiest way to get your marketing started is to use a professional. Just like a bride will utilize your wedding planning expertise, you should use a professional to help with your marketing plan. **The Wedding Planning Network** is a national advertising and marketing firm that specializes in the wedding industry, with special programs for wedding planners. To schedule your free marketing consultation, go to www.weddingplanningnetwork.com. They work small to mid-sized wedding businesses. Whether you need your business logo designed or a full marketing campaign and no matter what the budget, WPN can help. Their co-op marketing program starts at $100 a month for most areas, which includes monthly bridal leads, ad placement and bridal show representation. You can also check your local directory for an advertising agency in your area. Be sure to find out if they have experience in the wedding industry.

Now, let's address the smaller everyday things you can do to market yourself on a local level before tackling the larger mediums. No matter how small or large of a budget you have, marketing is a continuous investment that should NEVER be stopped. Stop marketing, and it will eventually stop the business.

Personal Appearance

We briefly touched on this before, but it's important enough to address again. Image is everything and can influence a potential client one way or the other. Your first impression will determine whether a bride or vendor feels comfortable working with you and having you represent them. Your personal appearance is like the packaging on a product. Many Fortune 500 companies spend billions of dollars on packaging because image greatly influences buying decisions.

You don't have to spend a lot of money on your appearance to look fabulous. Be sure to have a nice haircut and don't wear too much makeup or jewelry. You should invest in a nice suit or jacket, something neutral so that you can alternate your shirt/pants, shoes and accessories to create a new look.

When providing day-of services you will need to dress based on the time and type of wedding. If it's black tie, ladies should wear a conservative mother-of-the-bride type gown, preferably with a jacket top or a nice dark suit. Gentlemen should wear a tuxedo in this case but may also wear a dark suit at other functions.

Base your dress on the type of wedding and remember that you are NOT a guest. You are working and should not wear an outfit that makes you stand out in the crowd. Your role is behind the scenes. Be presentable and professional.

Business Cards

A business card is your first line of marketing and is an inexpensive essential marketing tool. It provides your name and all pertinent information to someone would need to get in touch with you. Keep your card simple and professional. If you have a company logo, make sure that it is on your business card as well as all of your marketing materials. Don't put too much information on your card; sufficient contact information includes the company name, business address, phone, mobile phone, fax, email and website address. If you plan on giving away a free gift to your brides such as a free wedding planning calendar, note that your card is "Good for a free wedding planning calendar". Maybe it also gives a discount on your day-of-services package, such as "Save 5% off my Diamond Package". Many companies allow you to print a short message or offer on the back of your business cards.

You can print very professional business cards on a good color printer and bring to Kinko's to cut for about $10-15. There are also many online printing companies that offer great deals. www.vistaprint.com is always giving away free business cards; you only pay the shipping charge. They are only one of many inexpensive business card companies out there.

Letterhead, Note Cards, Brochures and Envelopes

These are a very important part of your marketing efforts. Just as your personal appearance is a representation of your business, so is your stationary, note cards and envelopes. You do not need to spend a fortune on these items. There are many printing services that offer competitive prices. Even your office retailers such as Office Depot, Office Max and Staples have printing services. Group buying programs also offer competitive prices. For example, Wedding Planning Network members can benefit from discounted prices for all printing services for their consultants as well as promotional products such as pens, mugs, sewing kits, etc. You may even consider bartering for these items through a local barter company, which will really help to keep your overhead start-up cost low.

Note cards are extremely helpful when first establishing your company. You should announce your new business with hand written notes or announcements and include your new business cards. Let family, friends, business organizations and local churches know that you are starting your own venture and that you would appreciate their referrals and help. They might not need your services right now, but they may know someone who will need the assistance of a wedding planner in the future.

Networking

People want to do business with accredited individuals who have completed the required course work and experience that qualifies them as an expert in their field. You may earn your certification at the end of this course, ***but people really want to do business with people they know and trust.*** Your family, friends and church members are your inner circle of contacts and to increase that circle, you'll need to network with local business groups in your community.

The following organizations are just a few suggestions; you should take the time to find out what is available in your local area.

Barter Net- www.barternet.com

This is a wonderful business tool that can help your business conserve cash, generate new business and turn excess or unused inventory into the products and services you need most. It's called business-to-business (B2B) barter, a trusted method for trading products and services. Barter is the exchange (or interchange) of products and/or services without the use of cash. While barter has been used effectively around the world for ages, technological advances have made the process faster, more accountable, and available worldwide. Today, barter enjoys greater acceptance than ever before, especially in business-to-business (B2B) markets. BarterNet created the world's largest and most diversified barter marketplace by linking a global network of barter exchanges through the Internet.

BarterNet will promote your new company to other local companies that are already in their organization. You will also be able to utilize the barter services for local marketing efforts when available.

Chamber of Commerce- http://www.uschamber.org

The Chamber of Commerce is a wonderful way to meet and greet with other businesses in your community. A small business membership may be available, depending on your area. Take advantage of it when you can. You may not need to take on an annual membership, but be aware of business "after hours" or other events that non-members can attend. Showing your face once or twice a year will help build your credibility and give you an opportunity to pass out those business cards.

National Association for Female Executives- http://www.nafe.com

The National Association for Female Executives (NAFE) is the largest women's professional association and the largest women business owners' organization in the country. NAFE provides resources and services through education, networking, and public advocacy to empower its members to achieve career success and financial security.

Office of Women's Business Ownership Small Business Administration- http://www.onlinewbc.gov

OWBO promotes the growth of women-owned businesses through programs that address business training and technical assistance and provides access to credit and capital, federal contracts, and international trade opportunities. With a women's business ownership representative in every SBA district office and a nationwide network of mentoring roundtables, women's business centers in nearly every state and territory, women-owned venture capital companies, and the Online Women's Business Center, OWBO is helping unprecedented numbers of women start and build successful businesses. At every stage of developing and expanding a successful business, the Office of Women's Business Ownership is here to counsel, teach, encourage and inspire.

National Association of Catering Executives. http://www.nace.net

This organization offers an excellent opportunity to network. They are the National Association of Catering Executives. They have monthly meetings in many different markets across the country. They are not the only industry specific association out there. See what others you can find in your market. This specific group has monthly dinner meetings at local catering and reception facilities. It will allow you to introduce yourself to many business owners and you'll have the chance to see how a large event is done right.

Association for Wedding Professionals, International. http://www.afwpi.com

AFWPI is an international organization dedicated to providing quality service and a central source of information and referrals for those planning weddings and those who service weddings. Members receive benefits through networking and discounted services. Brides and grooms receive free referrals to wedding professionals. Members have agreed to a set code of ethics, assuring greater confidence in shopping with them. This organization is a MUST for any wedding planner.

Local Business Organizations provide a great way to connect with other businesswomen in your local area. The best part about these groups is the women attending are all aware of the importance of networking and referrals.

Here is a list of other business organizations:

American Business Women's Association (ABWA)

http://www.abwahq.org

Business & Professional Women / USA (BPW)

http://www.bpwusa.org

Business Women's Network

http://www.bwni.com

National Association for Female Executives (NAFE)

http://www.nafe.com

National Association for the Self-Employed
http://www.nase.org

National Association of Women Business Owners
http://www.nawbo.org

Office of Woman's Business Ownership
http://www.sba.gov/womeninbusiness

Center for Woman's Business Research
http://www.nfwbo.org

Digital Women
http://www.digital-women.com

SCORE
http://www.score.org

These are just a few of the hundreds of associations and business organizations you can be a part of. Use them wisely. Don't spread yourself too thin, but try and go to one function a month to keep up with what is going on in your community.

Keep Up With Current Events

How does this help your local marketing efforts? First, it will keep you abreast of what's happening on both the local and national levels and you will be better informed on where the industry is going. Local and world events can have a great effect on the wedding industry. Your knowledge will position you well amongst other consultants who don't keep up with the times.

Bridal Magazines and Websites

There is so much information out there, so stay in touch. Knowledge is your power. Use what you know to up-sell to your brides and keep the vendors on track. Subscribe to all national bridal magazines and any local bridal magazines. Modern Bride, Brides, Premier Bride, Elegant Bride, Martha Stewart Weddings, etc. Other national magazines also usually publish special wedding issues, so keep a lookout. The first place a bride will turn after she gets engaged is to a bridal magazine. Subscriptions are very inexpensive and qualify as a business expense.

Placing ads in these publications are also a very good way to spend your marketing dollars. Note that all national magazines, like Modern Bride, have regional advertisers, so if you live in Atlanta you would be placing an ad in the Southeast regional edition of Modern Bride. Your ad will not be seen in NYC. Rates are based on subscribers or readers. Display advertising is more expensive than running a classified ad, so even a small classified ad in the Pink Pages is a great way to get started if you don't have a large budget. Ask about discounts or specials if you run for more than three months. Don't place an ad unless you can run consecutively for three months, it will not be worth your time and you will not see results only running once. Research has proven that triple exposure of your marketing efforts will give you a greater return on investment or ROI.

WWW

Today's wedding planner is Internet savvy. Being a sophisticated online wedding planner means you're more productive in less time and you save your brides money while bringing them the best vendor services available. Utilize the web to do research not just for the brides but also for your business. In your travels, look for websites that will let you include your information for free if you are going to be placing ads. Have you found a neat wedding site that you know would benefit from your services? Take advantage of the web; most of today's brides and grooms will go there first. Weddingchannel.com and TheKnot.com, etc. are a few of the top wedding websites available.

It is also wise to include your business information with many websites. The search engine race is always changing and a site that was ranked 15 in one week can very easily rank as number 3 this week. You also need to remember "The better the searcher…the better the search results." Just because you can find your listing or website easily doesn't mean the rest of the world can. Many people are not educated on the best way to search for a topic. It is best to broaden your exposure by listing with many sites.

You'll also want to be sure that you invest in your own business website. Everyone utilizes a website when researching a business. Let your local brides find your simple yet elegant website so that your website can do business for you. You can sell invitations, wedding day makeup, gifts, favors, etc. in your online store. You can find businesses that design websites specifically for wedding vendors; they are not that expensive.

Email

Take advantage of your email. Utilize it to get in touch with brides and vendors whenever possible. We don't encourage spamming, but sending specifically tailored emails to brides and vendors can really market and move your business. It's a great way to keep in touch.

- Use Hyperlinks to promote an online service to your brides.

- Utilize the Subject Line. Catch the bride or vendors attention at first glance.

- Email signatures. Always have your email signature up to date and include all of your contact information.

There is a wonderful, and inexpensive online software called Constant Contact which allows you to create attractive email marketing pieces. It is very user friendly and it is free for up to 50 users or email addresses in your account. Their website address is www.roving.com. You can keep track and market to vendors or brides separately or together. You can create a monthly email newsletter, send out coupons or market a new service. It is a great marketing tool. www.roving.com

Do your research; there are many different emailing software packages available. To ensure you are not spamming people, you should use a software that has an unsubscribe feature so that a user can be removed from your list.

Voicemail

You've passed out your business cards and mingled at the local Chamber events and now your phone starts to ring. Great! So, what will the bride and vendor hear on your voicemail? Make sure you leave a professional voicemail message for your potential clients to enjoy when you are out of the office. Here is an example:

Hello, you have reached Suzie Sample, a certified wedding planner with Wedding's Are Us. I am currently unavailable to take your call, but your call is important to me. Please leave your name, short message along with your number and the best time to reach you and I will return your call. You can also email me at ssample@weddingsareus.com. Have a nice day.

Bridal Shows

Don't miss out on your local bridal shows. Find out when your local bridal shows will be held and reserve booth space. Bridal consultants are lucky in that there is a marketing event available that directly targets their clients: brides. Do no less than two bridal shows per year. They should be a staple in your marketing plan. They are worth the investment, as the brides will come to you.

January, February and March are the biggest show months because many couples get engaged over the holidays. Your market will dictate your bridal show schedule, but June, August, September and October will also result in successful shows.

If you don't have a booth at a bridal show, and you haven't attended one before, it will be worth your time to attend. Find out all the details ahead of time and bring your business cards. Bridal shows make their money from vendors and consultants buying booths and advertising.

They will most likely be fickle about you promoting your services to brides directly. Take this time to briefly introduce yourself to vendors, even it you just drop off a card and be sure to pick up as much information on the vendors as you can.

Bridal shows are one of the most important networking opportunities for any wedding planner. It's a great way to speak with many vendors in a short period of time. You have the chance to pass out your business cards to vendors and to also introduce your services.

When participating in a show, don't just walk around or sit behind your table. Introduce yourself to every vendor and bride. Once you have your vendor network established you will be ready to handle the high volume of clients that a bridal show can bring. A bridal show also lends credibility to your services. Only the premier wedding vendors go to bridal shows consistently. Please review the bridal show chapter for more information.

Press Release

This is an effective marketing tool. Intertwine your press release schedule to coincide with your marketing calendar. Your first release should be sent out to all local media to announce your new business. Review the PR chapter for more information.

On-Line Cross Promotion

Take advantage of your new business colleagues and vendor partners and cross promote whenever possible. Share Internet links on your website whenever feasible. If you chose to swap links with a national company, make sure they are active in your local market.

In-Store Signage

In addition to the online promotion, once you have established a solid relationship with your local vendors ask them to display your brochures, business cards, etc. in their store. Reciprocate by keeping their information in your store location or include them in your media kit. Every little bit helps, and the wedding industry is built on networking and referrals.

Specialty Items

For those consultants who are interested in investing a little more and adding to their presentations or giveaways, specialty items are a great way to promote your company with a "leave behind". Chose items that are useful and can include your company logo (i.e. pens, shirts, note pads, calendars, magnets etc.). There are many specialty item businesses out there, so shop around for the best price. Choose useful items that will display your company name.

No matter how you market your business, always uphold the highest standards as you start to build and market your business.

Chapter Fourteen

End of Chapter Suggested Assignments

First Objective

Start working on your annual marketing plan. Break down your plan quarterly, then monthly and weekly. Reference the website below for step by step guidelines on completing your marketing plan. Keep in mind that your business plan and marketing plan go hand in hand.

http://www.entrepreneur.com/howto/mktngplan

Second Objective

Order your business cards, letterhead and any other marketing materials you will need. Be sure to stay within your budget and that you have your legal business name on the cards, etc.

Third Objective

Research and join at least one local business networking organization.

Fourth Objective

Create your business brochure. Be sure to include your company name, logo, contact information, list of services and what you specialize in, i.e. what sets your business apart from all the rest.

You can use a variety of software programs to help you with the look and design of your brochure. For example, MS Publisher has many user-friendly templates to choose from.

Start now and do one thing every day to market your business!

Don't forget...The Wedding Planning Network offers FREE marketing consultations, so take advantage.
www.weddingplanningnetwork.com.

Chapter Fifteen

Marketing on a Local Level: Be a Social Butterfly

IN THIS CHAPTER YOU WILL LEARN:
- The secret to self promotion
- Unique ideas to help market your business locally
- How to organize and conduct a successful seminar or wedding planning party

Get Out of the Office

A bride cannot live on wedding cake alone, just as a wedding planner cannot survive by strictly working from her home office. Brides want to work with a wedding consultant who is known and respected in her community. Get out there and shake some hands, make eye contact and do some marketing to help make you stand out above the rest.

The Secret Ingredient:
Self-promotion…the life of a Successful Wedding Planner.

Having a bunch of prospective brides in your email box and a valuable group of vendors does not a successful wedding planner make. Self-promotion and how well you follow-up with your clients are what will make or break your wedding planning reputation and career.

Brides and vendors want to work with a wedding planner they've heard of…one with a name they recognize. Who is the fairest of them all?

Do you know who is recognized in your area as THE wedding planner to have? If not, you better find out and keep up with where she is networking and how she markets herself. Then go one step further and find a marketing niche that sets you apart. Offering your complementary service is a start, but getting the word out is the key!

Here are some suggestions of things you can do to market your services to bring in more brides and build the confidence of your vendors. Don't be shy; let people know what you are doing, who you are and how your services can benefit marriage bound couples looking for help. Almost everyone is only a few degrees away from knowing someone who is getting married.

Where to Begin

By now you've already started introducing yourself to brides and vendors through your email campaigns and over the phone. If you haven't stepped out from behind your desk and made some face-to-face calls, go NOW! People want to do business with someone they know and trust. Put a face to a name and set appointments with all of your vendors to start building your business relationships.

To really be certain a vendor is of exceptional quality you need to visit their shop, see examples of their work and get to know them personally. It's a lot to do when starting out, but you'll be laying the groundwork for success if you work your market right from the start. Once you have met all of your vendors at least once, future calls and email contact is all that is necessary for the majority of communication you will be doing with them.

You MUST sell yourself.

Vendors will even begin to send more brides your way! By touching base with your vendors every few weeks, you will notice an increase in your bridal referrals. Pick up the phone. Ask questions, talk specifically about your brides and wedding dates. This shows you are on top of what's going on and such action will build confidence in your vendors that you are promoting *their* business to your potential clients.

Now what?

You've pulled yourself away from you desk and you're ready to jump into being the best wedding consultant in town. Not sure what to do? Try some of these ideas on for size…they are sure to set you above the rest.

Wedding Planning Seminars (8-10 Couples)

A wedding planning seminar is a chance to meet newly engaged brides and an opportunity to display your wedding expertise. The bride and groom will benefit from the education and information you will provide by inviting a few vendors to explain their industry and services. Giving your vendors the opportunity to speak to a captured audience of potential clients is a unique way to get your name buzzing in the wedding community. Displaying your ability to organize and successfully coordinate a seminar will build confidence in your guests to book YOU for day-of-services once the seminar is over.

Utilize one of your best reception locations, or think outside the box and pick a unique location. Throw a Wedding Planning Seminar once a month or partner with a vendor and hold it at their place of business. This is great for hotels and reception halls as well as dramatic places like a photographer's studio or a flower shop. Make sure there is plenty of room and limit your guest list appropriately to insure proper accommodations.

Introduce What You Can Do!

This is your chance to shine and introduce your wonderful wedding planning assistance. Note that you are certified and that you're part of the local professional association or The American Society of Wedding Planners..

Vendors

Start by organizing your network of vendors. Chose one vendor from each category (i.e. photographer, caterer, florist, etc.) and have them discuss their specialties and guidelines as to what a bride-to-be should look for in a particular type of service or vendor.

Vendors love to promote their business and are always looking for new marketing venues. Each vendor will focus on what they do best; you can facilitate the introductions and keep the ball rolling. Limit each vendor to no more than 15-20 minutes, so you can stay on schedule- your seminar should not be an all day event. Brides will be excited to learn about everything, but don't let it drag. You want to show the bride you know how to keep your event on schedule and stay in control!

Scheduling these seminars once a month is reasonable unless you feel you can effectively handle more than that. Plan your wedding seminars to rotate between all of your vendors so that everyone gets a fair chance to promote their services.

Hint: Invite non-competing vendors each month; this will keep your vendors happy and avoid blatant competition. Keep in mind that you are doing this to network brides with your vendors. That's the bottom line. Your vendors are there to book those brides. This equals revenue for everyone.

How long should the wedding planning seminar last?

Keep the program no more than an hour to an hour and a half. Be sure those doing the presentations are prepared and professional. Use the remaining 30-45 minutes for the brides to socialize and ask questions.

Hint: Encourage your vendors to provide a small gift or sample of their services for the couple to take with them, such as a rose from the florist, a small jar of ring cleaner, a cake cutter or sample of cake. Don't be afraid to ask; vendors will usually be more than happy to show off their talents.

Should I pass out marketing materials?

Yes. Both you and the vendor should provide the bride with marketing materials and always have plenty of business cards available. Utilize your client profile forms and brochures. Put all of these materials together in a gift bag for the couple to take with them.

What about the wedding vendors that get left out of the seminar?

You should try and rotate between all your vendors; it's wise to plan your annual calendar. This will give the vendors an opportunity to pick and choose the best date and will give them time to prepare. Always confirm with your vendor the week and day before your seminar to insure they will be attending. Make sure you have an alternate, just in case.

If other vendors would like to provide coupons or giveaways, this is always nice, but make sure that it does not conflict with the vendor who is speaking at that particular seminar. Always have only one of each type of vendor represented at each seminar, regardless if they are speaking or providing freebies.

You will be the buzz of your wedding neighborhood when you start offering wedding planning seminars.

How should I promote my seminar to vendors?

First, map out your annual seminar objectives. Gather all the dates and decide if you are going to do any themes. You can focus your seminars around things such as etiquette, signatures, weddings on a budget, destination wedding locations, military weddings, holiday weddings, encore weddings, etc. The list is endless.

Decide what you want to focus on and create your calendar. Your next step should be to contact your vendors. Gather your list of vendors and send out a nice HTML marketing piece to them along with your calendar of events to encourage them to be a part of your wedding seminar calendar. You will be sure to fill that calendar within 48 hours.

How should I promote my seminar to brides?

Utilize your current database of brides or buy a list. There are many companies from whom you can purchase a marketing list. Send out invitations.

Have your vendors promote it to their customers. They will be happy to promote the seminars they are speaking at or sponsoring. You can convert their customers into bridal clients.

Contact your local churches and let them know what you're offering to newly engaged couples. We all know that there is money to be made in the wedding business, but what comes first? The marriage ceremony, and the majority of wedding ceremonies happen in a church. You may get a mention in a weekly bulletin or even in the sermon. Make friends with the local congregations and provide them with your annual calendar. Ask them to include it in their package of information for new couples.

Are you in a military market? Post a flyer on base or find out where soon-to-be military spouses get their wedding information in order to obtain those military brides as your clients. Military weddings are a wonderful focus for a seminar if you live in a military market.

Advertise in a local bridal magazine and provide your annual calendar. Send out a press release to promote your wedding seminars.

Seminar Tips

Always try to have a caterer who can supply appetizers for your guests to try. Use a florist or have a florist donate an arrangement and give it away as a door prize. See if all the vendors will donate their services at a discount to one bride who has the lucky number which will be drawn at the end of the event. Get creative.

Use wedding favors as gifts and always give away something. Have a local DJ or quartet play music to show off what they can do.

Bring your laptop and have your brides register with you online during the question and answer period. Set your next appointments.

Have your calendar open and ready to arrange your next meeting with each bride. If they like the seminar they should take you on as their "day of" consultant. Don't push your service, and be sure to let them know you are available for questions following the seminar. By keeping your seminar small and intimate, you will be able to give enough attention to each couple and will make them feel that they are just as important as the next couple.

Offer a discount on your day of services if the couples book your day of services that evening, or give them a week to decide.

Should I charge for the seminar?

You should try and offer the seminar for free or charge a small fee. This will encourage more new couples to attend. You and the vendors will make your money when they book. Be sure to be aware of the size limitations if you are holding it in a conference room vs. a church hall.

Maybe you want to ask for donations for a local charity if your seminar falls during a local charity event or do it in conjunction with a local event.

If you do feel like you have the need to charge a nominal fee for attending, be sure that you have something to give away.

Church Wedding Planning Seminars

We alluded to contacting your local churches to promote your wedding seminars, but why not throw a free seminar at some local churches. If you do this, be sure to focus on their religious traditions and see if the vendors and the church will let you hold your seminar at the church hall.

Limo Wedding Planning Parties

Sponsoring a "Limo Wedding Planning Party" is a mobile spin-off of your wedding planning seminar. A limo wedding planning party is pulled together by you and involves vendors donating their services to several brides who will win your contest. The key to this mobile seminar on wheels: a limousine.

You will want to create a contest and ask brides to register to win an afternoon/evening wedding planning party. Your main form of transport will be of course a local limousine vendor. Your limo will take you and a party of 6-8 brides or couples around town to meet the vendors who are sponsoring this mobile party. This can be great fun and usually draws some press.

Plan this event in advance, and if you can have vendors offer it at a bridal show you will be the most popular wedding planner in town. The vendors who donate their services should help promote it to their customers in their own shops.

Getting Started

Contact the limousine company first to see when they are willing to donate their time and see how long they are willing to cart you and your newly engaged couples around town. The incentive for the limousine company to donate a driver and a limousine for your event is that you will actively help to book the couples with the limousine company. The limo company has somewhat of an advantage because they are able to spend the entire event promoting their service and demonstrating their professionalism.

It is also good business to include a little something from each vendor you visit. For example, have a florist provide each bride with a small nosegay bouquet or single rose. The bakery can also provide cake samples or a mini-cake for each couple to take home. You also want to include ways to incorporate services. Take your brides on an afternoon adventure to look at reception locations, taste food at a local catering company or have a string quartet serenade them while they try on wedding gowns at the local bridal shop.

Make sure all vendors have marketing pieces to send along with your brides.

Promote your wedding planning services as part of the promotion and you'll be almost guaranteed to sign on all 6-8 lucky couples. Do this twice a year or once each quarter. Create anticipation and excitement so brides start to look forward to your quarterly event.

All vendors should donate their services. You can ask other vendors to donate coupons or freebies to encourage these wedding party brides to use their services. It is almost guaranteed that all of these brides will book with you and your sponsoring vendors.

What's the incentive for Brides?

It's a fun and exciting way to plan their big day! Who wouldn't want to be driven around in a limousine and treated like a princess? You'll have to work with your vendors on this one, but it is very possible to get your vendors to provide one or all of your brides with a give-away, free service or discount.

How do I promote my Limo Wedding Planning Party to vendors?

Simple. Put together a proposal and submit to all of your vendors. Detail how you envision the party to unfold and let the vendors know that it is first come first serve. Be sure to inform your vendors that each tour will consist of non-competing vendors. It will also help if you can reserve a limousine company ahead of time. It will show the vendors you are serious and have secured your transportation.

How do I promote my Limo Wedding Planning Party to brides?

The vendors that sign on with you will help to promote this wedding party to their clients. A mailed formal invitation is a direct way to get the attention of a prospective bride. You can also send out an email campaign to all of your brides announcing the contest.

Send out a press release to the media to get some attention.

You'll want to design a marketing piece to place in your participating vendor locations to help market the event. You can use registrations cards or have a fish bowl for brides drop in their name and number to "register to win".

If you are a member of The Wedding Planning Network, they can help market and promote your event.

Limo Wedding Planning Party Tips

Every bride in that limo should walk away with a new wedding planner. You! Make sure it's fun. Play your wedding music CD and have some extras on hand for purchases.

Create a generic Limo Wedding Planning Party invitation and use it for all of your winners for every limo event you coordinate; you need to plan ahead. Offer discounts and coupons to all of your participants if they make a purchase or place another type of order in a timely fashion. Get them while they are hot!

Market the wonderful YOU!

If you don't do it, no one else will. Getting the word out about your business when you're first getting started is the hardest part. But once you start you'll earn respect, and once the vendors and brides see that you can throw a great seminar or wedding party your dance card will be booked all year long!

Hint: Purchase car magnets with your company name and logo for the sides of the limousine so you will be sure to attract attention. You should also place a magnet across the back of the limo that says "WEDDING PLANNING PARTY". This will build momentum for your next party and create interest in your company in passers-by.

Chapter Fifteen

End of Chapter Assignments

First Objective

Schedule your wedding planning seminars and approach your local vendor partners to participate.

Second Objective

Schedule your wedding planning parties, coordinate with the limo company and then approach your local vendor partners to participate.

Chapter Sixteen

Bridal Shows

IN THIS CHAPTER YOU WILL LEARN:
- The importance of bridal show participation
- How to research bridal shows
- Essential elements of a bridal show checklist
- How to book a show
- How to work a booth
- How to conduct a post bridal show follow up

Bridal Shows are an amazing marketing tool for your business. With potential exposure to thousands of brides, the leads and the vendor contacts you gain from investing in a bridal show are invaluable. It is one of the best ways to build your business.

Every consultant should research the most successful and reputable bridal shows in their own area and attend at least one to two shows a year. Since the cost of a show can range anywhere from $300 to $1,000 it is important to know exactly what is involved in doing a show.

Steps to take when participating in a show:

Research

Book a booth

Prepare for the show

Attend the show

Do a post show evaluation

Objective

Set goals when participating in a bridal show to ensure you make the most of it. Your overall objective is to inform the public about your wedding planning business.

Some basic goals should be:

→ Inform brides about what YOUR business has offer

→ Introduce yourself to the brides as a certified wedding consultant

→ Introduce your business to your local market

→ Familiarize yourself with local vendors

→ Build a rapport and network with local vendors

→ Register brides to utilize your wedding planning services

→ Obtain updates on the latest trends in the industry

Researching Bridal Shows

The Internet is your easiest tool for researching bridal shows in your area. However, you may also want to talk to some of your vendors and see which shows they attend. National shows tend to be more expensive than locally held shows, and vendors have an inside track.

To start your research on the Internet here are a few sites to review:

http://www.afwpi.com

http://www.bridalshownearyou.com

http://www.bridal-show.com

http://www.weddingpages.com

http://www.greatbridalexpo.com/default.asp

http://www.bspishows.com

http://www.bestbridalshow.com

http://www.bridalexpos.com

http://www.osbornejenks.com

There are many more production companies that work regionally or by state so search specifically for your local area.

Always keep in mind the potential of partnering with the host of the bridal show, your vendors or another consultant in your area. This will help with the cost of getting a booth. You should also inquire whether the bridal show would offer a discount in order to promote their show on your own website if you offer a reciprocal link.

WHAT TO LOOK FOR

When researching a bridal show it is important to take into consideration a number of different factors.

Is it a national or locally held show?

National shows tend to be more costly than a locally sponsored show. However, local shows may offer you the same sort of exposure to potential brides, but they may offer less in the way of advertising and pre-show exposure.

What will the show offer you?

You will need to find out what the bridal show fee includes when you book a booth for the show. Questions to ask:

⇨ Will the show supply you with an Excel spreadsheet of all brides that register at the show and what information will be included?

⇨ Are email addresses included?

⇨ What size table is available?

⇨ Are table linens provided?

⇨ Are chairs provided?

⇨ Will a badge be given to indicate that you are a vendor?

⇨ Will there be hooks to hang your banner?

⇨ Will they provide the banner or do you need to bring your own?

⇨ What kind of electrical outlets will you have access to? (This won't be necessary unless you are planning on bringing a laptop computer.)

⇨ Is Internet access available?

⇨ What is the charge?

You can have brides register online, in addition to filling out registration cards.

Most bridal show Web sites will have a vendor page with these specifications. If the information you need is not there you will need to call and find out. It is important to know what to expect when you arrive so there are no surprises.

What sort of advertising will be done to promote the bridal show?

Many shows advertise before the event either via television, radio or newspaper. There are often additional advertising opportunities for vendors. For example, there may be booklet or bridal guide distributed to brides-to-be. You need to find out what kind of advertising they will do for you and for the show. Shows that invest a lot in advertising may be slightly more expensive than shows that do not advertise or print a bridal guide.

What is the cost?

The cost of a booth at a bridal show can range anywhere from $300 to $1,000 depending on the size and venue. Also, check on the possibility of reserving a half booth which they would offer at a discounted price. As a wedding planner there won't be too much involved in the set up, so it is possible to fit in a smaller space if they offer that as an option. Most shows require a deposit and the balance owed can either be paid closer to the day of the show or even the day of the show. When you are booking a booth, request a map of the booth set up and find out where your booth will be located. Also find out the cost of tickets to brides. If the cost of tickets is very high, it might deter potential brides from attending the show.

What is the set up time and break down time?

Find out how early you can begin setting up for the show. You may be able to go the day before the show and decorate your booth. If your show does not start until late in the afternoon, you can usually go early in the morning to set up. Find out what their policy is on breaking down. Do they have a time that you have to be broken down by? Keep in mind show producers usually discourage you from breaking down earlier than the specified time. For example, if the show ends at 4pm in the afternoon, they will not want you breaking down your booth at 3:30pm.

What is the location of the show and how much traffic will there be?

You want the show to be held in a reputable venue such as a convention center or hotel. Take into consideration that you will not get any additional traffic at the show other than the brides that are attending. If the show is held at a mall for example, you have access to more traffic that wasn't planning on going to the show. The bridal show should be able to provide you with a projected amount of traffic based on the previous year's bridal attendance. Make sure the amount of traffic will be worth the cost of investing in the show.

Will you receive a lead list?

A lead list is a list of all the brides who attended and registered for the show. Often shows will distribute these lists to vendors a few weeks after the show. It is important to email the brides on that list in addition to mailing a marketing piece and picking up the phone to call and introduce yourself. Even if the bride did not stop by your booth, still market to her. She may not have had the time to stop by. Here is a standard email template to refer to.

Dear New Bride-to-be,

My name is _____, and I am a Certified Wedding Planner. I received your registration from the Phoenix Bridal Expo and I wanted to touch base to let you know about our free wedding planning assistance to help you in planning your big day!

Looking at your wedding date, it appears you're at the beginning stages of your wedding planning. I would love to hear about what you've already accomplished in the planning process and how you envision your special day! It will help in personalizing my vendor research for your specific needs, so please let me know if we can setup a mutually convenient time to speak on the phone.

Please call the toll-free number below to contact me. If you get my voicemail, please leave the best time to contact you (and a phone number). Or you can just email me with more information on vendors you've already booked (or are considering booking) and what your ideas/themes are for your big day!

Congratulations on your engagement and have a great day!

Sample Sue
Certified Wedding Planner
1234 Maple Drive
City, State 55555
(555)555-5555
ssue@yourbusinessname.com
www.yourbusinessname.com

What other events will be happening at the show?

Often bridal shows will have a fashion show or some other kind of attraction for the brides. If there is some kind of special event it will help draw people to the show. Some shows will hold raffles; this is a good way to get additional exposure for your business. You can donate a gift package to the show to give away during the raffle. This can be anything from a wedding planning book to a Free Day of Service. Get creative…investing a little in a giveaway can go a long way towards promotional mentions at the show.

Don't forget presentation is everything; package your gifts in a pretty fashion. This is an area where you can be really creative and get your name out there. You will want to find out if there is a minimum dollar requirement for the door prize beforehand. Sometimes shows will ask that you have your door prize approved by them as well.

What other vendors will be attending?

It is good to know what other wedding professionals will be at the show. You may even request a list of participants. This is going to be a great way for you to network yourself and expose your business to many other vendors. The vendor list is also a lead list for potential vendor partners in your local market. Here is an example letter; you should feel free to submit your own copy as well.

Dear Wedding Professional,

I am writing to inquire about your services and available dates for next year's wedding calendar.

I am working with several new brides-to-be in your area and I am in the process of researching for quality vendors to include in my preferred vendor list.

Please let me know if you are interested, as this is a new area for me and I am looking to establish my preferred vendors to work with on a continual basis.

I will be happy to answer any questions and can be reached at the number below. I look forward to hearing from you.

Sincerely,

Sample Sue

Certified Wedding Planner

1234 Maple Drive

City, State 55555

(555)555-5555

ssue@yourbusinessname.com

www.yourbusinessname.com

CHECKLIST

Here is a checklist to ensure that you have gathered all the information you need:

- ✓ Name of Show and Name of Sponsor
- ✓ Date and Time of Show
- ✓ Location or Venue of Show
- ✓ Contact Name for the Show
- ✓ Contact Phone Number and Email Address
- ✓ Cost of Booth
- ✓ Booth Specs
- ✓ Booth Map
- ✓ Cost of Tickets
- ✓ Partnership Possibility
- ✓ HTML Coding Link for Their Web Site
- ✓ Lead List
- ✓ Set up/Break Down Time
- ✓ Other Vendors
- ✓ Traffic Anticipated
- ✓ Advertising Options
- ✓ Raffles or Door Prizes
- ✓ Bridal Leads

Booking a Show

Once you have researched the bridal shows in your area and feel confidant the one you have selected is the most cost effective show for your business and the amount of exposure you will receive, the next step is to book the show. Request a contract outlining the terms of your agreement. The contract should include the cost of the booth, when deposits and payments are due and the specifications of your booth. Many shows have terms and agreements including the use and distribution of the lead list as well as what you can and cannot promote at your booth during the show. Examples would include promoting other vendors who are not participants of the show. It is not fair to the vendors who have paid for the show if a competing business is promoted without paying to be represented at the same show. It is important that you follow the terms and agreements of all shows you attend.

Preparing for a Bridal Show

Now that you researched and reserved your booth, the next step is to prepare for the day of the show. The best way to avoid mishaps and to get the most out of your bridal show experience is to be prepared and to know what to expect. Don't wait until the last minute to prepare.

Decorations

Setting up your booth is imperative to attracting brides. You should use a company banner and by adding a few inexpensive decorations, it can really add to the attractiveness of the display. Remember to keep it simple though. A few decorations can go a long way and won't take you a long time to set up or take down.

Supplies

You will need additional supplies for the show. For the brides to fill out the registration cards you will want to provide a few pens and perhaps some clipboards for them to write on while they are standing, especially if you have a small booth. Nametags are given out for vendors to wear.

You will probably get a little hungry and thirsty from talking to so many people. It is a good idea to bring a small snack along with you and plenty of bottled water. The snack foods at the shows tend to be expensive and you may not get a chance to slip away to get something to eat. So be sure to eat a big breakfast or lunch beforehand so you have lots of energy to get through the day.

Dressing

You want to have a neat appearance and be dressed a step above what the brides will be wearing. This means business dress to business casual. You want to appear professional and confident to the brides.

We suggest anything from a business suit to a casual dress or skirt and blouse. Just remember to dress for success!

Remember also that you will be standing anywhere from six to eight hours, so it is imperative that you wear comfortable shoes. You can't smile and be friendly if your feet are killing you. Remember to bring shoes that can last you all day long, from set up to break down.

Suggested Bridal Show CHECKLIST

- ✓ Marketing Materials
- ✓ Business Cards
- ✓ Table decorations
- ✓ Flowers
- ✓ Florist Wire
- ✓ Scissors
- ✓ Vase
- ✓ Basket
- ✓ Banner
- ✓ Water
- ✓ Snacks
- ✓ Pens
- ✓ Clipboards
- ✓ Camera
- ✓ Comfortable Shoes

Attending the Show

The day of the show you will want to arrive early. If you have not already set up and decorated your booth, you will need to allow yourself about two hours for putting it all together if you are doing the show by yourself. If you have people who will be helping you at the show then allow at least one hour to get organized.

Once the decorations are in place and the tabletop is set up, make sure any trash that you have from set up is taken away. The show will usually make an announcement warning you that the show is about to start.

It is a good idea to get set-up as quickly as possible so that you have a chance to walk around the bridal show and look at the other booths and their set-ups. This is a prime opportunity for you to meet vendors and get their business cards and literature from their booths. Once the show starts you will most likely be too busy to walk around and if you are doing a show by yourself, you will never want to leave the booth unattended.

Greeting Brides (Working the Booth)

When brides walk past the booth you can either ask them if they would like to register for a free wedding planner or ask them if they have found a wedding consultant to help plan their wedding. At this point you will want to give the bride a registration card to fill out. While she is filling out the card, you can explain a little bit about your services and what you offer.

You will want to introduce yourself, and if you have time, ask the bride some questions about herself. Ask her when she got engaged, when the wedding date is, and if they have done any planning yet. You can also ask her whether she has ever considered having a wedding planner help her with the wedding. Do whatever you can to make them feel comfortable and get them talking to you. Create a connection with the bride and make her feel special.

After the bride registers, give her a rose as a gift from the Fresh Rose Club and also give her a postcard with your contact information and one of your business cards.

Breakdown

Packing up and taking down the both should not take very long at all. You will most likely have run out of your marketing materials and giveaways, so you will just have to worry about taking down the decorations. It is very important that you do not start breaking down your booth before the end of the show. Even though it tends to slow down towards the end, a few stragglers may be walking by and it doesn't look good to them to see you trying to get out of there as fast as possible. When the show is over, they usually give you an hour or so to clean up. Post show is another opportunity to interact with other vendors and hand out some of your business cards.

Post Show Evaluation

Almost as important as attending the show is the post show evaluation. Make sure the show was worth your while. You won't always know right away how successful the show was until you start booking your brides, but be sure to evaluate each show. Your return on investment should always be in sight.

Follow-up

After the show you will have a multitude of bridal registrations. Realistically, if the traffic at a show is approximately 1,000 brides, you will probably have time to collect and speak with 200-250 brides, depending on the length of the show and the number of people working your booth.

If you are partnering with someone else for the show you should divide up the leads. Remember that the brides will be bombarded with advertisements and solicitations after the show. However, you will want to begin following up as soon as possible.

Best of luck!

Chapter Sixteen

End of Chapter Suggested Assignments:

First Objective

Research the local bridal shows in your area and put them on your annual marketing calendar.

Chapter Seventeen

Online Marketing - Establishing a Web Presence. *Content provided by Sumantra Roy*

IN THIS CHAPTER YOU WILL LEARN:

- The importance of having an online presence
- The proper way to construct a web page for online marketing
- The importance of Keywords and placement
- Recommended Web Positioning Companies, software, websites
- Keyword Tools
- How to choose the right keywords for your site
- The importance of having your own domain name
- How to create keyword rich pages
- How to improve the Link Popularity of your site
- How to submit your site to the open directory
- How to become an Open Directory Project Editor
- About frames and how they effect search engines
- The top 10 search engine positioning mistakes
- Glossary of online terms

Google. What kind of word is that? Yahoo. Another word you don't hear everyday...or do you? So many unique words that when spoken make you think of the World Wide Web, the Internet and going online. Today's business owner has the world at their fingertips and so does the consumer.

If you are not computer and Internet savvy, please take the time to learn more. There is a great website that offers FREE online tutorials for web design and other programs:
http://www.educationonlineforcomputers.com

This web site covers the following programs: Microsoft Word, Excel, Access, FrontPage, Adobe Photoshop, Dreamweaver, Outlook, PowerPoint, Publisher, etc. To learn more about surfing the web...we suggest jumping in, clicking around and doing it. Many community colleges offer beginning computer courses, so check your local community college schedule.

The Importance of an Online Presence

It is amazing how much you can do from the luxury of your own computer. Modern day executives don't all wear Armani suits and have their driver pick them up in the Rolls Royce limo. Home-based businesses are the wave of the future. Wedding planners are part of this incredible phenomenon.

Whether you're a consumer or a business owner, utilizing the web as a resource helps make you more efficient, knowledgeable and keeps you ahead of the competition.

Beauty and the Beast

"Mirror, Mirror on the wall…who is the fairest of them all?" People do business with people they know and trust…but a first impression is what opens the door to building a long-lasting relationship. You need to look the part. Your marketing materials need to be top quality and your website needs to project your company's image just the same. Everything must all work together.

Image IS everything… website presence is the New Store Front of the technology age.

The web is the first place 90% of consumer's research before making a buying decision.

As a business owner there is no excuse for not having a website. It is a crucial part of your start-up costs and should not be put on the back burner. Your business will not survive without a website. Having a website doesn't have to be expensive. A website is an incredible way to keep your "store front" open 365 days a year.

As a wedding planner, you hopefully are utilizing the unique marketing ideas in this book, take it all the way and get your business on the web. Your competition is on the web…if they aren't…GREAT! You'll be one step ahead of them.

Today's bride and groom are web-savvy and they surf the Internet to find all their wedding needs and that includes their wedding consultant. They want to know who you are, what you offer, what makes you different and better from the other wedding consultants they have seen on web.

Weddings are big business and your image is everything…a website screams SUCCESS…that is if your site is professional looking.

Did you know that there are websites out there that have won "The Worst Website" award? Yes, there really is an award for having the ugliest website. There are chat rooms and websites dedicated to just that one topic. Don't let your business be one of them.

Website 101

Don't panic. Getting your website together is as easy as W-W-W. Let's talk about the importance of the website design.

Interactive Website Design and Template Creation

Developing a successful presence on the web takes a combination of quality content and powerful graphics. Take the time to identify your business objectives so that you and/or your developer create a simple, intelligent web solution. Interactive websites are an economical way to reach a potentially unlimited market. Also useful as a means of distributing information, a high impact site will compel customers to return time after time. Look for a company that designs specifically for wedding vendors. They will be familiar with your business and may be able to offer a savings by having website templates already designed. This allows for long-term savings as it provides our clients with the tools and instructions to maintain and update their web-presence without the additional cost of design changes. You should be able to add your own content (copy) and not have to worry about extensive labor costs that go into creating a "look and feel".

Brand and Corporate Identity

As we rush headlong towards the millennium, competition for available resources becomes increasingly fierce. To claim your slice of the pie means getting the word out - effectively and economically. Having a particular "look" signifies that your company is a key player in the game. Customers associate a distinctive logo with professional service. The elements of corporate identity selectively include Logo Design, Letterhead, Business Cards, Media Kits, Compliment Slips, Calendars, Postcard Mailers and Forms. In designing your website keep in mind your brand and corporate identity…all of your marketing should carry through and your website is no exception.

Building Your Own vs. Having a Designer

If you are web design savvy and are familiar with web design then it is in your best interest to develop the site on your own. It should be a piece of cake; you know your own business, mission and vision and should be able to convey that in your web development.

If you are NOT web design savvy and think that you'll save a few bucks by doing the work yourself…be sure you know what you're getting yourself into. Will you spend endless hours wasting time, only to then hire someone else? Bite the bullet and pay a designer/developer to do what they do best. Think of your website as a bride…should the bride plan her own wedding or should she hire an expert…YOU…the wedding planner.

Contact www.weddingplanningnetwork.com for website design. Members receive a discount, and they specialize in marketing for wedding professionals.

Building Your Own Website

OK, now that you have some idea of the computer basics, you're ready to get started building your own website. There are many "free" websites available out there. They are usually pretty user-friendly and will walk you through the entire process of building your website or page; however, they usually offer the "free" site because they will 1. Run banner ads on your web pages or, 2. Require that you pay them a monthly hosting fee to keep your web page(s) up on the web.

Be wary of these types of offers…if it's too good to be true, it probably is. They are not worth it. Another drawback is that you will not get your own URL (Uniform Resource Locator) or domain name (www.yourbusienssname.com) and will have to use theirs and be linked from their main page. Your business will never be found.

<u>Always have your own URL.</u>

Registering Your Domain

The first step in getting your website afloat is registering for your domain. Don't print up your marketing materials until you know for sure that you have the rights to your business domain name.

It is very inexpensive to register your domain name and can range from $10-50 dollars a year, depending on the company you use and how "in demand" your URL name is. With so many businesses online today, there are several extensions available. The most popular being **.COM** and **.NET, for commercial and business sites. .ORG and .EDU** are generally used for educational and non-profit institutions, **.INFO, .BIZ** are used for businesses and **.GOV OR .US** are used for government organizations.

In choosing your extension your first choice should be **.COM** and **.NET** as most people are used to typing those in following the company name.

Tip: Save your receipt, your domain registration fee IS a business expense.

Website Copy

You have your domain name www.yourbusinessname.com so now you're ready to come up with the copy. What do you say? Keep it simple. What is the message you want to get across? Are you selling your wedding planning services, day of, etc? Be sure to put your packages up on the site. If you are also selling products, invitations, wedding day makeup, gifts, favors, wholesale roses, etc. then you need to think ahead and include these items.

Here is an example of the basic five pages a wedding planner's website should include:

Home Page. This is your company face or front door. The first thing they will see when they click on your URL. The home page must include your company name, logo and a brief paragraph about what you do. It can simply be your tag line. Your other pages should also link to your other pages from here.

Services. What do you offer? Here is where you can list your different packages, rates, day-of-service offerings, and any other things you offer. Here is where you can sell your invitations, wedding day makeup, etc. Don't overwhelm your users with too many choices and keep in mind how you see your business growing so you can easily add on pages as you expand your offerings.

About Us. Who are you? Tell your visitors about yourself, brides want to know enough about your business to get in touch with you and learn more. Don't give away the entire cow, but give them just enough so they feel comfortable calling or emailing you.

Example: *"Weddings by Sue" was founded in 1997 by Susan Miller. Ms. Miller is a certified Wedding Planning University wedding planner and has continued her education with the Floral Design Institute. The staff at "Weddings by Sue" has planned and worked with some of Nashville's most exclusive brides. Their big budget experience has helped them to transform even the bride on the smallest budge. With over 450 weddings under their garter belts...they will help make your dreams come true!"*

You can also list your accomplishments, business organization memberships (BBB, Chamber of Commerce, Association For Wedding Professionals, International, local organizations, etc.). If you do annual charity events or have participated in local events, this is the perfect place to note this information.

Links. Here you can link back to other vendors you work with. Don't run out and give just any website a reciprocal link. There are many wedding websites that offer to swap links if you give them a link back. Be selective.

Contact. Provide your contact information, including your company name, business address, phone and email address. If you have a different contact for each department or customer support, this is where you should list this information.

The Tools of the Trade

Arm yourself with the tools the pros use before you start optimizing your site for the search engines.

The first and most important step is identifying the keywords that reflect the image of your site.

WordTracker.com provides a keyword research service and is the only one on the Internet that provides a comprehensive and powerful database of the most popular keywords in many industries.

Other sites:

Hitsnclicks.com   - This is a paid for site, but is very informative covering all aspects of search engine marketing.

Searchengineforums.com - These forums will inform you of everything you need to know about search engines. If you have a question that needs answering chances are it's been covered here. A very useful resource.

Searchenginewatch.com - This is one of the best sites on the web for finding information about search engines. This is the place to go if you need to find out exactly where to use keywords in your web page.

Searchenginegoldmine.com - Excellent site showing all the tricks and secrets you could possible need to gain high rankings within the search engines.

Self promotion.com - Attract more people to your website! Automatically register your URL to ALL the major search engines and indexes for FREE!

Seolist.com - A search engine optimization and search engine marketing pros directory.

Software

Search Engine Optimizer - http://www.se-optimizer.com/

Webjectives.com - Excellent free tool that analyzes the pages of your competition to determine the optimum density for your keywords.

Webposition Gold (http://www.webposition.com/)- Achieving those top rankings can be both time-consuming and challenging to attempt by hand. WebPosition Gold simplifies this process and saves you valuable time.

Marketing

Bizweb2000.com - A very useful business site. Full of articles to help increase your website traffic. Also offers a free newsletter with helpful tips for use with your marketing campaign.

Eboz - Eboz.com is listed as one of the Top 101 Best Business Sites by Windows Magazine. Eboz! offers webmasters & web marketer's free valuable resources to help them create & market successful websites.

Linking101.com - This site is dedicated to the website promotion technique of link building, reciprocal linking/link exchange, and link popularity.

Mybizmall.com - All types of marketing information including articles and books.

SiteSell.com - This Internet marketing book is only $24.95 and is packed full of incredible information.

Profitjump.com - Tips? Tricks? Secrets? Get them all. ProfitJump offers free tips and strategies for effective Internet marketing. Includes expert advice on web site promotion, traffic building, search engine positioning and more.

Web Stats

Clicktracks.com - ClickTracks displays website visitor behavior directly on the pages of your website. It's a completely new and much better approach to log file analysis.

HitBoxProfessional.com - With HitBox Professional, small and mid-sized businesses can get sophisticated, real-time Web traffic analysis without having to wade through Web server logs. There's no hardware or software to buy, and no reliance on IT personnel to run reports.

OneStat.com - OneStat.com tracks which search engines and key words drive the most traffic to your web site.

Recommended Web Positioning Companies

1stSearchRanking.com - specializes in achieving top placement in the major search engines for your company's Web site.

Arundel.net - Excellent company with extremely low prices

Esiteblast.com- Affordable search engine optimization and submission

Position-Builder.com - Search engine positioning firm

Position Solutions - PositionSolutions.com has a patent-pending 'turn-key marketing' system. It includes properly optimized doorway pages, automatic 'background' submission of pages, a new domain and ip address and 100% cloaking. Configuration for 30 keywords takes less time

Seolist.com - Find search engine optimization services

SubmitExpress.com - Ranked as the 3rd most popular search engine submission and optimization company in a recent poll by Iconocast.com

How to choose the right keywords for your web site (Resource 1stSearchRanking.com)

Keyword Effectiveness Index (KEI) - a mathematical formula which was developed by Sumantra Roy of 1stSearchRanking.com to help determine which keywords you should be utilizing for your site.

Step 1: Write down all the words and phrases that you might have searched for if you were looking for a company, which offers products and services similar to yours. For example,

Wedding Consultant Atlanta
Bridal Consultant Georgia
Wedding Planner
Wedding Director
Bridal Assistance
Wedding Expert

Hint: Stay away from single word keywords. Single word keywords tend to be hyper-competitive. A search for "wedding" or "weddings" in any search engine will probably generate hundreds of thousands of pages. While it is possible that you may get your page in the top 10 for such a single word keyword, it is unlikely.

Most search engine users have realized that they can get more relevant pages if they search for phrases rather than individual words. Statistical research has shown that most people are now searching for two or three word phrases rather than single words. Also, single word keywords won't get you targeted traffic. When people search for "wedding", they are not necessarily looking for wedding information in Atlanta - they may be interested in any other country or city in the world. Even if you got your site into the top 10 for nothing, you gain nothing from such visitors. However, when someone searches for "Wedding Consultant in Atlanta", they are your potential customer and it makes sense for you to try and get a top ranking for your site for that keyword.

Whenever you are trying to generate keywords, try to be location specific. Try to think of keywords which apply to the geographic area that your company and service is designed to serve.

A great way to obtain a list of keywords related to the ones you have developed in the first step is to use WordTracker's keyword generation service. Click on the "Trial" option at the top of the site. In the page that appears, type in your name and email address and click on the "Start the trial >>" button. In the next page, click on "Click here to start the trial". In the next page, type in the first keyword that you developed in Step 1, i.e. "Wedding Consultant Atlanta", in the text box. Click on the "Proceed >>" button.

In the next page, WordTracker will display a list of keywords related to the keyword that you had typed in. (Just scroll down the left pane to see the keywords). Now, click on the first keyword in the left pane, which is applicable for your site. In the right pane, WordTracker will show a list of keywords which, contain the keyword you had clicked on in the left pane.

Once you have added all the keywords in the right pane which are applicable for your site, click on the next keyword in the left pane which is applicable for your site. Once again, WordTracker will display a list of keywords in the right pane which contain the keyword you had clicked on in the left pane. Again, copy the keywords in the right pane which are applicable for your site and paste them in a document for future reference.

Repeat this process for each of the keywords in the left pane.

KEI - The Keyword Effectiveness Index is the square of the popularity of a keyword multiplied by 1000 and divided by the number of sites which appear in AltaVista for that keyword. It is designed to measure which keywords are worth optimizing your site for. Higher the KEI, the better the keyword.

And guess what - that's it! You now know the keywords which you should use for your site. You can now start implementing these keywords for your site one by one for each keyword, starting with the keyword with the highest KEI. Exactly how many of the keywords you choose to optimize your site for largely depends on the amount of time that you can spare from your normal business activities. But whatever the number of keywords that you target, it obviously makes sense to go for the most effective keywords first.

Tying up the loose ends:

The number of related keywords that WordTracker.com displays in the trial version is limited. In order to get all the keywords which are related to the keywords you had developed in Step 1, you would need to subscribe to WordTracker's paid service. We highly recommend that you do subscribe to WordTracker's paid service as otherwise; you will miss out on a lot of keywords that can prove to be extremely valuable to you.

Article by Sumantra Roy. Sumantra is one of the most respected and recognized search engine positioning specialists on the Internet. For more articles on search engine placement, subscribe to his 1st Search Ranking Newsletter by sending a blank email to mailto:1stSearchRanking.999.99@optinpro.com or by going to http://www.1stSearchRanking.net

Importance of having your own domain name
By Sumantra Roy

A question that I frequently hear is "Do I really need to have my own domain name?" The one word answer is "YES.". If you put up your site with some of the free web hosting services, the only company who benefits is the web hosting company. The last person who benefits is you. There are a number of reasons why having your own domain name is a must:

1) When you have your own domain name, the address of your web site will be of the form http://www.yoursite.com. On the other hand, if you put up your site on one of the free servers, the address of your web site will be something like http://www.somefreewebsite.com/yoursite/. Which of these two sounds more professional? Which of these two is smaller and is hence easier to remember? I leave you to make the judgment.

2) The only way to make money online is to build up credibility among your customers. Having your own domain name is the first step in doing that. Your customers will feel more comfortable buying whatever it is that you are selling if you have your own domain name. It makes your customers feel that they are dealing with a large, established company, rather than with some fly by night operator.

3) When you have your domain name, you can have multiple email aliases of the form alias@yoursite.com. This allows you to assign different email aliases to different functions, all of them pointing to your actual email address. Hence, for example, for questions related to the products and services that you sell, you can have an email address like sales@yoursite.com. For questions related to the newsletter that you publish, you can have an email address like editor@yoursite.com. For comments/suggestions about your web site, you can direct your customers to feedback@yoursite.com or webmaster@yoursite.com. Having different email addresses for different functions not only makes it easier for you to filter your email using your email client program (Eudora Pro, Pegasus Mail, Outlook Express etc.), but also gives your customers the impression that yours is a large, established company with whom it is safe to do business.

4) Many search engines give a lot of emphasis to the home page of a particular domain, i.e. other things remaining the same, a home page of a domain will often rank higher for a particular keyword than any other page. When you use some of the free hosting services, your index.html page is the home page of your site, but not of that domain. Hence in these search engines, your site will find it very difficult to make it to the top 20 or top 30, let alone the top 10 for some of the really competitive keywords. Just think of the amount of traffic that you will lose if this happens.

5) Some search engines are now refusing to spider the web sites which are hosted by the free web hosts. For instance, if you have a site hosted by the free web hosts, you would, until recently, have got the infamous error message saying that too many pages have been submitted from your site if you tried to submit your site to AltaVista. While AltaVista now says that "your URL has been submitted for processing" if you try to submit your site, rest assured that it will not spider any site belonging to many of the free web hosts even though it says that your site has been accepted. Can you afford that?

6) When your site is hosted by some of the free web hosts, you will find it very difficult to get it listed in a major directory like Yahoo!. Although Yahoo! will never admit that it won't add a commercial site which is being hosted in one of the free web hosts, in practice, it will be a miracle if you can get your site listed by Yahoo!!. Listing your site with Yahoo! is difficult enough even when you have your own domain. Don't make your task more difficult than what it needs to be.

If you do not currently have a domain name, are you convinced that you need one right now? The small fee that you pay per year for your own domain name is peanuts compared to the benefits that you get. You can check out the availability of domain names and register new domains here.

Article by Sumantra Roy. Sumantra is one of the most respected and recognized search engine positioning specialists on the Internet. For more articles on search engine placement, subscribe to his 1st Search

Ranking Newsletter by sending a blank email to
mailto:1stSearchRanking.999.99@optinpro.com or by going to
http://www.1stSearchRanking.net

Improve the Link Popularity of your site
By Sumantra Roy

Link popularity, i.e. the number of sites which are linking to your site, is an increasingly important factor as far as search engine placement is concerned. Other things remaining the same, more the number of links to your site, higher will be its ranking.

What is important is not only the number of links to your site, but also the types of sites which are linking to you. A link from a site which is related to yours is more valuable than a link from an unrelated site.

In this article, I explore different methods by which you can improve the link popularity of your site. I start with the methods that you shouldn't bother using, then go on to the moderately effective methods, and then end with the most effective methods you can use to boost the link popularity of your site.

1) Submitting your site to Free For All (FFA) pages
A common misconception among many Internet marketers is that while FFA pages may not directly bring in traffic to your site, it will help to improve the link popularity of your site, and hence, will indirectly bring in traffic through the search engines.

Nothing could be further from the truth. Most FFA pages can contain only a certain number of links at a time. This means that when you submit your site to a FFA page, your site will be placed at the top of the page. However, as more and more people submit their sites to the FFA page, your site will be pushed down, and finally, when it reaches the bottom of the page, it will be removed.

Now, since you can bet that plenty of other people are also submitting their sites to the FFA pages, your site will remain in these pages for only a short span of time. Hence, in order to ensure that the search engines see your site if and when they come to spider the FFA page, you will need to ensure that you submit your site to these FFA pages on a regular basis - at least once a week.

Even if you used an automatic submission program to do it, can you imagine a worse way to spend your time and/or money? Furthermore, many search engines recognize these pages which only contains links to other sites as FFA pages and may completely ignore them. And while I haven't yet seen any evidence that submitting to the FFA pages will actually penalize your site, there is every possibility that this might happen in the future.

Hence, when it comes to FFA pages, my advice is simple: don't even think about them.

2) Joining Reciprocal Link Services

Some people have recommended that in order to increase the link popularity of your site, you can join some reciprocal link services. The basic idea behind these services is that you add some pages to your site which contain links to other sites which are members of that service, and in exchange, these members will also add pages to their sites which will contain a link to your site. Theoretically, more the members of that service, more your link popularity.

However, I have plenty of reservations about using this method to boost the link popularity of your site:

i) Most of these services require that you add a visible graphical or text link from your home page to the pages containing the links. If they require a graphical link, it can completely destroy the general look and feel of your site. Even if they require a text link, how would you feel if a visitor to your site clicked on such a link and found one of your competitors (who is also a member of this service) right at the top of a page?

ii) Most of these services give the same pages containing the links to each of its members, i.e. the pages that you are required to upload to your site are exactly the same as the pages which all the other members of that service are required to upload to their servers. Even the file names of the pages tend to be the same for all the members. Most search engines are now able to detect such duplicate pages in different domains and may either ignore the pages or may even penalize all these domains for spamming.

iii) Instead of linking only related sites with each other, most of these services link all the members with each other. This means that lots of unrelated sites will be linking to your site. As I mentioned before, links from unrelated sites are simply not as valuable as links from related sites.

Hence, I don't recommend that you join any reciprocal link programs.

3) Exchanging links with other webmasters

Another way of improving the link popularity of your site is to exchange links with other webmasters who have sites which are related to yours, but are not direct competitors. Here's how you can do it:

First, open a database program like Microsoft Access and create a new table containing fields like FirstName, LastName, Email Address, URL etc. Then, make a list of the sites belonging to your competitors. Then, go to AltaVista, and type in the following in the search box:

link:somesite.com -url:somesite.com

where somesite.com is the domain name of one of your competitors. This will give you a list of all the sites which are linking to that competitor. Then, find out in what context a particular site has linked to your competitor. If this site is an affiliate of your competitor, then your chance of getting a link from this site is limited, unless you offer an even better affiliate program. However, if you find that this site has a Links page which contains links to other sites, one of which is a link to your competitor, then it is an excellent prospect for exchanging links. Find out the name and email address of the webmaster of the site and add them to your database. In this way, go through all the sites which are linking to your competitors, locate those sites which you think may want to exchange links with you, and build up your database.

Once you have done that, create a Links page in your site, and add the URLs of these sites to the Links page. Then, send an email to these webmasters, introduce yourself and your site, congratulate them on building an excellent web site, tell them that you have already added a link to their sites from yours, and then ask them whether they would be kind enough to add a link to your site. In your email, emphasize the fact that exchanging links in this way will be mutually beneficial for both of you because it will help both of you drive traffic to your sites. Wait for a month or so to see the response. Some webmasters will agree to link to you. Others will simply not respond. After a month, remove the links to those sites who are not interested in exchanging links and using the methods outlined above, try to locate more sites with which to exchange links.

When you send the email to the webmasters, make sure that you personalize each email. Don't begin every email with "Hello Webmaster", begin with "Hello Mike". If you want, you can use email merge programs to automatically personalize each email. You can check out some email merge programs by going to http://download.cnet.com and searching for "email merge" (without the quotes).

Another thing that you can do is to mention in your Links page that you are willing to exchange links with other web sites. This allows other webmasters who come to your web site to propose a link exchange.

4) Starting an Awards Program

A moderately effective method of improving the link popularity of your site is to start an awards program. You can have web sites which are related to yours apply for an award from your site. The sites which win the award get the chance to display the logo for your award. This logo is linked to your site, preferably to a page which contains more information on the award.

If you publish a newsletter, consider declaring the winners in your newsletter. You can also perform a review of the winners' sites in your newsletter. This adds useful content to your newsletter and also gives more webmasters the incentive to apply for your award, since you may review their sites in your newsletter. This also gives them the incentive to subscribe to your newsletter to see if they win the award.

Make sure that you give awards to only those sites which deserve to win. If you give your award to sites which don't deserve it, your award will have little credibility, which will, in turn, hurt the credibility of your company. Furthermore, make sure that the logo you design for the award looks professional. If it doesn't, not many webmasters will want to display it in their sites.

5) Giving testimonials

This may sound a bit unusual, but giving testimonials for products or services which you find useful can be another moderately effective way of improving the link popularity of your site. If you really like a product, simply write to the company and tell them why you liked the product so much and how it has helped you. Chances are, the company will write back to you to thank you for your comments and will ask you for permission to display your comments in their web site. Tell the company that you have no problems if they publish your comments, but request them to add a link to your site along with the testimonial. There is every possibility that the company will agree since publishing the URL of your web site gives more credibility to the testimonial.

Of course, please don't go about giving testimonials to every company you can locate just because it will improve your link popularity.

6) Posting to Message Boards and Discussion Lists

Another moderately effective method of increasing the link popularity of your site is to post to online message boards. At the end of every message that you post, you can sign off by mentioning your name and the URL of your web site. If the message board allows it, you can even include a short promotional blurb about your site at the end of your posts. However, make sure that the individual messages that are posted to that message board are archived in static HTML pages (i.e. the URLs for the individual messages should not contain a "?"). Otherwise, the search engines will consider these pages to be dynamic pages and may not spider these pages and hence, will not be able to find your link.

Email based discussion lists which are archived on the web in static HTML pages can also be used to boost the link popularity of your site in a similar manner. In this case, the signature file that you use with your email program should contain the URL for your web site.

7) Starting a Link Contest

A good method of improving the link popularity of your site is to give away prizes to other webmasters if they link to you. The prizes that you give out should ideally be something which other webmasters will find valuable enough to want to link to you, but which do not cost you too much. For instance, if you publish a newsletter, and have unsold ad inventory, you can give away some free advertisements in your newsletter to the winners. If you sell a software (or an ebook), you can give away a free copy of your software or ebook to the winners, since it doesn't cost you anything to produce an additional copy of digital goods like software and ebooks.

Link contests work best if you run the contest on a continuous basis and if you declare new winners frequently. If you run the contest for a few months, and then stop it, the webmasters who had linked to you will all remove their links. However, if you run it on a continuous basis, and declare new winners every month or so, the webmasters will have the incentive to keep their links to your site.

Also, make sure that you require all participants to have a link to your site either in their home page, or in an internal page of their site which is linked to their home page. Also ensure that the page which contains the link is no more than two levels deep from their home page (i.e. it should not take more than two clicks to go from the home page to the page containing the link). If they don't do this, the search engine spiders may not index the page which contains the link to your site, and hence, may not find your link.

8) Writing articles and allowing them to be re-published

This is by far one of the best ways of improving the link popularity of your site, and one of my favorites. Whenever I write an article on search engine placement, I first publish it in my newsletter and then I publish the article in my site as a separate web page. I also submit it to the following article submission sites:

http://www.ezinearticles.com/add_url.html
http://www.ideamarketers.com
http://www.marketing-seek.com/articles/submit.shtml
http://certificate.net/wwio/ideas.shtml
http://www.web-source.net/articlesub.htm

Many webmasters and ezine publishers frequent these article directories in search of articles. Submitting my articles to these directories gives them the opportunity of re-publishing my articles. While I have had some success with each of the above directories, by far the best among them is the ezinearticles.com directory.

Now, at the end of each article, I mention that people are free to re-publish the article as long as they include my resource box (i.e. my bio) at the end of the article. I always include the URL of my site in the resource box. This means that whenever someone publishes one of my articles in his/her web site, I have another site linking to my site. Also, many ezine publishers archive their ezines in their web sites. If they have re-published my article in a particular issue, I again get a link.

Writing articles is also an excellent viral marketing tool. As some webmasters and ezine publishers publish my articles, other webmasters and ezine publishers will read my article. Some of them, in turn, will publish my article, which will again be read by other webmasters and ezine publishers, some of whom will publish it... and so on.

Also, since only web sites related to mine would be interested in publishing my articles, all these links tend to come from related sites, which, as I mentioned earlier, are more valuable than links from unrelated sites.

Writing articles, of course, has another very important benefit - if you write good articles, it makes you known as an expert in your field. This helps to improve your credibility, which makes people more comfortable about buying your products or services.

Some notes about writing articles:

i)   I have learnt through experience that some webmasters will publish other people's articles and will display the complete resource box but will not link to the URL mentioned in the resource box. In order to prevent this, you need to explicitly state that the article can be published only if the URL mentioned in the resource box is linked to your site.

ii) Your resource box should not be too long - it should be no more than 6 lines long, formatted at 65 characters per line. Otherwise, other webmasters and ezine publishers will hesitate to publish your article.

9) Starting your own affiliate program

This is another excellent way by which you can improve the link popularity of your site. When you have your own affiliate program, you give other webmasters the incentive to link to you. In this case too, since most of these web sites will be related to the industry in which you are operating, these links will be more valuable than links from unrelated sites.

Now, when you start your affiliate program, you need to decide whether you want to run the program yourself, or whether you want to outsource it from a third party. While outsourcing your affiliate program has a number of benefits, doing so will not help you improve the link popularity of your site, because affiliates are going to link to the third party's site. In order to improve the link popularity of your site, you need to ensure that the affiliate links are pointing to your domain.

The affiliate program software that I highly recommend and have used for the affiliate program of our search engine positioning services is Kowabunga Technologies' My Affiliate Program. Although this software is hosted in a domain owned by Kowabunga Technologies, they give you the option of having the affiliate links pointing to your own domain.

10) Submitting to the directories

This is by far the most important step as far as improving the link popularity of your site is concerned. As I mentioned before, what is important is not only the number of links to your site, but also the quality of the links to your site. No links are as important as links from some of the major directories like Yahoo!, the Open Directory etc. However, Yahoo! currently requires a payment of $299 per year in order to list any commercial site. Paying them $299 per year just to improve your link popularity is probably not cost effective. But, the Open Directory is free, and you should definitely get your site listed in the Open Directory.

Also, you should submit your site to as many of the smaller directories as possible.

Article by Sumantra Roy. Sumantra is one of the most respected and recognized search engine positioning specialists on the Internet. For more articles on search engine placement, subscribe to his 1st Search Ranking Newsletter by sending a blank email to mailto:1stSearchRanking.999.99@optinpro.com or by going to http://www.1stSearchRanking.net

Chapter Seventeen

End of Chapter Assignments

First Objective

Map out a five page website that you can use for your wedding planning business.

Second Objective

Incorporate your website design into your marketing and business plan. Be sure to budget it for it!

Third Objective

Reserve your URL. www.yourbusinessname.com

The best place to register a domain is www.godaddy.com

Fourth Objective

Contact www.weddingplanningnetwork.com to have your business website professionally designed.

Chapter Eighteen

Public Relations

IN THIS CHAPTER YOU WILL LEARN:
- **How to approach the media and position yourself as an expert in your field**
- **The key elements of a press release**
- **How to get your press release out on the wire**
- **How to write your biography**
- **How to conduct editorial opportunity research**
- **How to create an editorial opportunity calendar**
- **How to contact local news and radio stations**
- **How to get your articles published**
- **How to create your business press/media kit**

In business, the old saying is true: "It's not what you know...it's who you know."

Media Relations /PR

Public Relations is image management for your business and the overall planning and research for dealing with the media. It can be the least expensive type of marketing and the most effective. Most people consider newsworthy stories to be more credible than any advertising. Getting a mention in a magazine is an endorsement from the magazine as far as readers are concerned.

When starting your business you will be networking and talking with many people promoting yourself and your services. This is public relations at its purest. Getting your name out there means you need to sing your own praises; if you don't, no one will. It is up to you to continuously network and follow-up with every contact.

Pitch Your Story

Your new business should be positioned as a hot new concept that is newsworthy and provides a service to the public. As your business grows, you will continue to inform the media on what you're doing and why your growth is newsworthy. Media outlets are always looking for unique stories that will interest or help their viewers/readers. And more importantly, every medium loves to say they got the story first! What do you do that sets your wedding planning business apart from your competition?

30 Second Sound Bite

Create a 30 second sound bite that you can consistently say when introducing yourself.

For Example:

"Hi, my name is Sample Sue and I am a certified wedding planner. I provide wedding planning services for the Houston area. My company, Signature Occasions, will be holding a traveling wedding planning party for 10 engaged couples next Saturday, June 15th. I would like to invite your news crew to participate. We will be traveling by limo to several different wedding vendor locations and providing gifts and samples from local wedding businesses. We will help each couple design their own signature wedding in one evening!"

You want to provide enough information to spark an interest and open up the conversation; however, you also want it to be short, sweet and to the point. All mediums look for the following six basics when writing a story:

Who? Tell them who you are.

"Hi, my name is Sample Sue and I am a certified wedding planner."

What? Tell them what you do.

"I provide wedding planning services. My company, Signature Occasions, will be holding a traveling wedding planning party for 10 engaged couples. I would like to invite your news crew to participate."

Where? Tell them where you work and the market you cover.

"…for the Houston area."

When? The "when" is when your event or special moment is going to happen.

"…next Saturday, June 15th…"

Why? Tell them the purpose of the event and "why" it is so special and unique.

"We will be traveling by limo to several different wedding vendor locations and providing gifts and samples from local wedding businesses. We will help each couple design their own signature wedding."

How? This is the sixth potential question that may need answering, so keep this in mind because this will be the question that will be asked after the first five questions have been addressed with your 30 second "elevator pitch".

"How can you offer an evening of wedding planning assistance to your clients and afford limo service?"

"Persistence breaks down resistance…the squeaky wheel gets the grease…the more you ask, the better your chances."

Getting PR attention requires tenacity and creative marketing. Just like you have a business and marketing plan, your company should have an annual PR schedule in place to coincide with the marketing and business plan. It will help maximize your exposure and keep you on track.

The media is flooded with requests and information from thousands of people, so you really need to be creative and set yourself apart. Most importantly, always, always, always FOLLOW-UP. Professional, prompt and repeated follow up is imperative to a successful business.

Media people rely on other resources to give them the scoop on what's new or up and coming trends. Stay in contact with your media contacts by sending them a hand written note, post cards or just leave a voice mail message every 2 – 4 weeks. You may not get a call back right away...but each message you leave re-enforces your name and your services with that person. In the future, that same person when in need of information for a story on weddings or related information may call you to get a quote or interview for their article and research.

Press Releases

A press release is the best way to introduce yourself and your story to the media all at once. It can be sent by fax and/or email to a list of targeted media contacts. Research to find out how the station or publication prefers to have a press release submitted. Some have very strict requirements and only read faxed in press releases, so emailing your press release to an editor will do no good if they are simply going to delete it.

On a local level, make sure to include your local business journals and trade publications, as well as your chamber of commerce and business groups.

When putting together a press release, be sure to keep your message brief and to the point. Today we are all bombarded with so much information that a short and simple announcement is more likely to be read then one that is several paragraphs long.

The following is a template to follow when announcing your service in a new market.

"Weddings by Sue" to Open the Chicago Market with Unique Wedding Planning on Wheels Services

(Chicago, IL)—Sue Miller, a professional wedding planner and mother of two here in the Chicago area, has opened her Chicago wedding planning business and will now offer free wedding planning parties on wheels.

Sue Miller has been a certified wedding planner for over four years and offers her services to all couples planning for their wedding, no matter what their budget is. "I believe that every couple should have the guidance and assistance in planning such an important and stressful event without struggling to afford it," say Ms. Miller. "My service fits every couple's budget and allows them to focus on the other details they would like to spend their budget on, such as a designer gown or exotic flowers."

Ms. Miller will be traveling around Chicago with 10 newly engaged couples, in two stretch limos, on an adventurous wedding planning extravaganza. The couples will be driven to a variety of vendors to learn about everything from wedding flowers to wedding music. Each vendor will have 20 minutes to present to the couples before they are whisked off to the next location. Each couple will receive a gift basket and "Weddings by Sue" will provide all of the pre-planning free of charge for each couple.

Ms. Miller received her certification from Wedding Planning University, is a member of the Association for Wedding Professionals, International and a contributing writer to various local bridal publications.

For more information contact: Sue Miller, (555) 555-5555 or via email at smiller@weddingsbysue.com.

Making Your Announcement

Sending a press release by researching and compiling your own list of media contacts is one way to get started, and the only cost is the time and effort it takes to do it. Other easier methods include using a service to put your release on the wire such as PR Newswire and Business Wire. The cost for sending a press release depends on the demographics and reach you are targeting and can range from $200-$100. You must be a member of the wire service providers which averages $125 and up for the year.

You will need to contact a local representative to get a rate card and determine if the cost is worth your time. However, before you think you are saving a buck by doing it yourself, consider the fact that if you fax a press release, the cost of long distance alone, in addition to your time spent compiling the information, could add up to the cost of a service doing it for you.

The easiest way to send out your press release is to use a PR firm or contact the Wedding Planning Network, as they offer PR services at a great rate and will even proof or write your press release if needed.

Here is a list of Distribution Services:

PR Newswire – www.prnewswire.com

Business Wire – www.businesswire.com

Internet Wire – www.internetwire.com

Internal News Bureau – www.newsbureau.com

EReleases – www.ereleases.com

PRWeb - www.prweb.com (free)

Press Kits

Take the time to put together a great marketing/press kit for your business. It is a very useful tool that can be tailored to your intended recipient. Customize the folder by adding your own bio sheet and press release.

Writing Your Bio

When writing your biography, approach it as if you are telling someone you have never met about yourself. You want to include information that helps people get a picture of the type of person that you are: where you are from and what type of things you do, etc. Assume that the reader knows nothing about you, so even the most basic information will be essential. The idea is to make you look good and come across as professional and experienced. You also want the reader to be able to identify with you.

Write as though you were someone else describing yourself.

For example, you could write "Sue Miller is an experienced certified wedding planner. She enjoys volunteering and playing with her dog, Tate."

Paragraph One: Introduce Yourself to the Reader

Tell who you are, how old you are, where you are from and where you live now. Also mention your family, if you are married, and if you have children. Give specific names and ages of spouses and children. Anyone else, or any pets that are important in your life, can be mentioned here.

Paragraph Two and Three: Background and Experience

Tell the reader things that give you credit as a professional businessperson, like where you went to high school and college and what degree you hold. Then list your work experience and different positions you have held in the past. Be sure to include any distinguishing awards or promotions or special distinctions you have received.

Paragraph Four: Hobbies and Habits

Write about personal things about yourself that you like to do. What are your past-times and hobbies? Where do you attend church? What clubs and organizations do you belong to?

Paragraph Five: Your Wedding Planning Business

In this paragraph explain what you are currently doing with your business in the first person. This is a section that will be used for quotes in the press release, so it needs to be from you. Tell the reader what types of services you offer and describe how wonderful you are as a wedding planner. Include reasons why you became a planner, why you like your work, how you got interested in the business, etc. Finally tell a little bit about why your services are special and how your company can be beneficial to a bride. You could also explain why you like working from home or being a stay at home mom (if you *are* a stay at home mom).

Example Biography

Angela Johnson is a 25-year-old upstate New York native currently living in Charlotte, North Carolina. She has two sisters, ages 22 and 14, who in Binghamton, NY with her parents Jim and LuAnn Johnson. She is single and lives in South Charlotte with her black lab, Tate.

Johnson graduated from Chenango Forks High School in 1996 and attended college at the University of North Carolina at Wilmington as a communications major. In 2002 she finished her degree in Journalism and Mass Communication at the University of North Carolina at Chapel Hill with a Public Relations concentration.

Johnson was a public relations intern for Advacon, the Carolina Union Activities Board as well as with Wedding Academy. In 2002 Angela was a recruiter for Wedding Academy and was July recruiter of the month. Currently, she works on public relations and marketing for Wedding Academy. Johnson is also a certified wedding planner through Wedding Planning University.

In her spare time, Johnson likes hiking in the Blue Ridge Mountains, working out, taking walks with her dog and spending time with family. She attends church at the United Faith Assembly of God in Charlotte and works with the youth group there.

"I began working with Wedding Academy as an intern over a year and half ago and I think that the Academy offers a unique and wonderful program to students planning on entering the wedding industry. I was certified by Wedding Planning University and enjoyed the academic program. Following graduation, I found a recruiting position with Wedding Academy and it has been a great combination, in addition to running my own wedding planning business, "Angel Weddings". The freedom that I have by working from home allows me to be my own boss and make up my own work hours. Not many people have that luxury, and I hope to someday have children and be able to continue to work and stay home with them."

Set Yourself Apart

When pitching an idea to the media plan ahead and choose one focus per quarter or month. It is easy with all that we offer to continue to keep your name on the media radar screen. Plan to send several releases scheduled over a 6 – 12 month period. Each one should have a different focus and provide informative, updated information to your list of media contacts.

Here are a few ideas to get you started thinking about how you would like to position yourself and your company with the media.

New Wedding Planning Business Comes to the market

Special story or contribution of your services to the community

Wedding Planning Party – Traveling bridal show style

Wedding Seminar

New Vendor Partnerships

Getting Started - Research

Contacting Local Media and Local Publications

The following information is a guideline for researching and contacting the media.

Editorial Opportunity Research

Local and national magazines targeting women and industry publications should be contacted to receive a media kit. The goal is to acquire the editorial calendar of the publication for the next 12 months.

When contacting a publication for the first time, it is best to start with the editorial assistant. The contact information for the editorial assistant is located in most magazines in the masthead. The masthead is the listing of people who work at and with the publication; it is divided into departments.

Notice the editorial assistant's name and contact information. When calling for an editorial calendar, ask the editorial assistant to send a media kit. If your company is interested in advertising in the publication also ask for a complimentary subscription (Comp. subscription) to evaluate the publication.

Here is a sample Masthead:

ıwalb

rer

tta

ɔneczyk

nishi

PRODUCTION DIRECTOR	Aysun Johnson
AD TRAFFIC COORDINATOR	Martin Magnusson
EDITORIAL & ADMINISTRATIVE ASSISTANT	Kathryn O'Brien
INTERN	Cybele Weisser

CONTRIBUTING WRITERS

Whit Andrews • Karen I Bannan

Once you start to receive the media kits and folders from several publications:

1. Pull the editorial calendars from each media kit.
2. Search for PR/interview opportunities related to our industry or any upcoming feature that may fit well with your company being researched for the article or interviewed for a quote.
3. Highlight all potential opportunities and create an editorial opportunity spreadsheet. Use the graph below as your guide:

Publication	Issue/Article	Closing Date	Writer	Contact Information
Working Mom	Feb. 2002 Family Friendly Companies	12/12/03	Tom Smith	555-555-5555 tomsmith@working mom.com
Bride's Mag.	Dec. 30, 2001 Online Wedding Planning	10/05/03	Dana Smith	
Business Journal	Home-Based Business	1/16/03		
Chicago Today	Wedding day stories	5/1/02		

Once an organized chart is developed it can easily be expanded as new information comes in and deadlines move forward. All the information collected should be entered into the spreadsheet. The contact information for the writer is imperative and should be given the status of writer for the specific publication/company. All contacts to the writer should be recorded in the notes section and follow ups scheduled into your calendar.

When pitching a story idea to a writer the key, is to know something about the publication you are emailing or calling beforehand. Writers like to have a scoop or be tipped off to a new trend. Many writers call PR professionals "Flack". This is because publicists trying to get their clients noticed or mentioned in a major publication, bombard writers everyday. However, the writer relies on the PR professionals to do his or her job, so it is a love-hate relationship.

When approaching a writer, be sure you angle is unique and you are able to reference past articles written by the same writer. Writers like to be acknowledged for their work and may pay more attention to your email if you are commenting on a past article or interest of the writer.

It is also important to find out from the editorial assistant how a writer likes to be contacted. Some only want email or faxes, others desire calls only or even no calls at all. Getting this information from the editorial assistant will help to avoid getting off to the wrong start with a writer. Make sure you are always polite and courteous when speaking with anyone. Even if a writer is rude or curt in their response it is usually because they are on a deadline and pressed for time. Keep this in mind and keep your conversation on track.

Types of Publications to Target

Wedding publications are a must, but think outside the box. If you are a woman, target some local women's magazines. Are you a work from home mom? Call a local parenting magazine. Whatever you can find that makes you interesting, different and "news-worthy" is what you should be pitching to your local/national media.

Contacting Local News and Radio Stations

Have you noticed that your local news reporters provide their email contact information when they do a story? In several markets news people are making their email address public in order to get the scoop on the latest news and stories. Finding this information is as easy as accessing the news station website or watching the news.

Take notice of which reporters do human-interest stories and which ones like to focus more on business. Pitch your stories according to the reporter who will be most likely to feature YOUR story.

The Assignment Desk

Every news department has what is called an assignment desk and the assignment editor is responsible for it. The job of the assignment editor is to choose what stories are going to be covered by the reporting staff. Stories are chosen by what is popular at the moment, what looks unique and of course, what is fresh and new. Press releases, emails and voicemail tips are followed-up and then a decision is made as to what will be "news-worthy" for that day.

Early in the morning a staff meeting will be called and the assignment editor, producers, directors and reporters will all be called in and told what they will be working on for the day. If someone can come up with something more interesting than what is planned for that day, the assignment editor can chose to pull one of his stories and replace it with another. In television and radio, this can happen moments before going live and in many instances, can change during the broadcast if "breaking news" happens.

Your goal will always be to get your story across the assignment desk and on the storyboard!

Television

When pitching your story to a television station, keep in mind what you have to offer visually. If you have something incredible to look at, that will give you an edge. The visual of a wedding planning party on wheels is a great human-interest story for a television station.

Once the TV station decides to do the story, remember that you will probably have the opportunity to do a "sound-bite". Be sure you are prepared and don't ramble on and on. Reporters are looking for individuals who are a "good interview". That means be professional, prepared, confident, and most of all, presentable. Dark blue is the most attractive color to wear on television, as it is the most flattering. Dark colors and solids are best; do not wear patterns and pastels as they will make you look washed out, and too much busy fabric doesn't work well with the camera lens.

Makeup: Wear foundation and natural colors; don't go crazy with the blue eye shadow. Red lipstick always works well, but stay away from too much lip-gloss.

If you get the press to use you once, you have a very good chance of them calling on you again, as an "expert". Be sure to send a thank you note to the reporter, photographer, producer and anyone else at the station that helped to get you covered. People like to work with people they like and those who are professional.

Radio

Pitching a radio station is much like television but without the pictures. They go through the same process in choosing which stories to cover. They have an assignment editor, producers, reporters, etc. The difference in pitching your story to a radio station is their format.

Format is what the radio station uses to get it's listeners to … well…listen. They can be Top 40, All News, All Sports, Easy Listening, Alternative, Classical, etc. You should target stations that will be interested in covering your story. One tip: stay away from the All Sports channels unless you're planning the wedding for a famous local sports professional or are targeting the groom.

AM Radio and FM Radio: what's the difference? Frequency. Frequency is the channel that you can locate the station on. WRDU 106.1 FM. Classic Rock. FM Radio will primarily have more music channels and AM Radio has more talk radio. AM Radio usually has a smaller reach or audience, but most talk radio listeners tend to listen longer and be more loyal than an FM listener.

Regardless, chose the proper format to pitch your stories to. If there is an easy listening station that does a noon lunch report and covers local events, be sure to get in touch. Radio stations like to be clever, and if you can get the attention of the station's DJ, you may get some free mentions or press. Just be sure you don't get on a DJ's bad side…you don't want them being negative about your business, although some say any press, good or bad, is still good PR.

AM news and talk stations will be good for you to promote yourself, and just like TV, they have different programs. Be sure to review their editorial calendars and focus on the reporters or show hosts who fit the best with your business.

When a radio station contacts you, you will probably do the interview over the phone. They may call you and tell you they are ready to do the interview right then and there. If you are in the middle of something, tell them when your next available time to chat will be. They may tell you they are in a rush and that they need a quick sound bite before the next show. Find out as much information about the story and when the story is expected to air. Keep your answers direct and to the point. Don't ramble; radio reporters and TV reporters are both looking for professionals who can speak well. Think before you speak and try to cut down on the "ums" and "uhs". If you don't know the answer to something, be frank and just say so. The worst thing you can do is to make something up and have the reporter come back to you to confront you after they have done more research and realized you were incorrect. Say what you know.

Print

There is something about having your name in quotes and down on paper that gives you credibility. If it's in print, it must be true. With TV and radio sound bites come and go, but when something is in print it can be quoted, photocopied, and emailed over and over again.

An advantage with print mediums is that they plan ahead so you will have their editorial calendars months and even a year in advance. What an incredible opportunity for you to plan ahead! Take advantage of it.

Each editorial calendar should include story or advertising deadlines. Deadlines are deadlines, and the print media allows no exceptions. Plan ahead and make sure you send out your press release that is tailored to what you KNOW they are looking for. If they are focusing on Wedding Planners in June, don't send them your stay-at-home mom press release in April or May. Tell them about your unique wedding planning party on wheels and be sure to keep with their deadlines.

Once you finally get the call from a print reporter, you will probably do the interview over the phone if it is a national magazine or you may meet with a reporter face to face if they are local. Print has more room and time to interview and may even do several interviews if it is a feature story. All the same rules apply: be professional, presentable and confident. Even the "ums" and "uhs" should be kept to a minimum, because once they're in black and white, they're forever.

Submitting Articles to Publications

As you build your consulting business you will build industry experience that eventually makes you an expert in your area and in your field of work. Use this knowledge to write wedding tips, ideas and stories and submit these articles to publications.

Publishing your knowledge of the wedding planning industry reveals your professionalism and legitimacy as an expert wedding planner. These are two of the most important aspects of your new career. Sharing your experiences, opinions and know-how with brides-to-be can open innumerable doors for you. Can't you imagine a mother dog-earing a page in a magazine or book marking a Web site to share with her daughter? Absolutely! If there is anything brides-to-be do, it is read, read, read about wedding trends and advice.

Did you come up with a clever way to incorporate the bride and groom's love of hiking into their reception? Did you figure out an ingenious way to include the bride's childhood nanny – more like a member of her family – into the ceremony? Are your bridal clients always gushing about your ability to control the groomsmen at rehearsals? Share this with readers.

"What readers?" we can hear you asking. Do your local vendors have Web sites with industry tips and testimonial pages? Utilize them to your advantage. Does your city – especially if it's a metropolis – or state have a wedding publication? Find out when it's published and what the guidelines for submissions are. Go to your local public library and check out their free publications section. It's usually by the door and it's sure to be packed with brochures, pamphlets and free women's and parent's magazines. Who publishes them? Is there contact information for editors and reporters? Use it; yours might be the expertise they're looking for. And don't forget your local newspaper. It's a rare one that doesn't publish wedding and engagement notices on Sundays. Many even print special wedding tabs on certain days of the year, especially in late winter/early spring when the wedding season kicks into full gear.

Another idea: major wedding magazines. Don't be afraid to send in an article or a tip you have for planning a wedding. True, they may not use your writing in its entirety, but don't be discouraged. You may get a mention in a story or a blurb on a 'Tips' page. It's always worth a try.

It's obvious that although professionalism and legitimacy lend a lot to your business, there is no comparison to getting your name out there. Try keeping a journal of what works well in your weddings and what doesn't; stay on top of the trends; get feedback from your brides. Then take it all and bring out the writer inside of you. Your business and career will benefit. If you can, get something published in a local publication, and always put your stories, tips and ideas on your own website.

Creating Your Business Media/Press Kit

A business media kit or press kit is usually a folder containing information about your business and services tailored specifically for the recipient. This folder is flexible in its use and content as you can add or subtract information from it as you see fit. For example, if you were providing information to a bride you would not also include pricing information intended for your vendors for ad space and vis-à-vis.

It is appropriate to include press releases, clippings or tear sheets of press you have received and a letter of recommendation or a list of testimonials from past clients.

Your kit should include different "one-sheets" or one page overviews about your business, history, services, products, etc. Provide a summary of each of your services and areas of the company so that anyone introduced to your business will have an understanding of what you do but will also want to learn more.

Entrepreneur.com has an outline of what should be included in a media and/or press kit.

http://www.entrepreneur.com/Your_Business/YB_SegArticle/0,4621,3 04700,00.html

Chapter Eighteen

End of Chapter Assignments

First Objective
Create an annual editorial opportunity calendar. Schedule when you will contact and follow-up with local and national publications.

Second Objective
Create your Bio using the guidelines in this chapter.

Third Objective
Create your 30-second sound bite.

Fourth Objective
Write a press release announcing your new business to the community.

Fifth Objective
Design your company media and/or press kit.

Sixth Objective
The Wedding Planning Network offers free PR consultation. Go to www.weddingplanningnetwork.com

Chapter Nineteen

Organization, Tools, Policies & Procedures

IN THIS CHAPTER YOU WILL LEARN:
- **Ideas to organize your business and streamline your daily activities**
- **How to plan your work and work your plan**

By now you realize that the lifeline of your business is staying connected. Your email is one factor that plays a major role in how productive you are each day. Let's talk about the tools needed to keep your business running smoothly.

Organization

Between your emails, faxes and voicemail messages left on sticky notes there are almost too many details that need your attention. Every bridal client is concerned with only one wedding, her own. What do YOU do to keep every wedding organized?

Keeping detailed records of your meetings with brides and vendors is crucial to your success. Detail management and adhering to deadlines will increase your productivity and insure a successful business. How do you stay organized?

Once you decide what tools to use, you'll be ready to get your business off the ground.

Calendars and Contact Management

All business professionals use some type of contact management software and/or day-timer to stay focused. Using ACT!, Goldmine, Outlook or another form of contact management software to keep track of your everyday tasks can increase your productivity. Work smarter. Not harder.

Every bride has her own calendar of events based on the date of her wedding and she will be counting on you for support and reminders as to when she needs to get things done. You are her expert!

If you miss just one item on the Bride's Checklist that she is counting on you to help with it could cost you her trust and potentially her business, not to mention your reputation. It may even damage your name with vendors. Everyone works differently, so do what works best for you.

Set reminders.

Alternate your follow-ups between email, phone calls and letters. Using snail mail can influence a bride's call to action and get her to book those vendors on schedule. Note phone conversations immediately following your calls so you have documentation to fall back on. This is important when speaking with brides and vendors because it cuts down on errors and misunderstandings.

Tools

Do you need to brush-up on your computer skills or would you like a refresher on how to use Excel or MS Word? Check out this website for FREE tutorials.

http://www.educationonlineforcomputers.com/

Monthly and Weekly Calendars

Create weekly or monthly calendars to keep you focused. When you first start working with a bride, schedule your own "to do" checklist right away; you can always adjust it as you go along. Set up client's reminders from the beginning and you will always be one step ahead of your bride.

Set your own reminders so that you stay on schedule with your marketing and business plan.

Wedding Planning Seminar Calendars

Map out your plan of attack and get your wedding seminars outlined for the next year. Start contacting local vendors to speak and have them sign-on in advance. This shows your vendors you are not a shot in the dark but a professional who is planning for the future and actively working to market their services. Preparing this calendar early on should guarantee you at least 8-10 new couples per seminar AND will keep your vendors booked.

Limo Wedding Planning Parties

Another annual objective should be to plan your mobile wedding planning parties. You can promote these during your seminars and be sure your couples will want to know dates ahead of time.

Chapter Nineteen

End of Chapter Suggested Assignments

First Objective

Create your annual calendars for your Limo Wedding Planning Parties.

Second Objective

Create your annual calendars for your Wedding Planning Seminars.

Third Objective

Organize your home office.

Chapter Twenty

Expanding Your Business Offerings

IN THIS CHAPTER YOU WILL LEARN:
- **How to incorporate additional services and products into your business**
- **Examples of complementary products and how to start expansion**

A business should never rely on one source of revenue if they plan on being successful. Does Wal-Mart retail only one product or category of products? Does Mercedes sell only one model of luxury car? Does Pfizer manufacture a single prescription drug? No, no, no. No business could survive with a single revenue source. There may be a few out there who do, but the majority of businesses have several products and service offerings to meet the needs of their customers. The same is true for your business. You must increase your revenue streams by adding additional products and services to your business offerings.

Expand your goods and services.

It's important to understand that you cannot be all things to all people. However, if you offer a variety of services you are more likely to increase the number of people you do business with.

When you are working with a bride, she will depend on you to guide her and provide professional advice.

In any business, people work with people they like and trust. As a consultant, you will be building a relationship with each and every bride as you help design her "perfect dream wedding".

Why not take more control over what your company has to offer while taking advantage of the financial benefits? From flowers to music to custom designed bridal jewelry, developing additional revenue channels helps your business grow in more than one direction. Take advantage of the financial rewards of marketing more than just your consulting services to the bride.

Do you find yourself taking more time helping the florist plan the details of the floral arrangements? Then maybe that is a sign that you should somehow incorporate a floral side to your business. There are many wholesale floral companies that offer no inventory business opportunities.

Flowers. The Fresh Rose Club, www.freshroseclub.com, is a wonderful rose distributor that works well with wedding consultants looking to offer a unique opportunity to their bridal clients. A bride on a budget can still have a luxurious wedding ceremony draped in roses for about a $1 or less a rose. Incredible!

Bridal jewelry. There are many independent bridal jewelry companies out there which can offer a bride her own jewelry designed just for her, or she can chose from a wide variety of already designed pieces that are Hollywood-style but without Hollywood prices. If you have a Tiffany's bride who can pay Tiffany's prices, good for you. Determine what you market is and plan accordingly.

Make-up. Do you already sell Mary Kay or Avon? Take advantage of your stock and sell it to your bridal clients!

Invitations. Carlson Craft, www.carlsoncraft.com, is a leader in the wedding industry for wedding invitations. They have a wonderful program where they will provide you with your own online invitation store. You can create a sample invitation in the store and send it via email to your couple to review. These are only a few simple ideas. It's easy to set-up your account. All of your couples will need invitations, and it's best for you that they get them from your business.

Wedding music CDs. Check out www.weddingmusiccentral.com to set up your wholesale agreement to purchase a series of CDs specifically for your bridal clients. They are a great gift for new clients as well as a unique favor for couples to distribute at the wedding.

The Possibilities are Endless

There are many ways in which you can expand your business. Talk with your vendors and see what other business opportunities are out there if the above ideas aren't what you're interested in. People are always looking for unique ways to grow their business; if you do enough research, you're bound to find something out there that is right for you.

The most important thing about adding additional revenue channels to your business is that you don't over extend yourself and you put them in your business plan. Most new opportunities, just like wedding planning, will require a small investment. Chose things that you're interested in and that work well with your wedding planning business. Your goal should be to bring in more revenue from each client and to add additional clients with your diverse menu of services. Don't put your eggs all in one basket.

Chapter Twenty

End of Chapter Suggested Assignments

First Objective
Create a list of ten ways you can bring in additional revenue to your business.

Chapter Twenty-One

Certification: To be certified or not to be certified…is that the question?

IN THIS CHAPTER YOU WILL LEARN:
- **What it means to be a certified wedding planner**
- **How certification can improve your business success**
- **What certification programs are available and what each has to offer**
- **How to earn your Wedding Planning Degree**
- **Career and job placement assistants**

What does it mean to be a certified wedding planner?

To be "certified" in any field of study means you have been trained by an accredited organization or educational institution.

Currently, the wedding planning industry is unregulated, meaning that each educational program, seminar, at-home study course, etc. are all based on the merits of each individual company's standards and/or local/state regulations. It does not matter which course you take since you can apply what you learn no matter where you are running your business.

As more and more people find that a career as a wedding planner is right for them, the industry will need to become more regulated. However, that does not mean that the current available programs are not worth the investment. When choosing a certification program for yourself, be sure that the organization you select, offers a program that fits your lifestyle and that the curriculum covers both etiquette and running the business.

Most wedding planners will go out of business within the first year because they have not taken the time to educate themselves and have no marketing, sales or business training.

Brides want to work with trained and educated consultants.

More and more brides are aware of the difference between a professional and novice wedding planner. Many marriage bound couples will be looking for a certified wedding planner to tap into her wealth of knowledge and experience. If you are serious about getting into the event planning business you will need to obtain the necessary education and training, not to mention a certificate to hang on your wall. Brides want to be assured that their bridal consultant has expertise and education. **Would YOU use a wedding planner for YOUR wedding that wasn't educated on the business of wedding planning?**

Is one program better than the other?

That depends on what you are looking for. Review each program's syllabus and determine what education is most needed by you. It is not uncommon for the most serious of wedding planners to be certified by more than one program. These consultants have the most well rounded educations. Most programs provide the basics of etiquette and wedding planning as well as information on the business side of wedding consulting. The rest is up to you. After the certification, you are on your own to use what you have learned to begin to grow your business.

Why should I spend all that money on certification?

It is an investment in your wedding planning education, your trade. Would you go to a doctor who hadn't graduated from medical school? If you trust your life's safety with just any quack, then go right ahead. It's the same thing for brides who are going to trust the most important day of their life to a wedding consultant. They will always choose a consultant who has been certified over someone who does not have any formal education.

If you are not willing to invest in your certification, then you're really not serious about this career decision. Many programs offer payment plans or accept credit cards. If you cannot financially afford the education right now, take what you have learned in this book and get your business moving and start saving up for that certification.

Taking a business course is also a wise choice. Many programs offer an education on how to run a wedding planning business, but having more knowledge on your local business laws and practices is always helpful, especially if you have never run your own business before.

Once you have completed your certification, don't think your studies are over. You will have to reinvest in continuing education over the course of your career. The industry will always be changing and you must keep up with the latest trends, etc.

Don't forget that the cost of the program qualifies as a business expense, so you can write it off.

The cost of a good Wedding Planning Certification education, will average $500 – 1,200.

It boils down to this: make your business the best and you'll stand out above the rest. Education is the key.

Certification Programs

Let's look at the certification programs available to you. A few tips to keep in mind when choosing a program:

- ➤ Don't let the cost of a program cloud your judgment. As they say, you get what you pay for. Go with a program that will help you grow and continue growing your business following graduation.

- ➤ Find a program that fits your personality; try calling the certification program director. If you need more help on the marketing side of the business, go with the program that offers more in that area.

- ➤ Note, just because an association offers a program, that does not mean they are superior to another program. Associations want their members to continually pay each year for their membership, in addition to paying for classes.

- A good certification program should come with some sort of continuing education requirement, to make sure that the student keeps their education current. Some programs require students to enroll in a new course or renew their certification every 1-2 years.

- Course format. What type of course options does the school offer? Home or self-study course, online classes, classroom or seminars? Select a course format that will best suit your learning style. If you have never used a computer before, do not enroll in an online class.

- No one organization can restrict you from joining another or limit how you market your business.

Here is an overview of the top certification programs available:

Association of Bridal Consultants

www.bridalassn.com

Association of Certified Wedding Consultants

www.acpwc.com

June Wedding, Inc.

www.junewedding.com

The International Institute of Weddings

www.instituteofweddings.com

Wedding Academy*

www.weddingacademy.com

Weddings Beautiful

www.weddingsbeautiful.com

Wedding Planning Academy*

www.weddingplanningacademy.com

Wedding Planning School*

www.weddingplanningschool.com

Wedding Planning University*

www.weddingplanninguniversity.com

How to use this book to become certified...

*These schools utilize the "How to Start a Wedding Planning Business" book as one of the text books in their coursework requirements for certification. If you are working through the suggested assignments at the end of each chapter of this edition of the book, you can contact each individual school for more information on how to obtain your certification and what additional projects are required.

Chapter Twenty-One

End of Chapter Suggested Assignments

First Objective
Do your research and find out which certification or career assistance program is right for you.

Chapter Twenty-Two

Relationship Education: Plan for a Wedding... Prepare for a Marriage

IN THIS CHAPTER YOU WILL LEARN:

- **The importance of relationship education before marriage**
- **How you can help change the rate of divorce in this country**
- **The Marriage Movement**
- **Suggested Programs and Websites**

Planning a Wedding is Tough... Planning a **Marriage** is Tougher

Sometimes it's the crash of six tiers of champagne glasses or the plaintive cry of bridesmaids popping surprising seams that steps to the forefront as the most important challenge to turning all of the wedding plans into perfect wedding memories.

While all of your focus and energy is being drawn toward completing the seemingly endless list of tasks that go into planning a bride's special day, it is very easy for the average couple to fall into the trap of leaving the details of their impending marriage to chance.

Married couples will avow that the wedding is only the beginning. Few couples take the time to actually plan their marriage prior to walking down the aisle.

Becoming engaged for the first time is something women consider being a right of passage; it is the beginning of a new stage in our life and couple-hood. It is truly an exciting and sometimes stressful time. Marriage is committing to another person…for better or worse, in sickness and in health, in good times and in bad, for richer or poorer, with or without children. Marriage is a merging of all assets and decisions, living under the same roof, accepting personal behaviors you have never seen before, discovering those little idiosyncrasies that will drive you crazy, and accepting blindly all the other fine print of the marriage contract that you never get to read and discover only after the deal is sealed.

Our society has become accustomed to a big celebration when two people legally commit to one another. We have also become influenced by the need to have the most unique or beautiful wedding day and have bought into the idea that it must be perfect. So much energy and fuss is poured into this one magical day that young brides-to-be are blissfully unaware of the reality before them.

Marriage is one of life's greatest rewards, but it is not easy. In fact, marriage is hard. At times, marriage can be the hardest thing you will ever experience. Our choice in a mate is influenced by our age, heritage, religion, family, friends, social status, and of course, love. Not all of us make it, but astonishingly, over 75% of divorced individuals remarry and give it a second try. Many learn from their previous experiences, do not repeat the same mistakes and end up very happy. Unfortunately, the added responsibility and stress of extended and blended families cause this group to have an even higher rate of divorce. It's a shame over half of us learn the hard way before we realize how to make a marriage work, proving the known fact that experience is the best teacher.

Why is it that so many people ignore their responsibility to educate themselves on the "How To's" of a relationship? Most people spend more time learning how to bake cookies than how to prepare for marriage. Many discover their relationship ignorance within their first few months of marriage. Those who don't understand, there is such a thing as relationship education usually end up as a divorce statistic among the number of first year failed marriages. Most people who have divorced within or shortly after the first year usually claim "We just didn't get along" or as the lawyers say, suffered from "Irreconcilable differences". Many others flock to the bookshelves or Internet to find information on how to fix what is "wrong", finally realizing that a marriage takes work. There is an entire industry built around relationship education and yet few discover it until they are in the throws of a struggling marriage or long term relationship.

Wouldn't it be interesting if our high schools required a course in marriage preparation? It would teach compromise, how to argue, and how to agree to disagree. It would drill into the minds of young people how to respect others, how to work together, and the responsibilities of a wife and husband. Most high school students are required to take driver's education, so why is relationship education any less important? Families are the cornerstone and foundation of our society. If our families are falling apart, what does that say about our communities and the basis of our culture?

Something has to change. We cannot continue to ignore the fact that getting married is a huge responsibility and requires relationship education prior to the "I do's". All engaged couples should take responsibility of the success of their future marriage and insist on learning the basics before the wedding day. Couples need to discuss things like respect, how to handle conflict, finances, control, decision-making, and setting fair rules the two can agree to live by in order to handle the reality of marriage as it comes to them. In other words, "Be Prepared". All marriages echo similar issues, and knowing issues to expect ahead of time can make all the difference for most couples.

Mainstream America is thirsty for knowledge on how to help their relationship. Shows like Dr. Phil are so popular because we all want affirmation that we are not different and that others are experiencing the same issues or problems.

We asked a few experts what they believed was most important to realize when entering into a marriage.

First, ignore the myths. Dr. Leslie Parrott of RealRelationships (www.realrelationships.com) says that the number one marriage myth is that a spouse should make us whole. This myth gives engaged couples unrealistic expectations. In other words, forget the whole Jerry Maguire "You complete me" thing. Both members of a relationship should work on personal wholeness first, not perfection, to achieve a self-awareness that brings individual satisfaction.

"Do I believe these myths?" is one of the seven questions to ask before you marry. These questions are the focus of the book *Saving Your Marriage Before it Starts* by Les and Leslie Parrot. The book says to enhance a marriage before it begins. In order to maintain a stable and loving marriage it is important to plan and learn marriage skills together.

Pairs (www.pairs.org) programs teach that a marriage takes skills. Their research shows that couples that learn a basic set of relationship skills develop a stronger marriage. Seth Eisenberg of Pairs says that only ten percent of engaged couples invest time into learning the skills they need for marriage. He says that couples must understand emotions and how to deal with conflict. Pairs teaches it's couples to always stand unified to find solutions to whatever problems they face. Learning these skills together gives couples a common language, the best way to deal with issues that will arise in their future.

As a wedding planner, your advice and guidance during this stressful time can help many couples as they move through their engagement to existing as a married couple. Use your influence during this happy time to encourage couples to participate in a relationship education course. Even small comments and suggestions can go a long way. Give your marriage bound couples a list of local classes as one of your handouts. This is a subtle way of giving them valuable information they may need at a later date. You can also include a great book entitled *Getting Ready for the Wedding* by Les and Leslie Parrott.

This book brings together some of the most respected experts in the areas of marriage, relationships and finance to explore ten topics. This book covers: Secrets of a Great Engagement, Getting Married Without Drowning in Debt, What To Do If Your Parents Don't Approve, How to Have a Great Wedding Night, and so on. Contributors include Norman Wright, David and Jan Stoop, Cliff and Joyce Penner, John Trent and others.

The Marriage Movement: A Statement of Principles.

Over 100 prominent scholars and religious and civic leaders have joined together to pledge that "In this decade we will turn the tide on marriage and reduce divorce and unmarried childbearing, so that each year more children will grow up protected by their own two happily married parents and more adults' marriage dreams will come true." The Statement has been the subject of numerous newspaper articles and radio talk shows. Most encouraging is that since its release on June 29, 2000 over 2500 individuals have added their names to the list of original signatories to state how important they feel marriage is in America. The list of names, a copy of the report, and the ability to join them, is available via http://www.marriagemovement.org/html/report.html

List of Recommended National Programs

Association for Couples in Marriage Enrichment (ACME)
www.bettermarriages.org

Catholic Engaged Encounter: Christian Marriage Preparation
www.engagedencounter.org

Interpersonal Communication Programs, Inc
www.couplecommunication.com

Couple Communication
www.couplecommunication.com

Family Wellness Associates
www.familywellness.com

IMAGO Relationships International (IRI)
www.ImagoRelationships.org

Marriage Enrichment, Inc -
www.marriageenrichment.org

MARRIAGE SAVERS & Community Marriage Covenants
www.marriagesavers.org

PAIRS: Practical Application of Relationship Skills
www.pairs.com

PREP: The Prevention and Relationship Enhancement Program
www.prepinc.com

The Cana Institute: Caring for the Soul of Marriage and Family
www.canainstitute.org

The Gottman Institute:
www.gottman.com

Marriage Alive International, Inc (MAI)
www.marriagealive.org

Marriage Builders, Inc.
www.MarriageBuilders.com

WORLD CLASS MARRIAGE
www.worldclassmarriage.com

Chapter Twenty-Two

End of Chapter Suggested Assignments

First Objective
Research your local relationship experts.

Chapter Twenty-Three

Philanthropy

IN THIS CHAPTER YOU WILL LEARN:
- **The importance of philanthropy in your business**
- **How to incorporate philanthropy**
- **Tips and ideas you can institute easily**

There is an important responsibility that every business owner takes on when starting a business. It is that of being a good philanthropist. Whether you own a small business that handles a few weddings per year or a large wedding planning dynasty, giving back to the community should be included in your business model.

If you have the passion to work for yourself, to create your own destiny…you have the qualities of a philanthropist. Being involved in your local community does not mean your efforts have to be all financially driven.

Here are a few simple ideas on how your business can be active in giving back to the community.

Intern Program

Offering an internship program to a young aspiring wedding planner is an excellent way to pass along your own knowledge and experience. Most local colleges and universities have internship programs. Contact your local career centers and let them know you offer a wedding planning internship program. Having a young marketing or PR student work with you is a great way to help the student learn about the local market and will help assist your local marketing efforts.

Be sure that you are committed to helping your intern learn the true nature of the business and follow all school requirements and guidelines. You should be in constant contact with an intern's career

advisor. You should require an interview, resume and cover letter.
Expect only the best from your intern.

Career Speaker

High schools also have career centers and internship programs, but
more likely a high school will be looking for career day speakers.
There are many high school students who will not be attending a four-
year college or university and will be looking for a career choice that
they can jump into with less time in school. Many young girls are also
fascinated with the idea of a career as a wedding planner. As a career
speaker, you have the opportunity to share your knowledge of the local
wedding market, the day-to-day life of a bridal consultant and what it
takes to run a business.

To get on the list of speakers, contact your local high school career
centers and they will put you on the list to call for their next career day
or guest speaker day.

Brides on a Budget

Not every bride-to-be has an average budget of $20,000 to spend on
her special day. Don't simply walk away from every bride who cannot
pay your rate card prices. If you can't help the couple, refer them to
someone who can.

Donate your services once or twice a year to a couple that needs your
expertise but cannot afford to pay for it. It will make you feel good for
helping to make their dreams come true.

Get Involved with a Local Wedding Organization

We covered the importance of being involved with a local wedding
organization for the professional relationships and status, but you can
also do great things for the community through your group.

Being in the wedding business, vendors have the ability to throw great
parties, and nothing's better than a charity function! If your local

association doesn't currently have a charity associated with it, then get the ball rolling and start a new committee. If they do work with local charities and put on events to raise money, simply get involved.

Wedding Giveaways

There are many couples in love that cannot afford to have the wedding of their dreams. Why not coordinate with your local vendors and organize a wedding giveaway promotion? Vendors donate their time and services. Expect everything, from the dress to the reception hall. Get the local media involved and have them donate the airtime or print space. The contest can be a surprise gift. Have family and friends write in to tell you why their engaged friend, sister, brother, son or daughter deserves a free wedding. The possibilities are endless. Make it an annual event and do it during the off-season.

Fundraisers

Did you know that the Fresh Rose Club has a fundraising program? You can sell roses and donate the proceeds to charity. They will help you organize the entire event! Think outside the box and incorporate a fundraiser into one of your wedding seminars or partner with a local church. Tell them you will organize the fundraiser and donate the proceeds to their favorite charity. Of course, you want to then have the opportunity to work with their congregation in the future, but this gesture is one small step in the right direction.

Give a percentage of your day-of-service fees to your own favorite charity. Be sure to note this on your marketing materials, or let the couple know that you will donate a percentage to THEIR favorite charity. Donations are also tax deductible.

Be a responsible business owner and give back to the community; it will come back to you tenfold.

Chapter Twenty-Three

End of Chapter Assignments

First Objective

Research your local area for charities and ways you can give back to your community.

Second Objective

Add one philanthropic event to your annual marketing calendar; perform one each quarter.

Chapter Twenty-Four

Wedding Day Mishaps

Congratulations... you are almost there!

Are you ready to take the wedding planning day challenge? Your ability to manage a realistic wedding scenario is what it's all about. One filled with unexpected surprises and small challenges to overcome gracefully. Review the following itinerary and then compare it with the "actual" day's events. This bride and groom are getting ready to face a wedding day made for bloopers television. How would you handle each of these mishaps and keep things running smoothly?

Wedding Day Itinerary

Plan your work and work your plan, as they say. Every successful planner knows to begin with a solid plan.

This following wedding itinerary will give you an overview of the entire day from a planner's perspective.

Wedding Planner Itinerary

12 noon Ceremony & 2PM – 6PM Reception

Day Before – Call to check with vendors on arrival times and drop-off information.

Rental Company – for linens and chairs – Reception by 9:15AM

Bakery – wedding cake – Reception by 12:30

Florist – Bride's House –10:30 AM, Ceremony-11AM, Reception-12:30

Video – Ceremony-11:30 AM, Reception – 2PM

Photographer – Bride's home-10:45, Ceremony-11:45, Reception – 2PM

Limo – Bride's home- 11:45, Ceremony to reception – 2:30

Caterer – Reception – 9AM

Musicians – Ceremony – 11AM, Reception (DJ) – 1:30PM

Wedding Day

9AM Meet with Caterer to oversee setup and decorations

9:30 Call Bride to check in and go to the ceremony location

10:00 Co-ordinate the flowers, decorations, musicians and videographer setup

10:45 Meet photographer at bride's house for photos

11:15 Go to the Ceremony location before the guests begin to arrive

11:30 Help with seating, boutonnières and corsages and extras (Bubbles)

11:45 The bridesmaids arrive

11:55 The aisle runner is placed after both mothers are seated

11:58 The Bride and her father arrive

11:59 Assemble bridesmaids to begin down the aisle, notify the groom to get ready

Noon The Processional

12:30 Ceremony ends

12:35 Recessional Begins

12:40 Receiving Line

1:00 Bride & Groom sign marriage license

1:15 Pictures of the bride & groom with bridal party

Direct guests to begin leaving for the reception

2:30 Bridal party leaves for the reception

2:45 Introduction of bridal party couples

3:00 Introduction of Bride & Groom

3:05 First dance

3:10 Bridal Party Dance

3:20 Celebration begins

4:00 Food is served

4:30 Best Man Toast

4:45 Dancing and celebration

5:00	Cake cutting
5:15	Father Daughter/Mother Son dance
5:30	Bouquet toss
5:45	Garter toss
6PM	Limo takes bride & groom to airport.

Amended Wedding Itinerary

Planning a wedding on paper is one thing... directing that wedding with the reality of life's little surprises is an entirely different experience.

Here is the itinerary with a few minor adjustments and insertions of reality. Use your good judgment and what you have learned so far to help you manage the mishaps, control the crises and deliver a beautiful wedding day to your clients.

Hint: Make every attempt to avoid upsetting or stressing the bride.

Wedding Itinerary with Realistic Challenges

Day Before – Call to check with vendors on arrival times and drop off information.

Rental Company – for linens and chairs – Reception by 9:15AM

Bakery – wedding cake – Reception by 12:30

Florist – Bride's House –10:30 AM, Ceremony-11AM, Reception-12:30

Video – Ceremony-11:30 AM, Reception – 2PM

Photographer – Bride's home-10:45, Ceremony-11:45, Reception – 2PM

Limo – Bride's home- 11:45, Ceremony to reception – 2:30

Caterer – Reception – 9AM

Musicians – Ceremony – 11AM , Reception (DJ) – 1:30PM

Wedding Day

9AM   Meet with Caterer to oversee setup and decorations

9:30   Call Bride to check in (*she tells you there are eight more guests coming to the reception than planned*) and go to the ceremony location

10:00   Co-ordinate the flowers, decorations, musicians and videographer setup (*The church does not allow video inside the church*)

10:45   Meet photographer at bride's house for photos *(The flower girl is disrupting the photographer and misbehaving)*

11:15   Go to the Ceremony location before the guests begin to arrive *(The video equipment is stacked up in the entryway as you arrive)*

11:30   Help with seating, boutonnières and corsages and extras (Bubbles*) (The florist is one corsage short in the delivery)*

11:45   The bridesmaids arrive – *(They all brought their purses and don't know where to put them when they walk down the aisle and are not comfortable leaving them in the side room alone and unattended.)*

11:55   The aisle runner is placed after both mothers are seated *(More guests arrive and need to be seated.)*

11:58   The Bride and her father arrive. *(The bride rips her dress seam at the waist when she emerges from the limousine.)*

11:59   Assemble bridesmaids to begin down the aisle, notify the groom to get ready.

       12 Noon – The Processional – Ceremony Begins (Guests arrive late during the ceremony)

12:30   Ceremony Ends

12:35   Recessional Begins

12:40   Receiving Line – *(Extends until 1:15 due to so many guests/you need to get back on schedule)*

1:00   Bride & Groom sign marriage license

1:15   Pictures of the bride & groom with bridal party

       Direct guests to begin leaving for the reception

2:30   Bridal party leaves for the reception *(The bridesmaids rode over in the limo and need a ride to the reception.)*

2:45   Introduction of bridal party couples

3:00   Introduction of Bride & Groom

3:05   First dance

3:10   Bridal Party Dance

3:20   Celebration begins

4:00 Food is served – *(During the celebration two women from the ceremony arrive to speak with the bride about a problem with the flower arrangements being taken and not left as part of her requirement to use the facility. They want to take two big flower arrangements back to the church.)*

4:30 Best Man Toast

4:45 Dancing and celebration – *(An intoxicated guest is not feeling well and needs to lay down)*

5:00 Cake cutting *(There is no cake knife on the table)*

5:15 Father Daughter/Mother Son dance

5:30 Bouquet toss

5:45 Garter toss

(The Bride & Groom did not get to eat their food)

(The Groom has a headache)

6PM Limo takes bride & groom to airport.

Answers:

Yikes! There are no perfect answers, as there are multiple factors that will help lead to a conclusion in every scenario. Use your head and never place stress on the couple. You can give them a follow-up report of what "really" happened when they return from the honeymoon.

Good Luck!

Glossary of Terms

Glossary

Familiarize yourself with these and other trendy wedding industry "buzzwords".

B2B: Bride-to-be

BM: Bridesmaid; acronym often used in newsgroups or email messages

Blusher: The part of the veil that covers the bride's face

Bomboniere: An Italian term for "favors" which are passed out to wedding guests as a keepsake in appreciation of their attendance.

Boutonniere: A flower arrangement usually worn on the lapel of members of the bridal party. French *boutonnière* buttonhole, from Middle French, from *bouton* button

Corsage: A tiny flower arrangement usually worn on the lapel of a jacket and given to special family members of the bride and groom, such as a grandmother or great aunt

Dowry: A gift; endowment. The money, goods, or estate which a woman brings to her husband in marriage; a bride's portion on her marriage

Encore Wedding: A wedding where either of the two people getting married have been married before

Fiancé: A *man* engaged to be married. French, from Middle French, from past participle of financer; to promise, betroth

Fiancée: A *woman* engaged to be married. French, from Middle French, from past participle of financer; to promise, betroth

FMI: Future Mother-in-Law; acronym often used in newsgroups or email messages.

G2B: Groom-to-be

Maid of Honor: An *unmarried* woman who stands by the bride's side

Matron of Honor: A *married* woman who stands by the bride's side

MOH: Maid of Honor; acronym often used in newsgroups or email messages

"Save the Date" Card: This informal announcement precedes the wedding invitations several months ahead and allows your guests to make the necessary arrangements to attend your wedding. "Save the Date" cards are ideal when your wedding date falls in close proximity to a major holiday

Trousseau: French, from Old French, diminutive of trousse; bundle.

The personal possessions of a bride usually including clothes, accessories, and household linens and wares.

Trunk Show: Usually held at a local bridal shop, a trunk show allows a bridal gown designer to "show off" her/his latest designs to the shop's customers

Traditional Terms

Glossary

Alencon: A mesh lace background that has been re-embroidered to outline the pattern. Traditionally used in wedding gowns, this lace usually has a scalloped border that can be used as an accent and along the hem

Ankle length: A dress that just barely reveals the ankles, a tad shorter than floor length

Appliqué: Lace or trim pieces that are sewn onto another fabric

Ascot tie: A wide necktie (almost like a scarf) that is looped over and held in place beneath the chin with a tie tack or stickpin. Worn with a wing-collar shirt and the daytime wedding cutaway jacket

Backpiece: A comb or a barrette that goes on the back of your head. The veil then attaches to the backpiece

Baguette: A diamond in the shape of a small rectangular stone. May be tapered at one end

Ball gown: A tight, fitted bodice and definite waistline with a gathered or pleated full skirt

Ballet: A veil that falls somewhere between the knee and the ankle. Also known as a Waltz veil

Band Collar: Collar that stands up around the neck and above the buttons; this is the most contemporary style

Band Neckline: A high neckline that circles the neck like a turtleneck but is shorter

Basket weave: A cake frosting technique that features interweaving vertical stripes and horizontal lines of frosting to look like a wicker basket

Basque: A neckline that follows the collarbone

Basque waistline: A waistline that is below the waist and dips down to a point in the front

Bateau Neckline: A neckline that goes straight across the shoulders with just a small dip in the front. Also known as a boat neckline

Beaded Alencon Lace: A re-embroidered mesh lace with pearls and sequins sewn onto the lace

Beidermeier: A nosegay made up of concentric circles of different flowers for a striped effect of rings (think of an archery target)

Best Man: Assistant to the groom and the head of the groomsmen, he is in charge of the bachelor party, getting the groom to the church, paying the official, signing the marriage license, holding the rings and giving a toast at the reception

Bias cut: Dress silhouette that is cut on a diagonal grain so that it gently curves to the body through the hips then falls into soft folds at the hem.

Birdcage veil: A veil that falls just below the chin and is worn at informal weddings. Also known as a Madonna veil

Blemish: An imperfection on the exterior of a diamond, such as a scratch or chip

Blusher: A short, single layer of veil material, it's usually worn over your face during the wedding ceremony and then flipped back over your hair when you kiss

Boat Neckline: a neckline that goes straight across the shoulders with just a small dip in the front. Also known as a bateau neckline

Bodice: The close-fitting upper part of a dress

Body Shapers: Term used to describe sheer or opaque hosiery providing more support and control in the panty and thigh portion of the garment with maximum support for stomach, hips, thighs, and butt

Boning: Flat plastic inserts sewn into a bodice's understructure. Boning gives shape and support. It allows for a smoother appearance around a body's curves because it stiffens the outside fabric and prevents creases at the waistline

Boutonniere: A single bloom of one or more buds worn by men on the lapel of their jackets. Usually worn by grooms, attendants, ushers, and the bride's and groom's fathers

Bow tie: A short tie shaped like a bow that can be worn with a wing or lay down collar. Most bow ties adjust to fit all neck sizes and are available in a variety of widths, colors, and patterns to match the vest or cummerbund, though black is classiest and doesn't scream 'high school prom'. Be sure to get a real bow tie and not a clip-on

Bridal satin: A satin with a shiny surface, sometimes used as an accent. Not recommended for an entire dress, as this fabric can be overwhelming

Brilliance: The white light that is reflected back from a diamond.

Brocade: An intricately woven jacquard fabric with a raised overall interwoven design giving an embossed effect. Contrasting metallic yarns often highlight the embossed effect.

Bunwrap: A band that encircles an up-do type hairstyle

Bustle: The way a dress with a train is lifted off the ground in a decorative way. There are several different bustle styles available; your seamstress will design a bustle for your individual dress using snaps and/or hooks

Butter cream: A light, creamy frosting made with softened butter, confectioners' sugar, egg yolks and milk or light cream. This uncooked frosting is beaten until light and creamy. It can be flavored and colored in many ways and is used both as a filling and frosting. It's very smooth and stays soft so it's easy to cut through, but it may melt in very hot or humid weather

Candelabra: A floral arrangement placed on a candelabrum

Cap Sleeves: The shortest sleeve style, it usually covers only the shoulder, though off-shoulder dresses sometimes also have small cap sleeves

Carat: The metric carat, which equals 0.200 gram, is the standard unit of weight for diamonds and most other gems. If other factors are equal, the more a stone weighs, the more valuable it will be

Cascade: Resembles a cascade or waterfall with the flowers flowing downward in a free-flowing, loose appearance. Traditionally made using white flowers such as roses, stephanotis, and white or calla lilies

Cathedral: The most formal veil, it's usually three and a half yards long. Also known as the 'royal veil'. Extends 6 1/2 to 7 1/2 feet from the waist

Certified Diamond: Diamond that has been graded based on an internationally accepted system for color, clarity, cut and carat weight. The grading is performed by an independent gemological organization, and the certificate details all of the characteristics that the diamond possesses, including an estimated retail replacement value for insurance purposes

Chantilly: Delicate bobbin lace design of scrolls and floral on a soft mesh background, often with scalloped edges. Good for all-over use on bodices and sleeves when a soft, romantic look is desired

Chapel: A formal veil that extends to the floor, the chapel veil is usually seven or eight feet long. Often paired with a blusher veil or another shorter veil. Extends 3 1/2 to 4 1/2 feet from the waist

Chiffon: A sheer, transparent soft-flowing fabric made from silk or rayon and used as an overlay for dresses. Also used as long neck scarves.

Chip: The place where a diamond has a tiny piece missing

Choker Necklace: A single strand of pearls worn around the collar; the most classic style of pearl necklace, it looks good with a jewel or bateau neckline.

Clarity: A stone's relative position on a flawless to imperfect scale; one of the four C's of diamonds. Clarity characteristics are classified as inclusions (internal) or blemishes (external). The size, number, position, nature, and color or reliefs of characteristics determine the clarity grade. Very few diamonds are flawless

Classic Hand-Tied Bouquet: Gives the illusion of a "just picked" bouquet of flowers; anchored in a bouquet holder, wired, or hand-tied

Cloud: A group of tiny white inclusions that result in a milky or cloudy appearance.

Collar Necklace: A necklace consisting of three or more strands of pearls fitting snugly around the neck; this style looks good with low necklines

Color: Grading color in the normal range involves deciding how closely a stone's body color approaches colorlessness. Most diamonds have at least a trace of yellow or brown body color. With the exception of some natural fancy colors such as blue, pink, purple, or red, the colorless grade is the most valuable. One of the four C's of diamonds

Comb: A headpiece that is held to the head with comb teeth; it can be decorated with either a veil or flowers and beads

Composite: A handmade bouquet in which different petals or buds are wired together on a single stem, creating the illusion of one giant flower

Control Top: Pantyhose with spandex in the top for soft girdle or "control" effect for thighs, stomach and hips

Corsage: A single bloom or a small cluster of blooms usually featuring a ribbon. They come in various styles, including those that are pinned on, held on the wrist with elastic, and hand-held. Usually worn by the mothers/grandmothers of the bride and groom

Crepe: A lightly crinkled textured fabric with a flowing hand; available in rayon for a more clingy dress or polyester for a less clingy look

Crepe-Back Satin: A lightly textured reversible fabric with crepe on one side and a high luster satin on the other. Very slinky and flows well

Crosswyck: This collar style crosses in front and is fastened with a shiny button.

Crown: The top of a diamond above the girdle. Consists of a large flat area on top called a table, and several facets below it

Crown: Similar to a tiara, but is a full circle rather than a half-circle. It sits on your head and is usually decorated with rhinestones, beads or pearls. Looks especially good with short hairstyles

Cuff links: Decorative jewelry used to close cuffs

Culet: The smallest facet at the bottom of the diamond

Cummerbund: These are pleated swatches of silk or satin worn around the waist and covering the trouser's waistband

Cut: The proportions and finish of a polished diamond (also called make). Cut can also mean shape, as in emerald cut or marquise cut. Proportions are the size and angle relationships between the facets and different parts of the stone. Finish includes polish and details of facet shape and placement. One of the four C's of diamonds

Cutaway: Jacket which tapers from the front waist button to a long, wide back tail; accessories include a wing-collar shirt with an ascot and a coordinating vest. Worn by the groom for formal daytime weddings, they're usually gray or black and come with matching striped trousers

Dais: A flower arrangement at the head table that usually hangs over the front of the table

Damask: Similar to brocade with raised designs, but of lighter weight

Décolletage Neckline: A deep, plunging neckline that reveals the décolletage

Detachable train: An extension of fabric that attaches to the wedding gown to make a trailing extension of the gown. It can then be detached at the reception to avoid bustling the dress

Dotted Swiss: A piping technique for cake frosting that makes tiny dots in patterns that resemble a dotted Swiss fabric.

Double Tier: A veil of two layers (either two veils or a veil and a blusher), usually of different lengths

Dragees: Round, edible sugar balls coated with silver or gold and used for decorative purposes

Duchesse: Lace with floral designs using a lot of raised work with irregularly shaped spaces between designs

Duchess Satin: A low luster satin with medium body. An elegant construction that is resistant to wrinkles and is machine washable. Available in polyester

Elbow Glove: Ends just above or just below your elbow and can have six, eight, or ten buttons

Elbow: A veil that's about two feet long and reaches to the bride's elbows

Emerald cut: Usually a rectangular cut of jewel

Empire: A waistline that starts just below the bust. An empire waistline can run straight across or curve down the sides to hit the small of the back

Euro tie: A long knotted, square-bottom necktie worn with a wing or lay down collar shirt

Extended Cathedral: Extends 12 feet or more from the waist. Also known as a monarch train

Facet: A plane; polished surface of a diamond

Fingerless Glove: Can be either long or short, and is good for when you're putting on those rings (you don't have to take off your glove or cut a slit in the finger)

Fingertip: A veil that falls just to the bride's fingertips

Firm Support: Support pantyhose that give more support because heavier weights of spandex are used

Fish bowl: A centerpiece in which flowers are arranged in a glass bowl

Fitted sleeve: A close fitting sleeve with no fullness or pouf at the top. There are various lengths: cap, short, above elbow, below elbow, ¾ length, and long

Fitted Sleeves: Sleeves that fit very close to the arm

Flaw: An imperfection of a stone

Floor length: The dress's hemline falls 1/2 to 1 1/2 inches from the floor

Flyaway: A less formal veil, it has multiple layers and reaches just to the bride's shoulders

Fondant: A sweet, elastic icing made of sugar, corn syrup, and gelatin that's literally rolled out with a rolling pin and draped over a cake. It's a smooth, firm base for gum paste flowers, decorative details, and architectural designs, and has a porcelain finish. A fondant cake should not be refrigerated

Fountain: A veil that is gathered at the crown of the head to create a cascading effect around the face; it usually falls to the shoulders or fingertips

Four-in-hand Tie: A standard long, knotted necktie worn with a lay down collar. Also known as a necktie

Fracture: A crack on the diamond's surface

French cuffs: Cuffs which are folded over and closed with cuff links

Full Dress Jacket: Usually worn at very formal weddings (read: evening), these jackets are short in front and have two long tails in the back

Full-Cut: A diamond with 58 or more facets

Ganache: A rich chocolate mixture made by combining chopped semisweet chocolate and cream, it has a consistency denser than mousse but not as dense as fudge. It can be used as a cake glaze or as a filling and will melt in very humid weather.

Garden: An airy floral arrangement featuring abstract wildflowers such as lisianthus, hollyhock, rambling roses, and foxglove

Garland: A woven rope or strand flower arrangement often used to adorn pews, staircases and doorways

Gauntlet Glove: Not as much a glove as it is a long sleeve that goes from wrist to elbow; does not even cover the hand. Sometimes they'll come to a point on the back of your hand

Gemologist: Someone who has been trained and certified in diamonds and colored stones

GIA: Gemological Institute of America, an organization that sets and upholds standards for grading diamonds and other precious stones

Girdle: The outer edge or the widest part of the diamond forming a band around the stone

Girdle Top: Pantyhose with a sewn-on girdle for the firmest possible tummy control

Glimmer: Sheer or opaque hose which have high reflection properties from the yarn; mainly from a trilobal yarn that provides the glimmer effect by reflecting the light

Gore skirt: Nope, this has nothing to do with Al Gore! It's a flared skirt that is fitted at the waist and full at the hem. There are no gathers or pleats at the top. All the fullness comes from the shape of the panels. A gore skirt has more flare than an A-line in the front

Graduated Support: Support hosiery that's more comfortable because there are no sudden changes in the tightness of the spandex going up and down the leg.

Gum paste: A paste made from powdered sugar, starch and soaked gum tragacanth that is used to make realistic-looking fruits and flowers for cake garnishes. Gum paste decorations are edible and will last for a long time if you want to keep them, but they don't taste as good as marzipan

Half Crown: Similar to a tiara but taller, it is a half-circle decorated with rhinestones or other jewels

Halter bodice: A bodice style that has a band that fastens in the back of the neck but leaves a lot of the back bare. Necklines for this style include round, v-neck, curved v-neck, square, curved square, and sweetheart

Halter Neckline: A neckline that scoops down in front and ties behind the neck, leaving the arms bare. Think of Marilyn Monroe's white dress from *The Seven Year Itch*

Head: (Diamond) The prongs that hold a diamond in its setting

Huppah: A wedding canopy decorated with flowers that is an integral part of the traditional Jewish ceremony

Illusion: Fine netting used for veils, headpieces, and on the sleeves and necklines of dresses

Inclusion: An imperfection internal (inside) to the diamond

Iridescent Taffeta: A shiny fabric that changes color from different angles and feels crispy. Looks good with velvet and in full dresses

Jacquard: An intricately woven shiny fabric with a floral or foulard design woven into the fabric

Jewel Neckline: A high neckline that follows the natural shape of the shoulders and neck

Juliet Cap: A skullcap (small round cap), often set with pearls or other gems, worn by women for semiformal or bridal wear. Usually decorated with pearls or semi-precious stones

Juliet-fitted sleeves: A tightly fitted sleeve with a small pouf at the shoulder

Karat: The measure of the purity of gold. 24-karat is pure gold, but jewelry is also made from 18K and 14K gold, which contain added metals for strength

Knee Highs: Short hosiery that comes up to just below the knee. They are styled with elastic tops and stay up without the help of garters

Latticework: A cake frosting technique that criss-crosses with an open
pattern

Leg o´ Mutton Sleeves: Sleeves that are very full at the shoulder and narrow to become very fitted at the forearm

Light Support: Pantyhose made with a low denier spandex in the leg to give light compression

Loupe: Magnifying glass usually of 10X used to look at jewelry up-close.

Madonna veil: A veil that falls just below the chin and is worn at informal weddings. Also known as a birdcage veil

Mandarin collar: A collar that stands up around the neck and above the buttons; this is the most contemporary style

Mantilla: A long, Spanish-style circular or triangular piece of lace that is draped over the bride's head. It is usually made of lace or lace and tulle and is held in place with a comb

Marzipan: A paste made of ground almonds, sugar, and egg whites used to mold edible flowers or fruit for cake decorations. It can also be rolled and used as frosting; similar to fondant

Matte: Hosiery with a dull finish

Mermaid: Slim-fitting dress silhouette that flares out at the knee

Modified sheath: Dress silhouette that is form fitting through the torso. It is narrow in the front of the skirt, like the sheath, but flares out below the hips in the back to finish in a small train

Monarch: Extends 12 feet or more from the waist. Also known as an extended cathedral train

Morning Coat: Jacket which tapers from the front waist button to a long, wide back tail; accessories include a wing-collar shirt with an ascot and a coordinating vest. Worn by the groom for formal daytime weddings, they're usually gray or black and come with matching striped trousers

Necktie: A standard long, knotted necktie worn with a lay down collar. Also known as a four-in-hand tie

Nick: A notch near the girdle or a facet edge of a diamond

Nosegay: Round in shape and usually smaller than the other styles, it's made using flowers all cut to the same length and usually made with one dominant flower or color. They're often wrapped with ribbon or lace

Notched lapel: A triangular indentation is cut where the lapel joins the collar; the least formal lapel style

Off-Make: A poorly proportioned diamond

Off-shoulder: A bodice style that stops just below the shoulder. Different neckline variations include straight, straight with notch in center, curved, sweetheart, and v-neck

Opaque: Stockings or pantyhose made of yarn that give them a heavier, less see-through appearance

Opera Glove: Featuring 16 buttons, this glove is worn only at formal weddings, usually with strapless or sleeveless or spaghetti-strap-style gowns. It goes all the way up to the upper part of your bicep

Organza: Crisp and sheer like chiffon, but with a stiff texture

Pantyhose: A garment that combines both panty and stockings into a one-piece waist-high garment that extends above the crotch, but not above the waist, to the toes, and is usually sheer rather than opaque

Pavilion: The bottom part of the diamond, below the girdle

Peaked lapel: A broad V-shaped lapel that points up and out just below the collar line

Pillars: Plastic or wood separators used in a tiered cake

Piping: Decorative details on a cake made with a pastry bag and frosting tips using frosting. They include flowers, borders, leavers and basket-weave patterns

Pocket Square: A small pocket-handkerchief tucked into the left breast pocket worn by groomsmen instead of a boutonniere

Poet sleeve: A sleeve that is fitted at the top and fuller at the bottom, where it is gathered into a cuff

Point: One-hundredth of a carat

Pomander: A bloom-covered ball suspended from a ribbon, sometimes carried by flower girls instead of the usual basket of flowers

Posies: Similar to nosegays but smaller, posies often feature silk ribbons

Pouf: A gathered piece of tulle or netting that fastens to a comb or headpiece to create height for the veil

Presentation: Flowers with long stems arranged so that the bouquet is cradled in the bride's arms (think beauty pageants)

Pulled sugar: A technique in which boiled sugar is pulled and stretched to produce flowers, ribbons and bows

Queen Anne Neckline: A neckline that is high in back and sides of neck, curving to a center front point

Reinforced: The stress areas such as the toe or panty portion have been strengthened with yarns of heavier weight

Round Brilliant Cut: The most common cut of diamond; contains 58 facets. Also the most brilliant cut, in terms of most efficient use of light to increase brilliance and fire, hence the name

Royal icing: A mixture of confectioners´ sugar and egg whites, it's a frosting that dries hard. It is often used to make filigree, beading and flower designs and should not be refrigerated

Sandal toe: This is a nude toe, meaning no heavier yarn in the toe than is in the leg. Good to wear with open-toed shoes

Satin-Back Shantung: A reversible fabric with a slightly irregular surface on one side and a high luster satin on the other. Available in silk and polyester

Seamless: Stockings knit in one operation on circular machines (one continuous operation) so that there is no seam up the back

Semi-cathedral: Extends 4 1/2 to 5 1/2 feet from the waist

Shantung: Similar to raw silk, it has a rough texture with irregular "nubbies" throughout the fabric

Shawl collar: A smooth, rounded lapel with no notch

Sheath: A modern dress silhouette with a narrow skirt that is form-fitting through the torso

Sheers: Hosiery that is see-through; dress sheers are hosiery to be worn for daytime glamour. Evening sheers are hosiery to be worn for special occasions

Sheer-to-Waist: Pantyhose without visible panty line or reinforcement in the panty portion. It is an all-sheer garment from waist to toe

Short Glove: Good for semi-formal or informal weddings. The end of the glove falls an inch or two above your wrist and is perfect paired with a long-sleeved dress. They often have one button, but there are two-button and four-button styles that end somewhere between your wrist and your elbow

Silhouette: The general outline and style of a dress

Silk: A strong, smooth fabric, it used to be a more expensive fabric, but is now available in less expensive blends

Sleeve band: A bodice style that has a band of fabric extending up from the bodice, going around the top of the arm. In some designs, this can be used in place of a sleeve

Sleeveless: A bodice style that doesn't have any attached sleeves. This style may end cut in from the shoulder, on the shoulder, or dropping down slightly off the shoulder

Slubs: The knotty bumps that can be found on natural silk. Often fabric will be referred to as 'slubby'

Snood: A netlike hat or part of a hat that encases the hair in the back, often made of lace or knitting

Stockings: Hosiery that go all the way up to the upper thigh and have to be held up with garters or a garter belt

Strapless: A bodice style that comes around from under the arms. Can be straight across in the front or in a sweetheart style

Stroller: For formal daytime weddings, attendants wear the stroller/walking coat, which is usually charcoal gray and is cut slightly longer than a suit jacket. This jacket is worn with a lay-down collar shirt and a four-in-hand tie

Suspenders: Two supporting bands worn over the shoulders to support the trousers. They can coordinate, in color or pattern, with a cummerbund

Sweep: The shortest dress train, it goes back 8 to 12 inches after touching the floor

Sweetheart neckline: A neckline that dips in "Valentine" fashion to the bust line

Taffeta: Crisp and smooth, good for full dresses. Can be matte or shiny

Tailcoats: Usually worn at very formal weddings (read: evening), these jackets are short in front and have two long tails in the back

Taped and wired: A technique for arranging flowers used to make them easier to maneuver. The head of a flower is cut from the stem and attached to a wire which is then wrapped with floral tape

Tea length: The dress's hemline falls several inches above the ankles

Thigh-Highs: Stockings that just reach the thigh and are held up by elastomer bands; can also be worn with a garter belt

Tiara: A semicircular headband of jewels or beads worn on top of your head

Tiffany: A simple 2-3mm ring setting with a head that holds a single diamond

Topiary: Flowers or foliage trained and trimmed into geometric shapes, often resembling miniature trees or animals

Torte: A dense cake

Train: An extension of the wedding dress that starts at the waist. Some dresses come with trains that are detachable

Trellis: A woven wooden frame used as a screen or support for climbing plants and flowers

Trumpet: Dress silhouette that is form fitting over the bust, waist and hips and then flares out at the top of the thigh. Fuller at the bottom than an A-line. Not the same as a mermaid style that flares out lower at the knee

Tulle: Netting made of silk, nylon, or rayon; used for veils and skirts

Tussy Mussy: A silver carrying cone for flowers made popular in Victorian times, often used by brides to carry a nosegay

Tuxedo: A single- or double-breasted jacket that is worn at formal or semiformal evening weddings and is paired with matching trousers

Ultra Sheer: The sheerest possible hosiery made with a fine denier fiber, which gives the ultimate in sheerness

Velvet: A luxurious napped fabric. Very soft and elegant. Can be used as a dress component to match crepes or satins or shantungs

Vests: Worn in place of a cummerbund to cover the trouser waistband. It's often worn with a coordinating bow tie. Some are adjustable at the neck and waist with an open back while others have a fully covered back

Waistcoat: Worn in place of a cummerbund to cover the trouser waistband. It's often worn with a coordinating bow tie. Some are adjustable at the neck and waist with an open back, while others have a fully covered back. Also known as a vest

Waltz: A veil that falls somewhere between the knee and the ankle. Also known as a Ballet veil

Whipped cream: Heavy cream beaten until very thick; it's not a good choice for frosting since it has to be refrigerated and can easily melt

Wide satin band: A decorative accent that uses a wider band of satin on the skirt's hem

Wing collar: A band that encircles the neck with turned-down points in front. The most formal choice and the collar style most often worn with tuxedo jackets

Wreath Headdress: A circle of flowers, twigs, foliage, and/or ribbon that sits on the crown of the head. Also known as a garland

Wreath Arrangement: A ring of flowers or other decorative materials that can function as centerpiece, headpiece, or door hanger

Wedding Industry Associations

Wedding Industry Associations

Association for Wedding Professionals, International

http://www.afwpi.com

AFWPI Corporate Office

2740 Arden Way

Suite 100

Sacramento, CA 95825

(800) 242-4461

Butterflies

International Butterflies Breeders Association

IBBA

PO Box 573

Winters, TX 79567

(915)754-4604

http://www.butterflybreeders.org/

Cakes

International Cake Exploration Societe

Mail Box Etc.

PMB 166

1740 44th Street

Wyoming, IM 49509

http://www.ices.org

Caterers

National Association of Catering Executives

5565 Sterrett Place - Suite 328
Columbia, MD 21044
(410)997-9055
http://www.nace.net

DJs

The American Disc Jockey Association

200 Corporate Drive

#408

Ladera Ranch, CA 92694

(888)723-5776

http://www.adja.org

National Association of Mobile Entertainers

Box 144

Willow Grove, PA 19090

(800)434-8274

http://djkj.com

Florists

American Institute of Floral Designers

Tom Shaner, Executive Director
720 Light Street
Baltimore, MD 21230
410-752-3318
http://www.aifd.org

Society of American Florist

1601 Duke Street
Alexandria, VA 22314

800-336-4743
http://www.safnow.org

American Floral Endowment

Steve Martinez, Exec. Vice President
11 Glen-Ed Professional Park
Glen Carbon, IL 62034
612-692-0045
http://www.endowment.org

International Freeze Dried Floral Association
Cindy Sheets, Director of Advertising
17955 S. Western
Canyon, TX   79015
806-355-5337
http://www.ifdfa.com

Gowns
Association of Bridal Retailers
2925 Pleasant Lake Dr.
Las Vegas, NV 89117
(800) 331-4472
http://www.aobr.org

Association of Wedding Gown Specialists
(800)501-5005
http://www.weddinggownspecialists.com/

Photographers
Wedding and Portrait Photographers International
PO Box 2003
1312 Lincoln Boulevard
Santa Monica, CA 90406-2003
http://www.wppinow.com

Professional Photographers of America
229 Peachtree St. NE
Suite 220
Atlanta, GA 30303
(800)786-6277
http://www.ppa.com

Videographers
Wedding and Event Videographers Association International
8499 S. Tamiami Trail, PMB 208
Sarasota, FL 34238
(941) 923-5334
http://www.weva.com

WEDDING VENDOR DIRECTORY

Company Name	EMAIL	CITY	ST	ZIP	PHONE
Charles Sides Photography	CSides2554@charter.net	Birmingham	AL	35243	(205) 822-1500
Soul Two Soul	soultwosoul@msn.com	Birmingham	AL	35208	(205) 426-8490
Bridal Video	info@Bridal-Videos.com	Roanoke	AL	36274	866-880-7787
Larry's Limos	larry@larryslimos.com	Springville	AL	35146	205-629-6642
Cakes by Sam	sam@cakesbysam.com	Little Rock	AR		
Full Circle Ranch	JLANGAN@FULLCIRCLERANCH.COM	Cave Creek	AZ	85331	623-465-7570
Photography By Elizabeth	bridalpix2000@aol.com	Chandler	AZ	85224	(480)821-1111
Jacqueline's Bridal and Tux	yongbloodcns@msn.com	Glendale	AZ	85308	(602) 547-9200
All About U Entertainment	drew@allaboutuentertainment.com	Mesa	AZ	85206	480-813-3877
Arizona Wedding Chaplain	myersjc@aol.com	Mesa	AZ	85213	480-890-0420
Memories By Marsha	questions@memoriesbymarsha.com	Mesa	AZ	85277	480-396-4983
Michael Monti's Mesa Grill	weddings@montis.com	Mesa	AZ	85210	480-833-7727
Capital Mortgage Banc	jlhughes1962@yahoo.com	Peoria	AZ	85382	(623) 204-3000
DJ 4 Hire	dj4hire@qwest.net	Peoria	AZ	85382	623-566-0617
Brides & Christmas by Carrie	carrie-er@mail.com	Phoenix	AZ		
Hurwitz Photography	harrison@hurwitzphotography.com	Phoenix	AZ	85018	602-971-7978
Azy's Photography	azy@azphotovideo.com	Scottsdale	AZ	85254	480-922-7422
Angel Flower Florist	ireneforsyth@aol.com	Sedona	AZ	86351	800-264-3538
Arizona DJ Music & More!	jeaniec@uneedspeed.net	Sedona	AZ	86336	877-283-3969
Canbys Camera	ropes24@earthlink.net	Sedona	AZ	86336	928-282-2069
Dahl and DiLuca	dahlanddiluca@sedona.net	Sedona	AZ	86336	928-282-5219
Lodge at Sedona	info@lodgeatsedona.com	Sedona	AZ	86336	800-619-4467
Red Rock Limousine, Ltd	redrocklimo@kachina.net	Sedona	AZ	86336	(877) 282-0175
Southwest Inn at Sedona	jg@sedona.net	Sedona	AZ	86336	520-282-3344
Taylor Card Company	sales@taylorcard.com	Taylor	AZ	85939	520-536-5006
AZMUSICMAN.COM	rankin@azmusicman.com	Tempe	AZ	85283	(480) 777-7323
Flowers Forever	flowersforever@cox.net	Tempe	AZ	85282	480-642-2133
Michael Monti's La Casa	weddings@montis.com	Tempe	AZ	85281	480-967-7594
Victoria's	vsbb@primenet.com	Tombstone	AZ	85638	800-952-8216
TLC Weddings & Gifts	tlc777@prodigy.net	Tucson	AZ	85746	520-908-2032

White Lace and Promises	Jocelebweb@aol.com	Tucson	AZ		520/ 572-2545
Studio Caroline Offering Cookie Lee Jewelry	studiocaroline@aol.com		CA		(866) 230-3686
Dale Bailey, THD	dale6050@pacbell.net	Albany	CA	94706	(510)526-1001
Delightfully Different Ceremonies	info@marryusnow.com	Aliso Viejo	CA	92656	800-270-2181
Portraits By Dawn	PBDawn222@Earthlink.net	Anaheim	CA	92804	(714) 220-1222
Over The Moon Jewelry	sales@overthemoonjewelry.com	Beverly Hills	CA	90211	(310) 289-0149
Spa 415	solutions@spa415.com	Beverly Hills	CA	90210	(310) 276-8018
Lakefront Occasions	ryan@lakefrontoccasions.com	Big Bear Lake	CA	92317	888-600-6000
Magical DJ's	magicaldjs@cox.net	Bonita	CA	91902	(888) 595-5867
A House of Engraving	awards@usa.com	Campbell	CA	95008-5046	408-879-9604
Floral Poetry	linda.lou@cox.net	Carlsbad	CA	92008	(760)212-3362
KINETIC Mobile Productions	questions@kineticdj.com	Cedar Ridge	CA	95924	(530) 913-0949
Enchanted Florist	nisiesenchanted@aol.com	Cerritos	CA	90703	562-865-2071
A Petal Company – Petals by Xavi	xvanegas@hotmail.com	Chino Hills	CA	91709	1-949-307-1918 Cell
JW Party Pictures, Inc.	jeff@jwpartypictures.com	Culver City	CA	90232	(310) 915-1640
Foto Arts Events	info@fotoartsevents.com	Downey	CA	90242	562-292-1154
World Class Marriage	hjtrainings@aol.com	Encinitas	CA	92023	(760) 436-3960
Boulevard Video	jaystein@sbcglobal.net	Encino	CA	91436	(800) 287-9985
Oak Creek Manor Luxury b & b	☐arline☐.c.zachbauer@gte.net	Fallbrook	CA	92028	1-877-451-2468 Toll
Custom Photography Inc.	custom.services@verizon.net	Garden Grove	CA	92841	(714)891-9859
Studio Caroline Photography	studiocaroline@aol.com	Garden Grove	CA	92841	(714) 893-FOTO
Georgio's Tuxedos	mkastelic686@msn.com	Glendora	CA	91740	(626) 963-3417
Portable Party Crew-West	portableparty@earthlink.net	Greenbrae	CA	94904	415.925.0955
The Magic of Steven Steele	info@magicsteele.com	Hesperia	CA	92345	760-956-2044
Angels Landing Country Inn & Resort	angels@angelresort.com	Julian	CA	92036	1-888-253-7747
Memory Lane Gown Preservation and Restoration	cvarbowtie@aol.com	La Cañada Flintridge	CA	91011	800-287-9085 (CA)
VIDEO MOMENTOS	jimcosta@videomomentos.com	La Jolla	CA	92039	(619) 823.4336
NOVA Entertainment	novalive2001@yahoo.com	La Mesa	CA	91941	619-337-NOVA
Pam's Productions DJ's	partypam@partypam.com	La Mesa	CA	91944	(619) 218-4783
Ron Brazil Photography	watercam@cox.net	Laguna	CA	92677-	(949) 249-9853

		Niguel		8885	
Hazy Meadow Ranch and Carriage Company	hazymeadowlinda@earthlink.net	Lakeside	CA	92040	619-561-7050/ cell61
Peter Horvath Photography	pzaxis@earthlink.net	Lakewood	CA	90713	562-712-3270
Obregon Photography	infokuz@aol.com	LaVerne	CA	91750	(909) 596-3638
Black Tie Professional DJ & Video Service	jeff@blacktiedeejays.com	Lemongrove	CA	91945	(619) 660-7800
Mane Street Hair Salon	Lrasmussen@aol.com	Loma Linda	CA	92324	909-796-0128
Violeto Trio		Los Altos	CA		(650)948-9366
AAA Wedding Photography & Video	pascalproduction@msn.com	Los Angeles	CA	90401	310-656-1155
Cherie Steinberg Cote Foto	cherie007@sbcglobal.net	Los Angeles	CA	90024	310-358-8133
Contemporary Catering & Event Services	cateringdirector@pacbell.net	Los Angeles	CA	90034	310-350-4639
Feet First Entertainment	feetfirst_dj@hotmail.com	Los Angeles	CA	90230	(800) 393-3338
Forever Yours Video Productions	forevervid@aol.com	Los Angeles	CA		888-84-4EVER
Geoffrey Gilmore Signature	arline@sigevents.com	Los Angeles	CA	90049	310-770-4502
Studio Caroline Photography	studiocaroline@aol.com	Los Angeles	CA	91401	(818) 909-0400
1A Wedding Photography & Video	pascalusa@hotmail.com	Los Angeles-Santa Monica	CA		310-656-1155
Garden Inn Hotel4me	tcsfousa@wans.com	Los Gatos	CA	95030	(408) 354-6446
Portrait Expressions by Maarqui	portraitexp@cs.com	Mentone	CA	92359	909-794-3378
All Seasons Catering	stan@allseasonscatering.com	Mill Valley	CA	94941	(415) 383-9355
Pianist On Call	pianistoncall@yahoo.com	Monterey Park	CA	91754	626-284-0036
Video Services Un-Limited	maurygo@aol.com	Northridge	CA	91324	(818) 727-7746
Classique Limousines and Transportation	chuck@classiquelimo.com	Orange	CA	92867	888-902-5277
Bode Photography	bodephotography@attbi.com	Orangevale	CA	95662	(916) 723-0787
Peloton Entertainment	pelontonent@aol.com	Pasadena	CA		626-794-8984
Weddings of Heart	weddingheart@hotmail.com	Petaluma	CA	94952	(707) 778-1382
R. C. Photography & Beauty Center	RCPhotoTwo@aol.com	Rancho Cucamonga	CA	91730	909-989-1165
Reining Romance	reinromc@verizon.net	Redlands	CA	92373	909-793-1218
Victorian Groves	Susieandfonda@msn.com	Redlands	CA	92374	909-794-1112
Flowers For You	flowers4u@flowers4u.com	Riverside	CA	92505	909-689-2711 or 1-80
GFM Digital Video		Riverside	CA	92507	909-683-6887
Video Images Productions	ACPROVID@aol.com		CA	94928	707-584-8781
		Rohnert			

		Park			
A Picture Perfect Image by Giovan	giovan@jps.net	Sacramento	CA	95864	(916) 482-5963
Christopher Kight Photographers	kightphoto@aol.com	Sacramento	CA	95821	(916) 484-1164
Clear Image Photography	info@clearimagephotography.com	Sacramento	CA	95814	916-553-4268
Mez Media	☐arli@mezmedia.com	Sacramento	CA	95828	916-689-6445
String Work Quartet	snemacd@aol.com	Sacramento	CA	95616	(530) 753-1938
Vintage Carriage Company	leilani@vintagecarriage.com	Sacramento	CA	95648	(800) 426-3321
A Mirage Dance Band	miragejazz@bigfoot.com	San Diego	CA	619-445-36	619-445-3616
Aaron Feldman Photography	afeldman@san.rr.com	San Diego	CA	92109	(858) 336- 5135
Bridal Beauty	lukeas@earthlink.com	San Diego	CA	92103	(619) 683-9206
Budget Bouquets	lori@budgetbouquets.com	San Diego	CA		858-829-4123
Cinderella Carriage Company	☐arline@cinderella-carriage.com	San Diego	CA	92101	(619) 239-8080
Disc Go Round	andy@discgorounddj.com	San Diego	CA	92109	(858) 272-8494
Entertainment Solutions West	berniek@tnl-online.com	San Diego	CA	92120	(619) 583-7265
Event Video	sales@myeventvideo.com	San Diego	CA	92111	(858) 715-0122
Humphrey Florist		San Diego	CA	92117	(619) 276-8319
Humphrey's Half Moon Inn	dmercer@halfmooninn.com	San Diego	CA	92106	(619) 224-3411, Ext
Humphrey's Half Moon Inn	dmercer@halfmooninn.com	San Diego	CA	92106	(619) 224-3411
Inviting Ideas	invitingideas@cox.net	San Diego	CA	92108	(619) 294-3032
Kosmicki Photography	mgk@cox.net	San Diego	CA	92115	(619) 583-2229
Music by Design	mgoldst1@san.rr.com	San Diego	CA	92121	858-457-9921
Photos by Cecilia	photosbycec@cox.net	San Diego	CA	92107	619-223- 2106
Putnam Travel	lctravel@san.rr.com	San Diego	CA	92109	(858) 488-2569
SilverWood	diane@silverwood-music.com	San Diego	CA	92120	(619) 286-4227
Tender Moments Photography	info@tendermomentsphotography.com	San Diego	CA	92128	858-487-2998
Vira-N-Company	vira92@hotmail.com	San Diego	CA	92121	(858) 695-9981
Zelman Studios	bil@zelmanstudios.com	San Diego	CA	92101	(619) 702-6345
Patrick Roddie Photography	quotes@webbery.com	San Francisco	CA	94109	415.928.1736
Alex Schoenfeldt, Photographer	alex@schoenfeldt.com	San Francisco	CA	94117	888 316 2539
AzzMazz Music	jean@jeanmazzei.com	San Francisco	CA	94134	(415) 467-9135
Helen Wills Brown	hwb@dnai.com	San	CA	94114	(415) 641-7691

		Francisco			
Oui, Three Queens Productions	evan@ouithreequeens.com	San Francisco	CA	94102	415.621.6877
The Joe Sharino Band	sharino@sti.net	San Francisco	CA	95120	(559) 658-7712
White Gloves Limousine Service, Inc.	whiteglvz@aol.com	San Francisco	CA	94109	877.929.5254
Flashback Band	mflashback@aol.com	San Jose	CA	95125	800.294.2677
Eagan Studios, Inc.	barbeagan@eaganpv.com	San Jose	CA	95110	(408) 295-6585
Newman Video Services	ea@newman-media.com	San Jose	CA	95119	(408) 362-0160
The Joe Sharino Band	sharino@sti.net	San Jose	CA	95125	831.722.4344
Wine Cask	abe@winecask.com	Santa Barbara	CA	93101	(805) 966-6750
Leonard Neil Productions	arline@leonardneilproductions.com	Santa Monica	CA	90403	(888)453-1137
Fleurs de France	js@fleursfrance.com	Sebastopol	CA	95472	707-824-8158
City Style Hair	citystylehair@inventivemail.com	Solana Beach	CA	92075	(858) 755-1202
Always & Forever Professional Disc Jockey	discjockey411@aol.com	Stockton	CA	95210	209-463-3472
Reel Memories	reelmemories01@aol.com	Studio City	CA	91604	818-752-0336
A Perfect Day Wedding & Event Coordination	sameyer@perfectdaywedding.net	Torrance	CA	90505	310-205-2646
Fly By Night	ross@flybynightdjs.com	Tustin	CA	92781	714.730.6070
Arbor Occasions	info@arboroccasions.com	Valencia	CA	91354	661-430-0062
Elizabeth Etienne Photography	eli@eephoto.com	Venice	CA	90294	(310) 396-8682
Venice Flowers	alan.flowers@verizon.net	Venice	CA	90291	(888) 408-3642
West Hollywood Florist	laflorist@earthlink.net	West Hollywood	CA	90046	800-991-0046
Wren Video Services	WrenVideo@aol.com	Littleton	CO	80122	(303) 347-9736
An Ovation Entertainment	Celebration@Ovation-Entertainment.com	Aurora	CO	80011	(303) 366-8649
Michael's Photography	Michaels_Photography@professionalphotography.com	Aurora	CO	80012	720-535-6073
Hudetz Photography	johnahudetz@bigfoot.com	Fort Collins	CO	80525	970 282-1798
Bear Paw Inn	bearpaw@rkymtnhi.com	Winter Park	CO	80482	(970) 887-1351
Angelica Farm Florals LLC	info@angelicafarm.com	Barkhamsted	CT	06063	860 379-7766
Victor's Video Productions	victorsvideo@aol.com	Branford	CT	06405	203-315-1342
Nifi's Wedding Planning	diane@nifiswedding.com	Coventry	CT	06238	(860) 614-2456
Begin With A Grin	sue@beginwithagrin.com	Danbury	CT	06810	203-792-6051

Camelot Creations LLC	Camelotcrafts@aol.com	East Hartford	CT	06118	411
The Hornets	1hornet@snet.net	Hartford	CT	06441	(800)423-4933
Music Unlimited, LLC	jcbazen@musicunlimited.com	Washington	DC		301-948-5419
Richard Basch Studio	richardbasch@mindspring.com	Washington	DC	20008	(202) 232-3100
Pat VanGelder	pvannc@aol.com	Bridgeville	DE	19933	302-337-9323
Florida Weddings Online	ecook41181@aol.com	Alva	FL	33920	239-728-2592
The Best of Times	dons.spot@verizon.net	Bradenton	FL	34203	941-742-3040
Diva D'Musica Entertainment	ddmusica@gte.net	Brandon	FL	33511	(813) 643-8353
Wyndham Palms Resort & Country	bazj@tempusresorts.net	Celebration	FL	34747	407-787-5627
All Pro Photo	dan@allprophoto.net	Clearwater	FL	33765	727-449-0610
Tutto Favoloso Catering	chefno1@gte.net	Clearwater	FL	33764	727-533-0222
Mario's Video Production	mariosvideo@msn.com	Coral Gables	FL	33134	305-461-1263
Janet Carlson – Lovegevity Consultant	jcarlson@lovegevity.com	Davie	FL	33324	(877)597-8166, Ext. 908
Variety Entertainment	variety1@tampabay.rr.com	Dundee	FL	33838	
Weddings By Joy	joy@weddingsbyjoy.com	Dunedin	FL	34698	727-771-7096
Aubrie's Photography	info@aubries.com	Edgewater	FL	32141	(386)426-2196
Rev. Elizabeth E. Berry	berrycounseling@hotmail.com	Fort Myers	FL	33913	239 225 0278
Mother And Daughter Photographers	arlin.young2@verizon.net	Hudson	FL	34669	727-379-0306
Catering By Altrovese, Inc.	altrovese@altrovese.com	Jacksonville	FL	32206	(904) 358-3262
Simple Pleasures	TamiL531@attbi.com	Jacksonville	FL	32216	904-805-8510
Chocolate Fountains by	kgift@aol.com	Kissimmee	FL	34744	407-935-9694
PolishPottery	tbpolishpottery@cfl.rr.com	Melbourne	FL	32936-2113	1(800)789-8430
A Petunia Flowers	weddings@petuniaflowers.com	Miami	FL	33137	305-576-0026
GooseMan Productions	arline@gooseman.net	Miami	FL	33178	305-205-3888
A Cut Above Catering	info@cutabovecatering.com	Orlando	FL	32878-0914	(407) 699-5400
And The Beat Goes On Productions	andthebeatgoesonproductions@hotmail.com	Orlando	FL	32743	407-873-6866
ArtzPhoto	artz@artzphoto.com	Orlando	FL	32824	407-856-5851
Cakes Via Maria	tonyviamaria@aol.com	Orlando	FL	32826	407-823-9059
Dixie Limousine	dixielimo@aol.com	Orlando	FL	32819	(407) 509-1710
Hunter's Creek florist	hcflorist2@aol.com	Orlando	FL	32837	407-855-3283
John Michael Catering	jmc@cfl.rr.com	Orlando	FL		407-894-6671

idnight Limo & ransportation	weddings@midnightlimousine.com	Orlando	FL	32812	407-306-0111
rlando Dream Weddings	arli@orlandodreamweddings.com	Orlando	FL	32835	(321) 287-9020
our Affair to Remember	remember9@earthlink.net	Orlando	FL		(321) 662-8372
he Wedding Duet	wedding.duet@verizon.net	Palm Harbor	FL	34685-4114	(727) 772-9423
hotography by Patricia	patsphotosfl@cox.net	Pensacola	FL	32507	850-492-2976
Mik'e'J Entertainment	mikej@mikejentertainment.com	Port Orange	FL	32128	386-788-2575
Digital Wave	chad@digitalwaveproductions.net	St Petersburg	FL	33710	727-345-9898
Elegant Occasions	bill@partydoctors.com	Sunrise	FL	33322	954-749-6764
CharlesBaisden.com	charles@charlesbaisden.com	Tallahassee	FL	32304	850-228-4806
Gordon Photography & Video Production	gordonphoto2@yahoo.com	Tampa	FL	33604	(813) 231-0931
Rev. Sharon Burnett	sharonburnett@ij.net	Zephyrhills	FL	33540	813.779.0508
IRD Photography	JRDphotography@cs.com		FL		1-850-609-3686
Lisa HandmanHarpist	Lhand30556@aol.com	Alpharetta	GA	30022	770-442-9172
Atlanta Corporate Events	gokingmichael@aol.com	Atlanta	GA	30314	770-399-0118
Awesome Blossom Weddings by Monique	escudie@bellsouth.net	Atlanta	GA	30101	770-529-3008
Chamber Music Atlanta, Inc.	david@chambermusicatlanta.com	Atlanta	GA	30345	(770) 496-1876
Ensemble pour Deux	barbarahood@juno.com	Atlanta	GA	30214	770-461-4595
Hayden Video Weddings	vpa77@hotmail.com	Atlanta	GA	30305	(404) 433-1769
Van Pragal Photography	vanpragal@earthlink.net	Atlanta	GA	30329	404-964-6258
Culinary Services, Inc.	joey@culinaryservicesinc.com	Conyers	GA	30094	770-929-3500
Capture It Graphics and Video	captureit@mail.com	Ellenwood	GA	30294	770-996-5323
Orphan Studios	milasking@orphanstudios.com	Ellenwood	GA	30294	678-289-0091
Cryxstal Video Productions	angela@southernbrides.com	Hiram	GA	30141	(866) 738-4828
2 Fun Entertainment	twofun@bellsouth.net	Lawrenceville	GA	30043	6783765775
ClassifiedEvents.com	chuck@classifiedevents.com	Lawrenceville	GA	30042	770-736-7647
First Class Second Plate Catering	firstclass@nc.rr.com	Lawrenceville	GA	30044	770-609-8985
Mike's Mobile DJ Service	mmdjs@mindspring.com	Lawrenceville	GA	30049	770-945-2621
The Soul Purpose Band	dhpenn@attbi.com	Lilburn	GA	30047	(770) 979-6180

A-STACPhoto/Video & DJ Entertainment	astac614@bellsouth.net	Lithonia	GA	30058	770-364-3745
Engraving Creations	info@engravingcreations.com	Loganville	GA	30052-5324	770-985-0405
Atlanta Holistic Ministries	rnz@smyrnacable.net	Marietta	GA	30067	(770) 850-9115
Bussey Video Productions	busseyvideo@aol.com	Marietta	GA	30008	770-439-5235
Carl By Request	carlbyrequest@att.net	Marietta	GA	30008	678-557-8718
Destinations Southern	berts431@aol.com	Savannah	GA	31401	912-232-3815
EverWord Media	nakin@everword.com	Watkinsville	GA	30677	770-725-8075
Down Home Fiddle	ted@downhomefiddle.com	Winston	GA	30187	770-942-3424
Bridal Bodies	bridalbodies@hotmail.com		GA		404-454-3178
Critical Focus Productions	⬜arlin@criticalfocus.net		GA	30318	404-964-2566
Music Express	rick@mxpentertainment.com	Ewa Beach	HI	96706	(808) 689-7579
A Special Moment Hawaii Photography & Video	vidsolve@hawaii.rr.com	Honolulu	HI	96826	866-591-2224
Island Disco	info@islanddisco.com	Honolulu	HI	96825	(888) 933-6248
Studio West, Inc. Hawaii	spower@aloha.net	Honolulu	HI	96813	(808) 593-9942
Pipi's Sound & Lighting	pipi@hawaii.rr.com	Kapolei	HI	96707	(808) 256-7474
Hideaway N' Paradize	aparadize@msn.com	Kihei	HI	96753	808-875-0356
A Simply Elegant Wedding	info@asimplyelegantwedding.com	Kihei, Maui	HI	96753	(808) 874-7447
Ghiselani wedding Cakes	ghiselani@hotmail.com	Kihei-Maui Island	HI	96753	(808) 874-9535
Anointed Weddings	anointed@maui.net	Lahaina	HI	96761	(800) 962-7622
Blue Hawaii Weddings	gmerald@gte.net	Waikoloa	HI	96738	1-888-311-2583
All Ways Maui'd Weddings and Ceremonies	lovegevity@maui-angels.com		HI	96784-0817	(877) 906-2843
Minson Photographics	cminson@sprintmail.com	Norwalk	IA	50211	515-988-0100
Hair Design by Joanne	laterza@mindspring.com	Bloomingdale	IL	60108	(630) 893-8459
Hair Designs by Deborah Ann & Co.	Ddesurne@aol.com	Brookfield	IL	60513	708-387-0791
M&M The Special Events Company	mberk@mmspecialevents.com	Carol Stream	IL	60188	(630)871-9999
Elegant Presentations	sales@WeddingChairCovers.com	Carpentersville	IL	60110	877-460-6239
Ben Lynn	lynnbj2@insightbb.com	Champaign	IL	61820	(217) 202-3603
Champaign Studio One Photography	bill@cuphoto.com	Champaign	IL	61822	217-352-3923
1800 Party Shop	smales4676@aol.com	Chicago	IL		(847) 830-8235
A Right Choice Limo	arightchoicelimo@aol.com	Chicago	IL	60611	312-654-5466

acchus Group Productions, Ltd.		Chicago	IL	60660-4798	(800) 767-6997
Ceremonies On Location	Rabrewin@aol.com	Chicago	IL	60643	(773) 881-4028
Chicago Producers	info@weddingvideochicago.com	Chicago	IL	60622	773-276-0694
va's Bridals of Chicago		Chicago	IL	60634	(773) 777-3311
olly Jim's Video	jollyjim@flash.net	Chicago	IL		(773) 589-9999
ORI –MAKEUP ARTIST	amaliax989@aol.com	Chicago	IL	60614	773-296-1476
MCG Beaute'	marcchristopher@attbi.com	Chicago	IL	60622	(312) 243-5258
Printboxstudio, Ltd.	info@printboxstudio.com	Chicago	IL	60614	(773) 388-0309
ProShots Photography	Hproshots@aol.com	Chicago	IL	60620	773-821-8779
SIM PRODUCTION COMPANY	simpro@aol.com	Chicago	IL	60617	(773) 374-9298
Wyndham Chicago Hotel	btanzil@wyndham.com	Chicago	IL		312/274-4426
Baking D'zine	ac@lmmkt.com	Glendale Heights	IL	60139	(630) 327-9222
Larry Eckerling & His Orchestra, Inc.	Leckerling@aol.com	Glenview	IL	60025	(847) 486-8181
Bever Photography & Design Studio	s.bever@attbi.com	Joliet	IL	60435	815-723-3051
The Original Mr. DJ	Mr.DJ@attbi.com	Joliet	IL	60435	815-690-6735
David Simm Photography	info@davidsimmphotography.com	Northbrook	IL	60062	(847) 803-9450
Millinennium Entertainment	jonas@millentevents.com	Oak Forest	IL	60452	(708)687-2772
Aspen Sound, Inc.	bruce@aspensound.net	Plainfield	IL		(800) 269-0075
B & B Video Creations	billa@bnb-video.com	River Grove	IL	60171-0627	708-453-6428
Flower & Flour Inc.	flwrflr@core.com	Roscoe	IL	61073	(815) 623-1333
Artistic Floral Design	info@artisticfloraldesign.com	Schaumburg	IL	60173	847-885-4532
Veni's Flower and Bridal	veniflowers@yahoo.com	Schaumburg	IL	60193	847-985-9550
Art40 Design	art40design@ameritech.net	Skokie	IL	60077	847.673.2828
Flawless Brides	mercierlady@aol.com	Skokie	IL	60077	(847) 322-8319
Blossom Basket Florist & Bailey's Fine Gifts	rlb@blossombasket.com	Urbana	IL	61802	(217) 367-8354
CruiseOne	ptyrrell@cruiseone.com	Wadsworth	IL	60083-9256	(866) 823-8570
"The Barn" at Arabian Knights Farm and AKF Entertainment	vci@vciconsulting.com	Willowbrook	IL	60527	(630) 327- 7399
Spiritually Bound	emontville@spirituallybound.org	Willowbrook	IL	60527	(630) 986-8891
Wings Like A Dove	wingslikeadove@aol.com	Woodstock	IL	60098	(815)337-4047
The Dance Machine Mobile		Bloomington	IN		(800)933-2980

DJ Service

Beach Bum Vacations	BeachBumHayley@aol.com	Carmel	IN	46032	317-748-5654
Bloomz	chrisatbloomz@aol.com	Fisher	IN	46038	(317) 570-0487
Andis Photography	rex@andisinc.com	Floyds Knobs	IN	47119	502-724-2630
Party Starters Entertainment Services	reserve@partystarters.net	Hammond	IN	46323	773-416-1237
AMS Entertainment		Indianapolis	IN		317-578-3548
Baby Boomer Sound	dcook@indyradio.com	Indianapolis	IN		317-823-3456
Brewster Photography	photographer@josephbrewster.com	Indianapolis	IN	46250	317-679-8895
Crawfords Bakery & Deli	rick@crawfordsbakery.com	Indianapolis	IN	46202	(317) 924-2494
Fashions & Custom Creations, Inc.	d-m-frey@iquest.net	Indianapolis	IN	46239	317 862 6931
Munchables & More Catering	Ljordanl@peoplepc.com	Indianapolis	IN	46240	(317)252-5875
Valley Branch Retreat	valleybranchretreat@yahoo.com	Nashville	IN	47448	(812)988-7750
Ehninger Florist	ron@ehningerflorist.com	South Bend	IN	46601	574-232-7976
The Ice Studio	theicestudio@yahoo.com	Yorktown	IN	47396	(765)749-2321
Benjamin Photography	bojobass@osprey.net	Emporia	KS	66801	620-342-1988
Mary Kay Cosmetics	angelamk@swbell.net	Lawrence	KS	66047	785-221-6650
Above & Beyond Wedding Consultants, LLC.	abovebeyond@everestkc.net	Lenexa	KS	66215	913-888-5554
ALL ABOUT LIMOUSINE	SBELL@ALLABOUTWIRELESS.NET	Mission	KS	66205	913-831-1939
Weddings by Chris	weddingsbychris@cox.net	Wichita	KS	67207	(316) 683-0344
CM Photography	dcreason@usa.net	Crestwood	KY	40014	502-241-5451
Associated Video	video@ka.net	Louisville	KY	40299	502-239-9149
Audio X-press llc	xpress@win.net	Louisville	KY	40216	502-449-0935
Artistry In Cake of Kentucky	gkidwell@iglou.com	Milton	KY	40045	502-268-5975
EARCandy Productions	tsnyder@earcandyproductions.net	Pewee Valley	KY	40056	502.241.9078
TVRock Productions	michelle@tvrockproductions.com	Shepherdsville	KY	40165	(502) 543-3338
William Boyd's Photography and Graphic Design	williamboyd@cox.net	Baton Rouge	LA	70808	(225) 387-2578
Extreme Elegance	info@extremeelegance.com	Metairie	LA	70003	(504) 466-0564
Best Western French Quarter Landmark	Chris_bonhagen@acihotels.com	New Orleans	LA	70116	(800) 535-7862
New Orleans Wedding Chapel	weddings@nowc.org	New Orleans	LA	70116	1-888-261-6787
Marty Gilman Band	mgband@charter.net	Auburn	MA	01501	508.752.4027

Walnut Hill Invitations	walnuthill@mediaone.com	Boston	MA		978-409-1211
LoveWorks	jrcd2@shaysnet.com	Deerfield	MA	01342	(413) 665-2971
The O-Tones	mwitt@gis.net	Florence	MA	01062	(413) 584-8760
DJ Michael Walsh	mwalsh@mwalsh.com	West Roxbury	MA	02132	781-958-2269
After Hours DJ Service	info@afterhoursdj.net	Westfield	MA	01086	800 782 3033
CustomWeddingVows.Com	love@customweddingvows.com	Worcester	MA	01613-0003	1-866-WED-VOWS
Stan Stearns Fine Photography	stearns@erols.com	Annapolis	MD	21403	(800) 585-4141
Borrowed Blue Photography	borrowedblue@borrowedbluephoto.com	Baltimore	MD	21212	(410) 532-0679
Ed's Personalized DJ Service	ed@djed.com	Baltimore	MD		(410) 382-3057
Ultimate/Events-4U	cmydjs@yahoo.com	Baltimore	MD	21138-4628	(410) 478-4683
Affairs Elegant Bridal Service	affairselegant@aol.com	Calverton	MD	20705	301-931-7900
Something Extra Cakery	sales@somethingextracakery.com	Gaithersburg	MD	20877	(301) 921-9194
S&S Candy Creations	Sscandycreations@aol.com	Pasadena	MD	21122	410-437-6846
Photography by Vicki Kelliebrew	kelliebrew@earthlink.net	Seabrook	MD	20706	301-552-2294
Night & Day Music	msuser@erols.com	Silver Springs	MD	20902	301-593-4209
Sounds Good Mobile DJ Service	SGDJKaptKirk@aol.com	Auburn Hills	MI	48326	248-802-2989
Party Cakes	CakeLady48072@aol.com	Berkley	MI	48072	248-541-2253
Detroit Weddings	info@detroitweddings.com	Dearborn	MI	48120	(313) 441-5258
Heavenly Bites	cakes@heavenlybites.com	Dearborn	MI		(313) 792-1206
eTuxedo	inquiry@etuxedo.com	Farmington Hills	MI	48334	(248) 865-9960
Suzabella's	sue@suzabellas.com	Lathrup Village	MI	48076	248-443-1546
Stealth DJ's Mobile	djmarkcone@stealthdjs.com	Romulus	MI	48174	(734) 753- 3755
Dave White Video Services		Saint Clair Shores	MI	48082	(810) 294-7635
DJ Mike Your Musical Slave	djmadmanmike@earthlink.net	Southfield	MI	48034	(248) 355-0863
K&R VIDEO PRODUCTION STUDIOS, INC.	recordav@knr.net	Southfield	MI		(888)802-0420
The Tapestry		Southfield	MI	48075	(245)356-5602
Blake's Photography			MI	78314	248-762-9055
Flutter-By Massage	flutterbymassage@hotmail.com	Crystal	MN	55428	(763)208-8800

Jenkins Photography	dave@jenkinsweddings.com	Eden Prairie	MN	55344	(612) 904-0404
Digital Moments, Inc.	info@digitalmoments.biz	Edina	MN	55343	952-930-0588
Club Dance Entertainment	info@clubdance.dj	Elk River	MN	55330	(800) 642-8647
Beauty Boutique- Beauty Consultant	sneisen@marykay.com	Maple Grove	MN	55369	763-493-8947
Sawyer Photography	sawyerphotography@hotmail.com	Minneapolis	MN	55418	612-387-5958
Greg Jansen Photography	gregjansen@yahoo.com	Minneapolis/ St. Paul	MN		612-825-1769
Inbeaute Photography	inbeautephoto@earthlink.net	Minneapolis/ St. Paul	MN	55407	612-729-0460
Radford Video Creations	jim@radfordvideo.com	Minneapolis/ St. Paul	MN	55126	612-677-3900
Calhoun Brass	2songers@prodigy.net	Minnetonka	MN	55345	952-401-3732
Joy Laansma	Joy@joysounds.com	Plymouth	MN	55441	736-544-6554
Twin Cities Music and Arts	tcmusicandarts@aol.com	Saint Paul	MN	55104	651-647-1459
Cadillac Catering INC.	cadicater@aol.com	Kansas City	MO	64108	816-221-3606
Evangelical Community Ministries	evcomin@mindsping.com	Kansas City	MO	64118	816-468-9691
Paul Phillips Formal Wear	sceniccleaners@aol.com	Springfield	MO	65803	(417) 869-1833
Team Steele, Coldwell Banker Gundaker	arline@teamsteele.com	St. Charles	MO	63303	1-800-203-5993
1st ProWeddingAlbums	george@proweddingalbums.com	Asheville	NC	28805	877-912-2229
Designs by Patricia	designsbypatricia@charter.net	Asheville	NC	28805	828 299 3135
Ice Sensations	icesensations@charter.net	Asheville	NC	28803	(828) 277-2763
Bridal Mart	Bridal@mindspring.com	Burlington	NC	27215	336-227-5500
City Videography	jpkvideo@hotmail.com	Burlington	NC	27215	(336)584-7714
Tables, Chairs & Staging	rental@netpath.net	Burlington	NC	27612-1957	(336) 437-0534
Capital Style Luxury Transportation, Inc	info@capitallimo.com	Cary	NC	27512-5664	919-460-1230
Crash & Coco Fine Lingerie	info@crashnet.com	Cary	NC		919.468.8668
Magic Happens Travel & Cruises	travel@magichappens.com	Cary	NC	27513	(800)824-4968
Mark Edwards Studio	Mark@MarkEdwardsStudio.com	Cary	NC	27511	(919) 467-3070
Tim Johnson	timjohnsonphoto@aol.com	Cary	NC	27511	919-467-4617
Carolina Inn	messercola@email.unc.edu	Chapel Hill	NC	27516	919 933-2001
Lance Richardson Photography	lrphoto@bellsouth.net	Chapel Hill	NC	27514	919 942-4044
MUSICA- Musicians for all	musicaplays@mindspring.co	Chapel Hill	NC	27516-	(919) 929-2477

...ccasions.	m			6284	
Occasions Engraving	signsnow353@mindspring.com	Chapel Hill	NC	27514	(919) 929-0702
Abbey Rose Florist	abbeyrose@perigee.net	Charlotte	NC	28215	(704) 531-7673
Body Awareness Center	info@bodyawarenesscenter.net	Charlotte	NC	28215	704-536-5001
Cake Expressions by Lisa	lisa@cake-expressions.com	Charlotte	NC	28269	704-560-2013
Capriccio By Denise	capriccio_2@yahoo.com	Charlotte	NC	28213	(704) 597-0400
Garmon Hall	nacaudle@aol.com	Charlotte	NC	28269	(704) 598-5450
Gift World Collection	gftwrldnets@netscape.net	Charlotte	NC	28227	(704) 573-0462
Hampton Inn & Suites Southpark	jsheppard@panoshotel.com	Charlotte	NC	28210	(704) 319-5700
Jerry Goodman Music		Charlotte	NC		(704)782-0913
Panos Hotel Group/Comfort Suites Charlotte North	gm.nc319@choicehotels.com	Charlotte	NC	28269	(704)598-0478
Studio 96	David@studio96photography.com	Charlotte	NC	28247-2593	704-544-0554
The Formal Touch, Inc.	Theformaltouch@aol.com	Charlotte	NC	28213	(704) 593-1961
Darrell Howell Mobile DJ	cwinslow@lovegevity.com	Cherryville	NC	28021	(704) 435-5175
Specialty Catering by	RFDUP@aol.com	Clayton	NC	27520	919-669-1149
Hampton Inn & Suites – Speedway Blvd/Concord Mills	wmiranda@panoshotel.com	Concord	NC	28027	(704)979-5600
Shear Image	bluebill71@aol.com	Concord	NC	28027	704-792-9191
Tina Turner	bluebill@aol.com	Concord	NC	28027	704-792-9191
Simply Thank You!	simplythnx@hotmail.com	Cornelius	NC	28031	704-987-8469
AZMUSICMAN.COM	rankin@azmusicman.com	Durham	NC	27713	(919)806-4929
Double Tree Guest Suites	dtgsrdu@aol.com	Durham	NC	27713	919-361-4660
Jean-Christian Rostagni	jeanius@artmessengers.com	Durham	NC	27707	(919) 416-1111
John Elkins Photography	jkephoto@aol.com	Durham	NC	27701	919-286-4049
Millennium Hotel	rusales@gte.net	Durham	NC	27612	919-383-8575
Montgomery's The Florist	staff@lovegevity.com	Durham	NC	27707	919-489-3361
Museum of Life and Science	rentals@ncmls.org	Durham	NC	27704	(919) 220-5429, Ext.
Season Creative	e.darling@verizon.net	Durham	NC	27713	919-824-1188
JiL Companies, Inc.	toni@jilcompanies.com	Graham	NC	27253	336-570-9262
A & A Disk Jockey Service	partypros@aandadj.com	Greensboro	NC	27427	1-800-742-1683
Cavin & Stovall Photography	csphoto@bellsouth.net	Greensboro	NC	27408	336-292-2701
Personal Touch Bridal Consulting	LilLori1976@aol.com	Greensboro	NC	27407	336-299-2924
Kelsey's Café and Catering		Hillsborough	NC	27278	919-732-1155

Abigail's Florist	abagailsflorist@hotmail.com	Holly Springs	NC	27540	919-303-8777
Bob Servatius-Photography	servati716@aol.com	Matthews	NC	28105-5505	704-847-1603
By Invitation Only	BY_INVITATION_ONLY_1@HOTMAIL.COM	Morrisville	NC	27560	919-388-7143
The Flour Shop	flourshp@bellsouth.net	Morrisville	NC	27560	919-319-8634
Hampton Inn & Suites Pineville	asailors@panoshotel.com	Pineville	NC	28134	(704) 889-2700
Hilton Garden Inn, Pineville	asailors@panoshotel.com	Pineville	NC	28143	(704) 889-3279
Antique Limousines Inc	vintagecar@nc.rr.com	Raleigh	NC	27609	919-876-0060
Bunn DJ Co.	joebunn@nc.rr.com	Raleigh	NC	27609	919-785-9001
Danamare Productions Mobile DJ	danamare_prod@hotmail.com	Raleigh	NC	27604	919-212-3566
Dazzle and Lace	info@dazzleandlace.com	Raleigh	NC	27603	(919) 662-0018
Doug Pitts' Photography	dspitts@mindspring.com	Raleigh	NC	27608	(919) 821-5673
Laurence Lynn Photography	LlynnPhotography@aol.com	Raleigh	NC	27609	(919) 981-0890
Musical Athlete		Raleigh	NC		(919)878-7270
Rev. Kayelily Middleton	kayelily@mindspring.com	Raleigh	NC	27612	919-844-1844
Wedding Reflections dba Marlin Events	marlinevents@earthlink.net	Raleigh	NC	27615	919.874.0370
Zeb Starnes Creative Photography	zebstarnes@mindspring.com	Raleigh	NC	27704	(919) 477-6715
Girgo Media LLC	info@girgomedia.com	Salisbury	NC	28145	(704) 633-1237
A Sound Entertainment	soundent@statesville.net	Statesville	NC	28625	704-873-1386
Clay Russell Photography	crphotography@yahoo.com	Stokesdale	NC	27357	(336) 706-2086
The Manor House at Waxhaw, Ltd.	themanorhouse@connectingpoint.com	Waxhaw	NC	28173	(704)843-7514
Treasured Reflections	wforbis@triad.rr.com	Winston-Salem	NC	27103	336-723-5853
DONNA BOWLES PHOTOGRAPHY	d242b@aol.com		NC	28115	704-799-7711
Party Unlimited	jeff@weddingpartydj.com		NC		(800) 789-0851
Four Star Entertainment	stevedj02@yahoo.com	Grand Forks	ND	58201	(701) 792-2924
The Cake Specialist	hunter32pt@aol.com	Bellevue	NE	68005	(402) 733-2253
Terryl's Flower Garden	Terrylvae@aol.com	Omaha	NE	68114	(402) 393-3131
The Scoular Building Ballroom	lroth@scoular.com	Omaha	NE	68102	402-449-1424
Art Of Flowers	aof3459191@aol.com	Atlantic City	NJ	08401	(888) 306-0035
Mix Master Disc Jockeys	dave@mixmasterdjs.com	Dover	NJ	07801	973-989-0787
Digital Memories Forever	arline@dmforever.com	East Windsor	NJ	08520	609-548-2778

Dynasty Entertainment – Jack Goodman Orchestras, DJ's, and Ensembles	jackgmusic@aol.com	Edison	NJ	08818	732-985-7577
Pictorial Parlor Photographers and Video	pictpar@aol.com	Edison	NJ	08817	(732) 572-5773
Gforce Band	jgrillo@gforceband.com	Ewing	NJ	08628	609-883-3492
A.J. Elbaroudy Photography	aj_photography@yahoo.com	Franklin Park	NJ	08823	732-940-6864
Carlo's Bakery	info@carlosbakery.com	Hoboken	NJ	07030	201 659-3671
Riviera Limousines	rivlimo@earthlink.com	Leeds Point	NJ	08227	888-625-9448
Music Affair Productions	DJ@DiscJockeysOnly.com	Little Falls	NJ	07424	973-345-1286
Distinctive Entertainment	service@distinctiveent.com	Marlton	NJ	08053	1-800-400-7124
HANK JOEL MUSIC	hankjoel@aol.com	Mountainside	NJ	07092	(800) 449-1444
Fresh, The Band	fdagos4971@aol.com	Neptune	NJ	07753	(732) 502-0813
Oromi, Inc.	servello@oromi.com	North Bergen	NJ	07047	201-868-1114
Derek Fowles Photography	info@derekfowlesphotography.com	Northhampton	NJ	01060	413-584-7756
Shoe Chic	Gdsshoes@aol.com	Paramus	NJ	07652	201-291-9373
The Domesticated Jungle	abbe@abbe-m.com	Paramus	NJ	07652	(201) 707-0587
Monday Morning Flower & Balloon Co.	mondaymorningflowers@yahoo.com	Princeton	NJ	08540	609-520-2005
Alex V. Entertainment	alexvm@vipdiscjockeys.com	Springfield	NJ	07081	(973)467-7911
D-Vision Video Inc	bonnie@dvisionvideo.com	Succasunna	NJ	07876	973-927-1588
Soular Rhythm Music and Entertainment	info@soularrhythm.com	Union	NJ		888-414-4499
VINCENZOS TUXEDOS	formals@vincenzostuxedos.com	Wayne	NJ	07470	973-633-8881
Calligraphy by Jennifer	calligraphybyjen@aol.com	West Orange	NJ	07052	(973)736-6845
John Christian Entertainment	jcola78359@cs.com	West Orange	NJ	07052	(973) 669-8848
Michele's Harp & Vestments	arline@cybermesa.com	Albuquerque	NM	87106	505-765-1288
The Galisteo Inn	galisteoin@aol.com	Galisteo	NM	87540	(505) 466-8200
Bradley Studio	info@bradleystudio.com	Santa Fe	NM	87504	(505) 989-7743
Southwest Healing Sanctuary	draryana@cs.com	Santa Fe	NM	87508	(505)466-6887
Taos Video Works	pierce3@taosnet.com	Taos	NM	87571	505-758-4404
A Ceremony to Remember	revjule@hotmail.com	Las Vegas	NV	89110	(702) 320-1123
A Las Vegas Wedding & Rooms	arline@lasvegasweddings.com	Las Vegas	NV	89109	800-488-6283
Abbey Group of Las Vegas	abbeygroup@lasvegas.com	Las Vegas	NV	89119	877-264-8255

Homes or Loans	BRENNA@HOMESORLOANS.COM	Las Vegas	NV	89128	702-768-9544
Rent-A-Dress & Tux	rentadress@earthlink.net	Las Vegas	NV	89104	1-800-375-2931
Sierra Elegance Photography	sierraelegance@charter.net	Sparks	NV	89432	775-673-9520
Christine Austin Photography	info@christineaustin.com	Astoria	NY	11105	718.721.6437
Weddingreels.com	weddingreels@weddingreels.com	Bayside	NY	11361	(718) 225-7185
Annique Lambe Designs	annique@anniquelambe.com	Brooklyn	NY	11211	646-325-3615
Boulevard Video	sugarart@earthlink.net	Brooklyn	NY	11231	(718)923-1004
Claudia Mann Photography	claudiamann@earthlink.net	Brooklyn	NY	11217	(718) 488-7549
Horst Staudner Photography	info@hsphotography.com	Brooklyn	NY	11218-1213	(718) 369-2514
Miranda DJ Entertainment	mirandadjent@yahoo.com	Brooklyn	NY	11234	(718)763-0431
Dalsimer Florist and Event Decorators	dalsimer@aol.com	Cedarhurst	NY	11516	(516) 569-2100
SOULSYSTEM ORCHESTRAS	Rob@soulsystemorchestras.com	Gardiner	NY	12525	800-466-SOUL
Victor Talbots Formals of New York	info@victortalbots.com	Greenvale	NY	11548	516-625-1787
Enhance Face & Body Spa	info@enhancespa.com	Hartsdale	NY	10530	914-997-8878
Ultra Denmark Limousines	ultradenmarklimousine@yahoo.com	Hempstead	NY	11550	(516) 292-5466
Sugarberries	info@sugarberries.com	Jamaica	NY	11435	(718) 526-9371
Queens Bridal Center	qbcgeu@aol.com	Lindenhurst	NY	11757	6319577700
Sheer Expressions Lingerie	Sheerexp@aol.com	Lindenhurst	NY	11757	631-957-3708
Gina Limo	ginalimo@aol.com	Staten Island	NY	10304	(888) 345-GINA
Reverends Irwin & Florence Schnurman		Long Island	NY		631-345-3606
Sound on Sound Music		Long Island	NY		(516)374-2707
Memorable Moments Photography	moments@optonline.net	Nanuet	NY	10954	845 627-1435
Alfonse Pagano Photography	apagano.shootokill@verizon.net	New York	NY	10038	212-425-8853
Eclectrix Inc.	eclectrix@eclectrix.net	New York	NY	10034	(212) 569-9246
Grandma's Secrets	info@grandmasecrets.com	New York	NY	10031	(212) 862-8117
Home Sewing Association	dpierson@sewing.org	New York	NY	10018	212-714-1633
Philip Seaton Photography	pseaton@pseatonphoto.com	New York	NY	10014	(718) 757-7553
REVLES.com	revles123@aol.com	New York City	NY	10017	212-949-9529
Flower Barn	sandipots@aol.com	Penfield	NY	14526	586-5195
Laurie Studio-The Art of Photography	ken@lauriestudio.com	St. James	NY	11780	212-942-5839

ox Video Productions Inc	charles@foxvideoinc.com	Staten Is.	NY		718-351-2400
ead Over Heels Band	Nfeddy@aol.com	Staten Island	NY	10302	718-981-2188
remier Party Network	premierpartynet@aol.com	Staten Island	NY	10312	(718) 356-7863
ic Anthony Productions	ric@ricanthony.com	Staten Island	NY	10305	(718) 816-5412
Itra Express Coach	etelmany@ultraexpress.com	Staten Island	NY	10302	1-800-437-0711
weet Music	msweet@sweetmusicensembles.com	Tappan	NY	10983	800-229-7763
uartet Quintessence	gcubed@peoplepc.com	Williamsville	NY	14221	(716)689-3172
he Elegant Chef	info@theelegantchef.com		NY		516-496-7971
oneymoons Two Travel	sherry@honeymoonstwo.com	Canfield	OH	44406	330-538-3006
akes By Linda	thecakegoddess@aol.com	Groveport	OH	43125	614-830-0600
igital Wedding Videos & ilms	erek@digitalweddings.com	Hamilton	OH		513-897-4441
ugarcraft, Inc.	proicer@one.net	Hamilton	OH	45015	1-800-400-7124
hristopher Norris Wedding Portrait Photography	erek@christophernorris.com	North Royalton	OH	44133	440-237-0008
lajestic Sound	majesticsound@alltel.net	SagamoreHills	OH	44067	330-467-2830
& R Photography	lk@lkramme.com	Bethany	OK	73008	405-789-6600
ove is Carriages	sbowers@aol.com	Guthrie	OK	73044	405-833-4557
)J Dance Entertainment	djdance69@hotmail.com	Tulsa	OK	74134	918-639-8102
ro Sound Mobile Music	dj@tulsawed.com	Tulsa	OK	74133	(918) 232-4087
ulsa DJ	paul@tulsadj.com	Tulsa	OK		918-625-7068
Rosewaters Weddings-N-Flowers	egalasso@harborside.com	Floreance	OR	97439	541-902-7609
mageWise Productions	rob@imagewiseproductions.com	Hillsboro	OR	97124	503-439-8282
As You Wish Concierge Service	asyouwishconcierge@msn.com	Portland	OR	97223	503.805.5526
BridalVeilInvitations.com	rsvp@bridalveilinvitations.com	Portland	OR	97236-1925	
KTVA Productions	mail@ktvavideo.com	Portland	OR	97269	(503) 659-4417
Jorning Star Gift Baskets	renee@morningstarbaskets.com	Portland	OR	97229	(503) 466-0491
/ideo Theater	john_videotheater@yahoo.com	Allentown	PA	18104	610-395-1321
Rev. Ellyn Kravette	light@epix.net	Brodheadsville	PA	18322	(570) 992-0465
ce Craft Enterprises	icecraft@isrv.com	Butler	PA	16001	724-285-4402
Kaminski Studio	kamcorp@salsgiver.com	Cheswick	PA	15024-1449	(724) 274-8171
A. Gerard Sound	agerard@comcast.net	Harrisburg	PA		1-800-536-3629

Entertainment

Cherubs-N-Chocolate by Michelle	michellekhouri@aol.com	Harrisburg	PA	18052	610-799-4596
Colonial Country Club	rpierce@colonialcc.com	Harrisburg	PA	17112	(717) 657-3212
Journeys of the Heart	BethOfJourneys@aol.com	Hollywood	PA	19046	215-663-1494
Precious Petals	precpetals@aol.com	Huntington Valley	PA	19006	215-357-3870
RIX Limousine/Johnstown Limousine Service	rastan@microserve.net	Indiana	PA	15701	724-463-3992
Music Productions Entertainment, Inc.	TheMusPro@msn.com	Kennett Square	PA	19348	(610) 925-3260
Sweet Wrappings	sales@sweetwrappings.com	Mount Joy	PA	17552	800.449.3948
Barry Warren Orchestra	barwarren@aol.com	Phila	PA	19111	215.885.7019
Bob Abramson Photography	bob@bobabramsonphoto.com	Pittsburgh	PA	15210	(412) 881-8900
DJ Raw-Z	djrawz@attbi.com	Pittsburgh	PA	15131	412-418-9887
Reverend Diana Wyne	revdwyne@earthlink.net	Scotrun	PA	18355	800-594-3527
Absolute in Catering		Charleston	SC	29414	843-556-6995
Creative Catering of Charleston, INC	creativecateringofcharleston@att.net	Charleston	SC	29414	(843) 529-0004
Matthew Scott Photographer, Inc.	matthew@scottshot.com	Charleston	SC	29407	(843) 766-8866
Upstate Bridal Service	staci@upstatebridal.com	Clemson	SC	29631	864-624-9066
Cathey Cole Productions	catheycole@cs.com	Fort Mill	SC	29708	(803) 802-2695
Jean-Paul's Creative Cakes	Jpcc29406@aol.com	Hanahan	SC	29406	(843)744-6791
Raffisson Studio	matthew@hiltonheadphoto.com	Hilton Head	SC	29926-1297	(843) 689- 9113
Carolina Bridal Images	chris@carolinabridalimages.com	Lexington	SC	29073	(803)356-1178
Gene Ho Photography	gene@geneho.com	Myrtle Beach	SC	29572	(843) 692-9565
Rev. Dr. Alden Marshall	alden.marshall@att.net	Gatlinburg	TN	37738	877-851-5507
Germantown Mobile DJ	grebec@bellsouth.net	Germantown	TN	38138-2201	(901) 755-7676
G & G Productions	gandgproductions@comcast.net	Hendersonville	TN	37077	615-826-6404
Memphisjam.com	haveyourparty@memphisjam.com	Memphis	TN	38125	(901) 757-4709
Nashville Party Authority	npa@comcast.net	Nashville	TN	37214	615-391-2322
Prime Source Entertainment, Inc.	sbeck@primesourceproductions.com	Nashville	TN	37204	(800) 737-1662
Mountain Valley Properties, Inc.		Pigeon Forge	TN	37863	1-800-644-4859

moky Mountain Wedding hapel	smokywed@nuvox.net	Pigeon Forge	TN	37863	865-428-5177
i-Class Limousines, Inc.	hiclasslmo@aol.com	Strawberry Plains	TN	37871	(865) 932-1990
KE Productions	DJLKE@hotmail.com	Arlington	TX	76012	(817) 905-1841
uality Entertainment	erek_hughes_76017@yahoo.com	Arlington	TX	76017	(817) 695-5427
pple Creek Productions	mike@applecreekproductions.com	Austin	TX	78759	(512) 338-4699
s It Develops Photography	cari@asitdevelops.com	Austin	TX	78720	512-431-0837
looms	blooms@austin.rr.com	Austin	TX	78613	866-873-7552
ictures Perfect	sandy@picturesperfect.com	Austin	TX	78767	1-888-272-5536
elley's Flowers	kelleysflowers@sbcglobal.net	Bellaire	TX	77401	713-664-5559
entral Texas DJ Service	dj@centraltexasdj.com	Cedar Park	TX	78613	512-785-7165
ustom Invitations and ddressing	paula@custom-invitations.com	Cedar Park	TX	78613	512-259-4547
uture Sounds DJ Service	info@future-sounds.com	Converse	TX	78109	210-945-9601
PL Entertainment	djjeff@jplentertainment.com	Cypress	TX	77429	832-237-5125
The "J" Team Dj Service	jhornok@earthlink.net	Dallas	TX	75287	972-307-1683
indy Davis Designs	cindydavisdesigns@sbcglobal.net	Dallas	TX	75220	(214) 357-4714
lite Gatherings	elitegather2@earthlink.net	Dallas	TX	753764675	2143754525
eller Williams Realty	tandag@aol.com	Dallas/Ft. Worth	TX	75254	214-549-4525
Taste of Europe	inquiries@atasteofeurope.com	Fort Worth	TX	76103	(817) 654-9494
lphorn Konditorei	hobiusa@aol.com	Houston	TX	77019	(713) 650-3262
avarian Bakery, Inc.	cakes@bavarianbakeryinc.com	Houston	TX	77098	713-524-7100
eautiful Memories Studio	fotos@ev1.net	Houston	TX	77022-6006	(713)691-6542
hamber Music Unlimited	cmu@houston.rr.com	Houston	TX	77070	281-469-2496
J Connection	music@djconnection.com	Houston	TX	77043	(713) 461-7309
ouston's Uptown Banquet acilities	tamma@houstonuptownbanquet.com	Houston	TX	77379	7135422333
ilworth Manor	kilworth109@aol.com	Houston	TX	77006	713-520-5526
imShannonPhoto	kimshannonphoto@ev1.net	Houston	TX	77041	713-896-1936
al's Fine Catering	info@ralsfinecatering.com	Houston	TX	77055	713-688-7257
ussell Catering Inc	weddings@russellcatering.com	Houston	TX	77090	281-587-0012
uperior Video Productions	niles@svproductions.com	Houston	TX	77009	713-523-8006

Inc.

Vendor	Email	City	State	Zip	Phone
The Dunstan	info@thedunstan.com	Houston	TX	77005	713-942-7711
Weddings By Jan	jan@weddingsbyjan.com	Houston	TX	77084	7137745645
Hackberry Creek Country Club	ana.farrand@ourclub.com	Irving	TX	75063	(972) 444-4534
Bedazzled Entertainment	bill@bedazzledentertainment.com	Lancaster	TX	75146	(972) 218-7590
Cakes By Miriam	cakesbymiriam@aol.com	League City	TX	77573	(281) 334-2103
Wedding Elegance	weddingelegance1@aol.com	Lubbock	TX	79414	(806) 791-4547
Kristen's Wedding Cakes	queq131@cs.com	North Richland Hills	TX	76180	(817)427-9697
Hayden Video Weddings	vpa77@hotmail.com	Plano	TX	75025	(214) 641-6559
Tux 4 Sale.com	sales@tux4sale.com	Richardson	TX	75080	972-783-4TUX
The Pictures	Picbyron@aol.com	Round Rock	TX	78664	512-339-9234
Michael Gaston Photography		Rowlett	TX	75089	214-510-0904
Agustin's Photography	L97991@aol.com	San Antonio	TX	78245	210-827-0480
Gingiss Formalwear	rentatux@wireweb.net	San Antonio	TX	78218	210-654-1330
Masquerade DJ	adjdj@connecti.com	San Antonio	TX	78213	210-377-DJDJ(3535)
Real Audio Entertainment		San Antonio	TX	78212	210-381-7325
Rolls Royce Limo	tommydaniels@yahoo.com	San Antonio	TX	78209	210-930-3907
San Antonio Wedding Professionals Association	info@sawpa.com	San Antonio	TX		
Alana Padgett – Lovegevity Consultant	apadgett@lovegevity.com	Spring	TX	77379	877-597-8166 x. 978
Danny & Amy's Video	drunnels@hotmail.com	Spring	TX	77373	281-350-6810
Happy Needle	onehappyneedle@hotmail.com	Spring	TX	77373	281-355-5310
True Commitments	onehappyneedle@hotmail.com	Spring	TX	77379	713-298-4719
Wedding Video Productions	mastervideo@ev1.net	Spring	TX	77388	281-350-3733
A Simple Indulgence	marie.travis@simpleindulgence.com	Sugar Land	TX	77478	281-772-8139
Suzanne's Flowers	suzannesflowers@aol.com	Sugar Land	TX	77497	(281) 265-0048
The Knights of Dixie Orchestra	knightsofdixie@ev1.net	Sugar Land	TX	77479	(281) 265-8410
Ann's Specialties	annve@earthlink.net	Sugarland	TX	77478	(281) 980-4467
Lone Star Freeze Dry	info@lonestarfreezedry.com	Waco	TX	76712	254-716-1898
Carriages Etc.	samparker@carriagesetc.com	Waller	TX	77484	713-319-0727
JJJ Photography	jjjphotography@aol.com		TX		(860) 582-8363

Schopke Photography	schopke@attbi.com	Provo	UT	84601	1-800-SCHOPKE
Michael Lucarelli Classical Guitarist	Michael@Lucarelli.com	Saint George	UT	84117	801-274-2845
Universal Joy Ministries	weddings@weddingswedding s.com	Saint George	UT	84770	877-235-9457
Clayton Chase Photography	love@claytonchase.com	Salt Lake City	UT	84108	801-58-Chase
Tuxedos By Lee	TuxbyLee@aol.com	West Valley	UT	84120	(801) 966-7825
Celebrate! Celebrate!		Lake of the Woods	VA	22508	(540) 972-0612
Best Choice Catering	bchoicecatering@aol.com	Annandale	VA	22003	703-437-7177
Pampered Chef	sandyputnam@adelphia.net	Ashburn	VA	20148	(703) 723-1014
Ashland Flower Depot	ashlandflodepot@aol.com	Ashland	VA	23005	(804) 798-2034
Mike Topham Photography	mike@miketopham.com	Aylett	VA	23009	(804) 285-1979
Daria and Angel & Aces	daria_mat@msn.com	Burke	VA	22015	703 455-5232
Teatime Delicacies Inc.	teatime@teatimeinc.com	Burke	VA	22015	(703) 323-1607
Suh's Formal Wear	info@tuxedoshop.com	Centreville	VA	20121	703-802-9636
SOTA Weddings		Chantilly	VA	20151	(703) 345-0100
The Wedding Florist		Chantilly	VA	20152	(703) 385-0830
Blooming Dale's Florist	duckbutter517@aol.com	Chesapeake	VA	23322	757-482-5686
Peachtree Video Productions	peachtrvideo@aol.com	Chesapeake	VA	23322	757-482-8170
Holiday Inn Express	chesterhie@aol.com	Chester	VA	23836	(804) 751-0123
Homewood Suites – Chester	saunakamin@aol.com	Chester	VA	23836	(804) 751-0010
A Slice of Creation, LLC	cwilli7718@aol.com	Chesterfield	VA	23832	(804) 717-5243
Comfort Suites – Innsbrook	saunakamin@aol.com	Glen Allen	VA	23060	(804) 217-9200
TigerLily Floral Design	tigerlillyfloral@aol.com	Leesburg	VA	20176	(703) 669-9402
Heaven on Earth Wedding Flowers	linheavenonearth@aol.com	Manassas	VA	22110	703 791-6585
Goodstone Inn	information@goodstone.com	Middleburg	VA	20117	540-687-6115
RSVP	rsvpvirginia@erols.com	Midlothian	VA	23113	(804) 794-9440
Amber Grove Inn	agrove@Comcast.net	Moseley	VA	23120	804-639-7717
Radisson Hotel Norfolk	sales@radisson-norfolk.com	Norfolk	VA	23510	(757) 627-5555
Kingston Plantation Inn	missann@villagepop.com	North	VA	23128	804-725-5831
Specialty Cakes by Karen	sweetsheltons@aol.com	Prince George	VA	23875	(804) 452-4123
Capital Club	nancy.bass@ourclub.com	Richmond	VA	23219	(804) 788-1400
Everyday Gourmet, LLC	everydaygourmet@attbi.com	Richmond	VA	23230	(804) 873-5156
Hampton Inn - Midlothian Turnpike	ricmd_hampton@hilton.com	Richmond	VA	23236	(804) 897-8099
Mark Meitz	mmeitz@hotmail.com	Richmond	VA	23226	800-291-9545

Media Arts Events	weddinginfo@mediaartssolutions.com	Richmond	VA	23230	(804) 257-7360
Mosaic Cafe	holland804@aol.com	Richmond	VA	23229	(804) 288-5915
Pretty Paper	prettypaper@att.net	Richmond	VA	23226	(804) 288-0747
Stewart Limousines	info@stewartlimo.com	Richmond	VA	23228	(804) 264-1129
The Renaissance Conference Center	harry@dominioncafe.com	Richmond	VA	23220	(804) 649-3373
Triple "R" Horse & Carriage	triple-r@corlink.com	Richmond	VA	23231	(804) 222-8264
Vogue Flowers & Gifts. Ltd.	steve@vogue-flowers.com	Richmond	VA	23230	(804) 353-9600
Will's Disc Jockey Service	djwillthrill@earthlink.net	Richmond	VA	23230	(804) 353-2207
Jeri Rogers Photography	info@jerirogers.com	Roanoke	VA	24108	540-342-9900
Homewood Suites - Richmond Airport	saunakamin@aol.com	Sandston	VA	23150	(804) 737-1600
Marco Polo Caterers	info@marcopolocaterers.com	Vienna	VA	22180	((703) 281-3922
Astro Disc Jockeys	astrogm@yahoo.com	Virginia Beach	VA	23455	757-460-2224
Caton Video Productions	dcaton@cox.net	Virginia Beach	VA	23452	757-486-2084
Mary Kay - Lee Goldman	leegoldman1999@yahoo.com	Virginia Beach	VA	23505	757-489-9077
The Rhondels	rhondels@msn.com	Virginia Beach	VA	23454	(757)486-3311
Fooph!	jenniferburgara@attbi.com	Vancouver	WA	98683	360 903 9627
The SoapMeister	ange@cameodesigns.com	Ardenvoir	WA	98811	888-291-5607
Blooms to Twigs		Bothell	WA		425-806-8598
TMK Entertainment	Todd@tmkentertainment.com	Federal Way	WA	98003	206-953-7135
Mareel - Music of the Celtic Harp	Mareel@earthlink.net	Issaquah	WA	98027	(425) 235-7087
Geoffrey Gilmore Signature	gilmore@sigevents.com	Kenmore	WA	98028	425-488-8171
Fleur de Joie	info@fleurdejoie.com	Kenmroe	WA	98028	(206)234-7678
Werner's Photography	admin@weddingphotog.com	Lakewood	WA	98499	253-207-2806
Enchanted Flute Productions	kim@enchantedflute.com	Oak Harbor	WA	98277	360-675-7593
Maricel's Floral Design	maricelsfloraldesign@comcast.net	Redmond	WA	98073	425-466-8767
Northwest Gift Company	sales@nwgiftco.com	Redmond	WA	98053	(206)948-4438
FOX Music	hfox@foxinternet.net	Seattle	WA	98133	206-363-7742
Mortgage Market Inc.	snowmansteve88@hotmail.com	Seattle	WA	98116	(206)371-5785
All 'N Digital Photography	mr_stein@msn.com	Vancouver	WA	98686	(360) 241-6585
Escape Massage Therapy	ajdcollier@yahoo.com	Vancouver	WA	98664	(360) 944-6692
Top Hat Productions, Inc.	tophat@pacifier.com	Vancouver	WA	98664	(360) 694-5985

AC Silver Images	adamcastelo@aol.com	Yakima	WA	98901	(509) 453-6884
The Brides Oasis			WA		425) 823-2273
A Special Request	mydj@asrdj.com	Green Bay	WI	53189	(262) 662-5DJ1
Frame Your Day	dana@frameyourday.com	Green Bay	WI	54304	920-362-6531
Yellowdog Productions	info@yellowdogproductions.net	Madison	WI		(608)848-6258
Allen Jones, 'The Ultimate Disc Jockey'	ajtheultimatedj@earthlink.net	Milwaukee	WI	53219-4836	(414) 545-4700
A Crossfading Technique 2 Dance 2	crossfadersdj@cs.com	Milwaukee	WI	53223	(414) 371-1353
Allen Jones, 'The Ultimate Disc Jockey'	ajtheultimatedj@earthlink.net	Milwaukee	WI	53219-4836	(414) 545-4700
Top Shelf Bartending Services LLC	joangroh@juno.com	Muskego	WI	53150	414-422-9868
Wishes Come True LLC	wishescometruellc@yahoo.com	Neenah	WI	54956	920-428-7216
Dragonfly Studio	signex@frontiernet.net	New London	WI	54961	715-752-3096
Chi-Town Productions	Mobiledj101@aol.com	Pewaukee	WI	53072	(262)369-1409
EZ Rock Entertainment	danceez@aol.com	Pewaukee	WI	53072	(888) 455-3307
Zamba Studios	larry@larryzamba.com	Union Grove	WI	53182	(262) 597-9610
Jackson Hole Stationers	karenv@sprynet.com	Wilson	WY	83014	307-733-3763